MW01288976

QUANTUM ASCENSION

By PETER COLLA

A Companion's Guide to Ascension in
Health, Wellness, and Healthcare amidst the
Shadow of the Cabal, Fake News, Pandemics,
and Butterflies

ISBN: 9781795563901

FORWARD

CONTENTS

Acknowledgments i

1 The Beginning of Ascension 1

2 Simple Truths 5

3 Prisons 15

4 Intro In To Ascension 21

5 I Was Alive But Really I Died 27

6 The Whirlwind Of Our Lives 39

7 Social Ascension 53

8 Peace, Ascension, & The Plandemic 63

9 A Single Step In Ascension 75

10 Critical Mass Reaction 83

11 Why Masks 93

12 Quantum Descension 105

13 Riots, What Is Going On 117

14 Tower Of Babylon 123

15 Ascension & Evil Eliminated   129

16 The Dam Has Broken   137

17 Vaccination To Light   147

18 Bricklayer   161

19 The Mark Of The Beast   179

20 Light Seed   189

21 The Hunted Become The Hunters   197

22 The Descended   205

23 Boo-Boo The Scary Stuffed Bear   223

24 Water Fall? No Water Ascension   241

25 Bread   253

26 Ascending Sounds   271

27 Viral Whispers   283

28 Fade From View   291

29 Ascended And Descended Vibrations   297

30 Meester; I Can Fly   315

31 **Garden Of Pigments**   321

32 **Fighting Goliath's**   333

33 **Flying In The Fourth Dimension**   349

34 **Ascension Out Of Spiritual Enslavement** 369

35 **Grace Is The Sound My Eye Sees**   391

36 **Q**   403

ACKNOWLEDGMENTS

This book is dedicated and would not be possible without the contributions of all the great men and women who risk their lives revealing Truths, taking down Strongholds, and setting Captives free throughout the world, in the air, and in the deepest recesses of our souls. This great band of End-Time Warriors led by our Great President Trump; These are the Remnant, Star Seeds, Researchers, Truth Seekers, Prophets and Seer's, men and women all the behind the scene soldiers who with ascended voice bring light into hearts of all those willing to listen.

Any you who have listened know their names; they are The Anna's and The Charlie's, The Michael's and Mel's, some Peter's and Paul's, David's and John's, Simon and Eva, Ben and Rob's, Judy and Janet, an Alex, a Christen, a Santa, a Sidney, a Lin, and a Juan. The Real Generals and The True Fighter's, Teachers, Patriots all, an Isaac, a Ronald, some who have risen and others who fall, those who said yes without fan fair, praise, or payment at all, stepping up because it is right lifting voices when in danger they are called.

On the final day this book was completed January 18, 2021 I heard the voice of the Lord say;

"Behold the Great and Mighty Day of the Lord, it is upon you, and it is... Vengeance."

By Peter Colla

THE BEGINNING OF ASCENSION

In the beginning, God created the Heavens and the Earth, creating all things He created men and gave them the Earth so that they could experience the majesty of Him through it.

And the Light came into the world, and the Light was Good, so that the men in the world could see and experience the light, and the light could experience men and the world through a man.

Men saw the Light and for many they recognized it and came unto the Light, thus taking the Light into themselves, and the Light dwelled within them and they were good.

But for some when they beheld the Light they turned away, and fled, for darkness dwelled within their hearts, feeling the shame for the evil things they had done. They hid their hearts from the light, afraid the Light would reveal what darkness had formed within them. For darkness flees from Light, and as so do also the followers of darkness turn and flee.

So began the great division of darkness and Light, ever fighting for the souls of men.

And darkness began building and maneuvering forces throughout the

1

world, strategically scheming from the shadows and secretly whispering curses in the dark, stealing the best for itself but also enslaving the many to its end. Ever plotting for its final goal and that is to take the whole world for itself, destroying and polluting all the men therein so that none would come to the light.

A war began slowly to build over the millennium between forces of dark and Light, a great war that ultimately would lead to either Light or the dark being vanquished from the world forever. A great war, not one of only blood and bones, or even minds and sanity, but of spirits. The same spiritual beliefs that decide if a man will choose the Light or not in his or her soul.

Then God sent His light again into the world, this time not only to call men to Himself but to illuminate the truths that had been hidden from them. Those who were willing to look up from the ground suddenly saw the light and realized the truth, this even would become Revelation.

Men saw the truth that was hidden by the lies he had been told, and he realized himself not only that he was lied to, but by whom and for what end? This was the first step up the mountain of enlightenment and freedom.

An apocalyptic revelation was suddenly realized that all of mankind was already in an epic battle between good and evil, and this war would be the war to end all wars, for it is not a simple war between men, or gold, or even countries, but a war for the souls of mankind.

This is the End of Times War, and it is upon us.

By Peter Colla

SIMPLE TRUTHS

The simple truth about health care is simple; we have been systematically lied to about just about everything when it comes to our health and health care treatment. People have been slowly and completely brainwashed in their belief regarding their own health for years and this belief has systematically been altered to a point of complete fear and loss of hope.

I feel like a caterpillar who wakes up one day and realizes its whole world is defined by the few small inches of dirt he or she has been allowed to dwell on, the few dry blades of grass or fallen leaves presented to us like another meager bowl of gruel clutched in the hands of a starving peasant, displayed as the mere crumbs from the table of some dark and sinister overlord, reluctantly granted from where I am not quite sure? As my senses reach out from beyond the few morsels in my hands I seem to hear the never-ending voices and echoing repeated chants of others who are increasingly desperate to tell me how the world is defined or exactly what I am supposed to do especially with others. "Only the ground is important!"

"And no matter what you do, don't look to up, keep your eye on the ball, only the job is important," those little voices in my dreams of little green men with pointy ears telling me, accusing me, belittling me; "You are always looking to the horizon, never keeping your mind on where you are, and what you are doing!" But the more I seem to look, the more that I am realizing the truth is not buried in the dirt, not in the cold metal of sand and pebbles before me, but lay up in the climbing of what feels like slowly ascending ground? How can this be they keep telling me to stay firmly with all of my feet on the ground, the ground is real, spinning, hurtling through space at incredible speeds, up is nothing only space?

I have learned as a health care practitioner with over thirty years of experience and treatment history of thousands of souls, the simple truth about health care is that unless a person looks to the cause of an issue, all the causes, and then applies a subsequent treatment to include this causation information revealed within the plan to fight the affliction, they pretty much have a "blind man in a boxing match" chance of overcoming the problem?

The manipulation of the mind regarding this deceit is all around us, constantly coming at us in every possible form, presenting a complete bombardment of the poisoning of our bodies through our eyes, ears, mouths, minds, and bodies with one purpose, to manipulate and dumb us down, stimulate a negatively affect, weaken our body or drive us to an evil end, while at the same time confuse and lie to our minds, distract us from the truth, and eventually manipulate our beliefs towards this evil agenda, one that has the ultimate purpose to direct us towards the point where we give up all freedom to make decisions for ourselves and become slaves to their system, giving up any chance health or hope.

First and foremost the present health care system, with its heart the basic pharmaceutical insurance model seems from this health care providers standpoint to be driven caring nothing about curing anybody of anything, they are merely interested in the perpetuation or approval of treatments of the symptoms of the afflictions we suffer from, making money, and enslaving us into a belief system of total dependency as well as hopelessness. The basic fact is, there is not a single medicine on the market that cures anybody of anything, they all merely reduce the symptoms that the injuries or sicknesses cause, while we sit back and hope even pray that sickness will finally just go away. And if you examine the waste that is distributed in overpricing and useless treatments it would seem even money is not truly a concern, though they would tell us all that it is the only reason they inflict their increasing controlling measures.

In a time not so long ago if a person started suffering from an illness they did just that, there was a belief that they "Suffered" from something, they may have "Came Down" with, were afflicted with this or that, suffered from an attack or problem, or caught this or that bug? But in the last couple of decades people have been told with more and more regularity; they "Are Sick," they have something, it resides is inside them, it has somehow developed within them, evolved, or it is something they were created with, like a flaw? Instead of just suffering from sicknesses as our ancestors have for millennia, the more advanced people of today have even started taking on for themselves the names of the sicknesses they perceive they are afflicted with such as; diabetic, alcoholic, schizophrenic, any one of the numerous "ic's" or "ism's" that have sprung up to redefine or help us realize who we are.

This is a very slight and mild form of manipulation of the mind and most significant to the persons physical status because if a person now believes they "Are" or have become something 'Ism" within themselves instead of merely "suffering" from something, they tend to give up hope, relinquish power, much easier to manipulate, setting aside their own willingness to fight, as a result, they will just sit there and take it as these abusive attacks continue. By just taking it, they suffer hopelessly, give up any resistance against future attacks' that may follow, and worse, they are ultimately led to believe God doesn't love them, somehow has allowed it to happen as a punishment, or that He may even be angry with them, and worse yet, created them flawed in order for them to now suffer.

As I have said, I have been a medical practitioner for over thirty years, and as such has been an active participant in a sense, with this senseless brainwashing of helplessness that we are being dowsed with through the media continually, but this most recent worthless and forgotten social manifestation is truly a new occurrence pressing into the forefront over the last ten or fewer years. I remember only just a few years ago, people would come to me with a preconceived notion that they were suffering from this or that issue, often because of things they had seen on television, or read on the internet, attributing a much more morbid outcome on the few symptoms than they had experienced. Often much of the therapy would then consist of convincing them first that there was hope, things were not as bleak as they had been told, and contrary to what lies the public was told, there could be belief for healing.

It didn't even matter if the conceptual self-diagnosis was a direct orthopedic dramatic event such as a break or injury, or if they were suffering from a more complex systemic affliction such pain in the back, a total knee replacement occurrence, a heart attack, an amputation procedure, or an affliction name such as Lupus or High Blood Pressure, even all-dooming cancer, they felt dammed by this increase in the information they had literally drowned in?

But at this same time, I also began noticing when delving into the origins of injuries and not just symptom analysis, almost every person I spoke with could almost exactly pinpoint in most cases the exact day the issue started, what they were doing, and in most cases what they were dealing with in their spirit or emotions thus lending to a possible examination as to the spiritual cause with its own possible specific and subsequent cure. This revelation demonstrated to us over and over, that when the cause was examined in the body, mind, and spirit spiritual healing took place, it often could even be coupled with likewise physical healing. I wrote about many of these examples in my previous books and will not at this time reanimate these, but if the reader wishes they can see plenty of examples in the book Heal Yourself; "For God's Sake."

Now today people seem to be more resolute in their assessment and conclusion of their own physical ailment often coming in and saying; "I have this or that", "I have a Rotator Cuff", "I have pain", "I am a cancer patient", "A Diabetic", "Disabled", "An Amputee", "A Schizophrenic", "I AM SICK!!!" having concluded themselves to the belief that the sickness is a part of who they are, who they were created to be, in most cases, and along with this have given up all hope to a possible cure, merely seeking treatment to help them function or ease suffering with this new life's sentence.

Well, I am here right now to tell each and every one of you, that you are not these diseases, these afflictions, these ailments, these injuries. You are not predisposed or destined to suffer from this or that, and you certainly are not a slave to anyone, including the fool doctors who tell you differently. Certainly not to the insurance companies that just want to control every aspect of your health care authority, put you in fear, or suck from you all aspects of self-decision regarding your own health. Let's not forget the pharmaceutical companies that want to give you one poison for one ailment while possibly causing three others that further push you down a rabbit hole of despair, until you end up with an entire list of so-called medicines, continually dumping money at the feet of their god's, ultimately resulting in a loss of every gift you have ever received, as well as the bonus; complete enslavement as the ultimate slap in the face of God.

For thousands of years, when people would suffer from ailments, they would search out the most learned member of their society and seek advice. Often this was the oldest most experienced person, like a grandmother, a "Meester," or Wiseman. What would qualify such a person? Three things; experience in either overcoming the same or an alike issues in the past, helping others with similar issues or a broad base of education in the area of identification and subsequent treatment options for like issues.

The problem with the majority of the health care providers of today is they have only a very limited ideology regarding treatment options, specifically one-directional educations into the possible aspects and treatment options of the ailments they treat, and at the same time, they have very little if any personal experience in the feelings and specific situations of the people they give advice to. I have seen uniform driving factors for health care in most cases being money or busy waiting rooms, and not primarily the health enrichment of the person they are treating. What is sad is in most cases many health care practitioners would not render the same treatment they give to others to their own mother, father, or family member, speaking very specifically to the essence and quality of what they believe they are delivering?

These days people go to the doctors so they can be told what is "wrong" with them, the doctor does his examination within the limits of his training or his experience, and then sets up his treatment course of action using the tools or medicines he has been told he must use. The testing, the diagnosis, and the course of action must all be authorized by the insurance company before a person can receive their so-called healing, and the course of action must be narrowly observed without any deviation, no matter what a particular person might find they need unless again consulted with the doctor and cleared by the higher-ups.

Now mind you, these authorizing agents, these are the same people who are profiting the most by limiting a persons care, directing them into treatment facilities they might own, and profit by, recommending the use of one pill that might lead to a lifetime of usage rather than merely a short-term or natural use option. Why would they possibly do that; easy they either own the pharmaceutical companies, owned by them or controlled by the same entities that would profit the most by this deception, at the very least, they are in league with the same snake-pit as they, this is the only plausible deduction?

There is not a single medicine or medical application out there that can make a person heal, become a better human being, or give any person a single day in their single life, not one, not anyone, that function comes completely and solely from God. Pills, chemicals;

they all just reduce the symptoms in our bodies that are the result of the initial injuries or attacks, the same symptoms that are designed to warn us something dangerous is occurring.

I know this fact is true because I have seen it with my own eyes, over the course of tens of years, and with the direct experience of treating patients, repeated revelations do not lie, they merely speak the truth. There is one simple fact, when you look at all of them collectively, in our now present health care model; some get better, some don't, a few almost miraculously, a few drastically fail and even tragically, but the only real person in control is God. There seems to be no rhyme or reason to this, or is there?

The Initial Goal of True Health Care Ascension; is to realize the lie, a lie, any of them, then start looking at the why's and by whom, it is only then a person can move on to real effective treatment options.

The first and foremost in the treatment goal must be to identify what exactly is afflicting the person seeking help, and then formulate advice as to the best way to move forward through his or her immediate days, how to avoid further issue or reoccurrence. This can be done on an almost immediate basis by adjusting what they might eat or drink, how they might rest or move, or basically what slight but subtle immediate changes need to be made to move the life of the person towards the positive healing result.

The goal must be to examine all possible causes of the original issue, fight back any way possible, and become better or well, and to then take on a future course of action as to not suffer the same attack again.

If people would consider taking a God-given course of action whether it be good food, a good reflection of all the natural and wonderful options we have already been given, or merely a combination of herbs and teas, (of which most of the present-day medicines are based and synthesized from), implement a remedy or action that has worked in the past, and facilitate a plan that moves them away from what is harming them, they would, in fact, change their lifestyles that may have precipitated the injury in the first place, they would in the process of overcoming the injury actually lay the ground for a better life and in getting better become better.

Over the course of the next few chapters of this book, I am going to demonstrate to you how to accomplish this very thing, demonstrate how people can be healed merely by changing their perspective of thinking. We are going to examine together from a Quantum level how all these things are possible and predictable. I know this fact is true because I have witnessed it firsthand in the treatment office of my Physical Therapy clinic but more importantly, because it is The Truth as already spoken to us in God's Word for centuries. These parallels will be clearly demonstrated and hopefully applied.

PRISONS

At the beginning of my practicing physical medicine, I had just begun with my own small office sharing space with other doctors, one of which volunteered his work often on weekends, we will call him Dr. Mike. Dr. Mike, by the way, was one of the finest Doctors I had ever had the honor of meeting, what made him a true Doctor in every sense of the word, was the fact that he truly cared about the wellbeing of all of his patients, always wanting to give them everything in his ability and knowledge he could to help them recover from whatever issue they happen to be suffering from.

Dr. Mike had such a love and concern for his patients that he would spend every lunch sitting at his desk, with a simple sandwich he would collect from a nearby fast-food establishment, calling every patient he had seen the day before to ask them how they were? A real and true family doctor, who, in my opinion, personified the Godly manner in which doctors should practice.

On one particular weekend he asked me if I wanted to come with him, he was volunteering for a few hours at a local prison working in their infirmary? He stated to me that he looked at it more like a mission to God helping these unfortunate souls who found themselves there then the actual medical advice he may present. I had never seen the inside of a prison being curious, so I decided to meet him there.

After a brief tour by one of the prison administrators, Dr. Mike excused himself and then went off to the infirmary to begin seeing anyone who happened to be there. I continued talking to the administrator in his office, who himself was a man of faith complimenting continuously Dr. mike and his wonderful soul, the spirit he brought when he visited.

After a short while, Dr. Mike popped his head back into the office and said to me; "There is a guy in the infirmary who hurt his knee, maybe you could do some physical therapy, or there is something you could offer him to help him with his injury?"

I looked at the administrator and he gave me an agreeing nod so I said; "absolutely" and got up to follow Dr. Mike.

The Doctor informed me a brief history hurriedly as we walked together; "Apparently this patient was involved in some kind of scuffle yesterday, a fight or something, I'm not sure if he was directly involved, or someone just fell on him, but the guards assured me he was not dangerous, merely a bit bruised and battered. He is in the last examining table sitting on the table wearing a knee brace." Dr. Mike explained as he hurriedly walked down the corridor back to the infirmary, making a reference to the other end of the room and finally turning directly to someone else waiting for him.

I continued down the long row of examining tables each draped in old fashion curtain separating them from each other. A few resting patients/inmates watched me with inquisitive looks as I passed by, some were sleeping, others merely curiously looked up at me as I smiled, few smiled back. The only comforts these men seemed to enjoy in the small individual rooms the patient had where the private old fashion examination plinths they rested on with each a simple pillow, a bit of privacy the curtained off little make shift room the simple cloth curtain that hung from the ceiling gave.

Other than the eight or ten tables all occupied, and the Doctor, the only other person in the room was one of the guards standing in the middle of the room half watching the men on the tables, for the rest watching the television set that silently displayed images over in the corner up against the wall.

As I came to the last little room, sure enough a man was sitting on the edge of the table, middle-aged, pleasant enough looking, he looked up at me with a simple smile seemingly expecting and waiting for me to appear. With the exception of a few minor scrapes and a couple of small bruises on his arms and one on his cheek, he didn't appear to be in much distress. He was although wearing a knee brace on his Left Knee which, I immediately noticed, was placed completely wrong lending no support or even comfort, placed much too far off the knee and in the wrong direction to do any good.

After the briefest greeting, I immediately began to loosen the knee brace so I could adjust it for the man and examine his knee. He then looked at me and with a confused look on his face asked; "What are you doing?"

"Sorry, I thought the Doctor told you, I am a Physical Therapist," I said, "I am going to see if I can help you with your knee injury. I will first need to look at it and then maybe I can help you with it."

Then he said the most bizarre thing that has stayed with me all these many years later, as clearly and concisely as if it was just yesterday; "Can you help me escape from this prison?"

The statement startled and confused me enough to have me suddenly freeze from loosening the straps of the brace and look over my left shoulder at the guard who was clearly now looking directly at us, he too obviously heard the prisoners question.

"Because if you can't, there is nothing you can do for me," He continued, "So you might as well leave me alone."

I glanced again back to the prisoner who also was looking at the guard, an obvious look on his face he knew the guard heard the prisoner's words. As he again looked at me, I realized by the look on his face he wasn't trying to hide his comments merely stating them almost as fact.

"I can help your knee to feel better, at least put this brace on the right way so it will do what it's supposed to do rather than just sit here doing nothing? I can't help you get out of prison, but I can at least help you get out of the infirmary, feeling better." I offered with my own smile almost feeling I was part of some joke waiting for the "punch-line."

"Well, that it isn't it?" he said with the slightest laugh, "I am not in any hurry to get out of the infirmary, back out there with those animals, that's the place that did this to me. What, just feel a little better, and then go right back to it? I have no desire to go right back in that hell."

"If you can't help me get out of here, out of this prison, then there is nothing you do to really help me." He said with a smile, not angry or aggressive, but merely resound as he pulled his leg back away from my reach. Smiling back to me in an almost wise understanding of a man who truly understood the situation he was in, and the "what" he truly needed for the issue he was suffering from.

"Listen, you seem like a nice guy, but if I go back in there with this brace on my knee, I am more of a target than I was before. If I look weak, or afraid, they will attack. They are Animals, they sense fear, almost like they feed on it. It is the nature of this place."

I looked back at the guard who turned his attention on the other prisoners up the row of tables, and back to the TV on the wall.

It took almost thirty years for me to understand the truth of the instruction that man had given me all those years ago. The majority of the people I treated in the current health care system really are prisoners of this system, and all we seem to do, at least for the most part is treat symptoms, treat people in the prisons they have fallen into. Patch them up, make them feel a little better, and then send them right back into the prison yard so they are exposed and vulnerable for another or even greater attacks.

If I want to really help people, then I need to help them get out of the prison of the health care system they find themselves in.

INTRO INTO ASCENSION

Ascension of awareness, looking up to God, prayer, meditating in the spirit, or simply hope for relief from afflictions, these are all basically the same things. Even though organized religion has told us for ages it is ungodly to meditate, and at the same time we medically trained individuals are schooled into the belief of separating medicine from prayer, I would state the contrary, from my own experience seeing the promise, power, and value practicing these similar activities when it comes to where we focus our attention, it is only through such endeavors a truly heavenly and spiritual explosion of consciousness and likewise, healing can occur.

Yet forever there seems to be an itch, a seemingly soft nudging to turn this way or that bringing the caterpillar with each turn again with a choice to do what is right or good or again fall to the hard ground below as with each step, each truth up into the unknowns of the heavenly his attention seems to be brought.

Oh, how many times do I crawl like a blind caterpillar, up those slow sloping grades, the inclines of what appears progress, in life as well as within one? The crescendo of images popping into the mind of the caterpillar, are the dreams, the seeming assembly of colorfully painted brush strokes, bright hues with pleasant-sounding views, shuttered silences as dark pieces of shadowed memories unfold, they lay across a table of my mind spread out through what seems millennium of time, thoughts and words whispering softly into the mind of a young baby all tend to remind only just the beginning her first few steps of a now great anticipated journey untold?

Health or healthcare is a tender subject especially among two groups of individuals in our society; those who suffer the most in health, and those who profit the most in care of health. Both groups have bought into the fallacies of healthcare the "system" that feeds them, along with its narrow-minded point of view as to how and why to treat a person a certain way. Any further information that could either positively affect the outcome or alleviation of their afflictions, discourage the participants from participating fully, or possibly steer them into a more alternative treatment method that is outside the common media-driven accepted solution, is not only strictly withheld from them but if know even more ruthlessly forbidden.

The person group suffering or in this case, the patient, feels, for the most part, they are powerless to do anything about the situation they are suffering in, accepting the projected treatment course as the only trusted, affordable, or authorized choice, this is the first lie they have been brainwashed us with.

The second group believes they have been given all the knowledge, authority, and options to provide medical assistance to the first group, and as the full authority spokespersons for the care regiment, no other course of action should even be spoken about. Whether they know this is a lie, or choose to participate in exchange for lucrative payouts, purposely providing health when they know either there are better options out there, or perhaps what they are providing really doesn't help, or yet worse; they do know that the options they are presenting actually are harming those individuals they have sworn to help, all fall into the category or not only unethical but immoral.

I have witnessed in my own practicing of health care that there has been increasing pressure by the powers to be, which in my case happens to be the insurance industry coupled with the pharmaceutical industry, these entities which I believe are also owned and ruled by the same that control the Deep State, have little interest in the actual healthcare of the people being treated, as a matter of fact, their desires, authorization, or recommendations often are increasingly more directed toward keeping people sick as a means to keep them in the system rather than help them eventually leave healthy.

Yet in the last couple of years, there has been a resulting manifestation in the present vibrational dimension in which we currently reside, especially over the course of the last year, an astonishing revealing of truths that have until recently been suppressed, at least for those willing to open their eyes, minds, and search. When people do make that choice to look up, search the answers themselves, fact check, or consider options counter to the media-driven narrative, the results are nothing short of bliss. I have increasingly seen evidence of miraculous healings when people merely engage the act of belief or essences of the spirit in their daily perceptions.

Again, as I have already been stated in the past writings; why are all forms of healthcare seemingly designed to isolate, numb, confuse, or concentrate the injured person's attention onto the smallest single part of the physical life. It would only mean that they, the powers who have the secrets, are desperate for the truth not to get out, perhaps they themselves know the truths about greater spiritual energies are the only Truth, and they want us all dumbed down and just obedient, silent and masked.

So how does a person Ascend in their Consciousness especially regarding their overall health and wellness regardless of what affliction they may be suffering from? The answer is simple; "They merely need to start with the admission they have been lied to, then begin upon a wonderful journey for the discovery of Truth."

Over the course of the next few chapters of this book, I will discuss not only the means by which ascension in health and wellness can be obtained by everyone and anyone who wishes to reach out and grasp it, but I will also correlate "why" it is possible on a physical level, how it has been promised by God for centuries, and finally make correlations to the present worlds system so clarity can be witnessed as to what the dark motivations are, the designed evil seeded within their prescribed system, and the many ways it has been purposely manipulated to impede the Children of today in their journeys as Ascending Spirits as God intends for all of us.

By Peter Colla

I WAS ALIVE, BUT REALLY I DIED

Oh, how many times have I woke in this cocoon wondering what is a dream and which is a joke, an impersonate sense that sanity may dispense, leaving young traveler in wonderings dawn, of how many days have gone wrong, yet a new light with hinder flight may commence? Dreams of dark days gone by, spread before him like the many glistening wonders of river filled sparkles lie, the cool rivers waters cascading along a grass-lined shore, many droplets caress her skin, for all the ages of memories begin, to the life that one smiles at no more.

I thought I was alive but really I died! Now that I have died, it was only then I could be borne! Yet now that I know that I am dead, I realize finally I truly live!

The day I died:

One day I awoke as a health care provider and realized a portion of what I was doing, teaching, preaching, presenting was not true; the Health Care I was giving, while it seemed to help with symptoms, for the most part, treated only the bodies reactions to them, the specific illnesses the people were suffering from and did little if nothing for that actual cause of the affliction. There seemed to be a decreasing interest by the "System" in any evaluation information regarding the

27

actual causes of the injuries only an ever-narrowing interest in identifying the exact location, tissue, or base chemical system in the body affected by the person's symptom to then put in place a counter chemical in to basically reduce this effect. I guess I saw the light?

These many symptoms; swellings, allergic reactions, sudden weakness, even pain, if they are in our body for a reason, and clearly to warn us about some kind of danger or attack that occurred against the whole, why was there such an increasingly blind interest in needing to dumb them down, stifle or muzzle them to the point where a person could barely feel them?

This approach seemed in many cases to even contribute to the prolonging of the actual issues or possible facilitation of others, these standard treatments certainly seemed to be only enough to ensure a person felt just a little better, yet retained enough of an issue to assure the same person would return again, perhaps in a couple of days for another treatment.

I noticed this ideology seemed to be coupled with increasing faith in a system that promised the only ensuring way, of the Insurance way, that waiting rooms would be busy enough to pay bills was conforming to the desires of the authorizing agents controlling the payments of the care. Some of the same said bills, actually issued by the same entities that were responsible for paying the costs of that same care for the individuals I treated in the first place pushed the majority of the people to the facilities or companies that seemed to give the worst care.

Participation contracts began to pop up throughout the industry where fees or seemingly taxes were assessed yearly, in essence, the insurance industry was paying me for care and I was turning around and handing them back at least a portion, laying my alms at its feet, but that is another story to be discussed later. With this increasing participation contract, more and more regulations were included such as verification of benefits, authorization of care, mandatory collecting of copays, more and more the system pressed for ever-increasing control over every aspect of the health care situation, always on the threat of as a provider or patient for that matter, if any participating person didn't do exactly what they said, in the manner, they said it, as well as in a timely fashion the way they mandated, no payment would be made, no care would be grated and a person even risked being excluded from future participation with them at all.

"Do as we demand or you will be kicked out of the system." They believed they own the health care system!

I decided then and there that the care, the advice, the direction of the treatment, needed and deserved to be, no, it was the "Right" of the patient to be included in the examination process; the actual cause of the injury at hand, the whole injury, and not just the after-effects or few symptoms that present itself this day at this time. Treat the cause not just the result.

Now that I was dead, time to be born:

Examining the issue at hand allowed one to see so clearly what actually was going on in this person's life (their very soul). When I would ask a person what were you doing at the time you felt the injury, the first moment of pain, or the very first symptom, but more importantly what were you thinking, in each and every case the person knew with the most distinct and almost supernatural clarity the answer, and if they didn't they merely needed to ask their own spirit and it seemed almost out of thin air the answer would be revealed to them.

This period of my life happens to coincide with a real introduction to God, (another story for later), basically it resulted in the dedication of myself and my office to attempt to place God into the treatment process. Exactly how, I wasn't sure yet, but all I knew I needed to open up to this idea any way possible in order to truly honor the patients and their potential healing process.

The caterpillar meanders along the base of a tree, the gradual ascend seems more like a climb than a normal walk. She still passes many every moment seemingly in every possible direction, yet to the ascending caterpillar there is only one true way up and that is up. Lifting her head to the heavens suddenly there is a warmth that bathes her face warmer and more loving than any he had ever experienced before.

When eyes are closed or one experiences blindness there is a common occurrence whereby entities of great energy are clearly perceived appearing lighter in colors of reds, oranges or lighter colors still bringing with them the unmistakable assurance not only are they good but they are true. This new world of color matches that one hidden within the soft whispers of her dreams. For our ascending little caterpillar, a single truth has been revealed laying ground to the steps before her, leaving little doubt where the next step will be and more affirmatively what direction it will be.

As Obama Care spread its tentacles throughout the healthcare providing industry, ever-increasing its red tape, reducing payments, increasing the co-pays made by the patients, steadily ramping up authorization and controls making it almost impossible to survive with the increasing administrative costs unless an office was full, we saw the slow strangulation of the small company practice, not only in my own case but across the entire healthcare environment. Insurance companies began buying up healthcare providing companies, primary care doctors offices, but also many of the auxiliary providers whereby the majority of the patients were told they must go, regardless of whether the care was poor or not.

In my case the pushing of people away from the cause-based ideology had the opposite effect and actually precipitated a direct consideration in treatment for the actual issue at hand and it allowed many of our clients to, as it were, put an eye on the actual cause of the issue. In addition, what I also witnessed was nothing short of miraculous, not only did symptoms immediately cease but in some of these cases, the actual physical afflictions left altogether, resulting in seemingly miraculous healing to occur.

Issues that may have lingered for years vanished, abilities that were thought gone suddenly reappeared, and afflictions thought incurable suddenly and magically began to flee, even tissue thought long dead seemed to spontaneously regenerate, this was especially true in children. But the most remarkable fact was that bodies thought permanently changed or damaged by these issues like scared battlefields, suddenly, almost instantaneously, revert back to their previous, undamaged, and in some cases even better status than they had been prior to the event that causes them injury in the first place!

Many people, myself included were eager to bring these realizations not only to the doctors but to the insurance agencies directly figuring they would no doubt be interested in at least seeing their health care cost reduce by less care? Yet this was the opposite of what occurred, especially from the authorizing agencies when they found that the person actually was maybe getting better, an almost aggressive effort began to set in to halt all care, benefits were dropped, contracts with us were immediately canceled and we were immediately ordered to send the person to the more unethical companies on the threat of complete denial of all payments. Even when I would complain to supervisors or management the repeated final statement was a casual; "Then sue us!" before they would laugh and hang up.

An anomaly developed inside my own observation; this factual truth realization was in direct conflict with the belief system I had been taught or programmed my entire life, causing me then to wonder about perhaps what other parts of what we were taught as absolute truths perhaps were not?

Now that I have died I realize I am borne:

These healing events, I needed to write about them, speak about them, study and understand them, even publish them. But one thing was sure in me as a health care practitioner it had two results; one, I knew at that moment I must investigate if these seeming miracles were flukes, why they occurred now, were they replicated in other individuals, but more importantly, what does it mean especially towards my belief in the actual treatment process I had been engaged in; what was I to do with this information that I had witnessed?

But more importantly; two, I felt that not to share this information, especially with every person who presented themselves before me in pain, other therapists I worked with, my friends, family or anyone, not saying so liked unto denying a thirsty child a simple drink of water in a scorching desert, especially when the water had been redly and freely given to me, seemed in my spirit to be no different than Peter the Apostle denying Christ at the burn-barrel.

You would think such information, such revelation would be welcome, even lifted up for all to see, especially by the very organizations that have pledged their support to the people who have come to them for help, but the opposite seemed so. The moment a person or persons seemed to experience an almost miraculous ceasing of affliction, especially when it was clear a long time client would suddenly not need the services moving forward, the institutions whether companies, owners, or the medical insurance agents at hand, would envelop the event, remove it from sight, (under the guise often of further investigation), later deny the occurrence ever happened, and in many cases often seek to destroy the very participants of said "Miracle." Certainly, they would separate the participants, denying us contact upon threat of denial of future services, or even ruination? Sometimes even direct actions were instigated to eliminate them altogether, discredit them, slander and destroy them, rather than let any word that such a process of healing actually could or did exist.

And now that I have died:

But what can a person do? Are we not all as health care practitioners swore to do our "Utmost," everything in our limited power, ability, or knowledge to help other individuals with the afflictions they happen to be suffering from? That is the "Hippocratic Oath," at least I thought it was?

Do we actually do everything we can to help, but more importantly, not withhold but share, pass on to those in need the knowledge we ourselves have learned or certainly was given to us, especially when we are being asked and paid to? Do we give them what they need to heal or merely enough to feel better and come back?

What can a person say, when another person in tears asks, pleads for their ailing child or spouse, even begs you "what you would do," if you actually know what they can do to find some relief, overcome this issue at hand, even defeat this "bully" that has been harassing them for so long, and seems not only scary but so permanent?

How do you say no, withhold information, or bite your tongue, to the mother, the child, the brother who is pleading with their eyes, suffering? You can't, I can't, especially if I fear to lose my own soul in the process. What, deny one to make a buck, as I seem by so many to be told to do? If a person does that; how about ten, well then, why not a thousand, by this time a person seems to be brought to that same question more and more frequently until it would become so blurred you would have a hard time even remembering any truth, and life in the first place?

You look around and see how people are paying for care and being dealt out the minimal, most cost-effective crumbs, or profitable for someone but not them, the few "bowls of gruel," and it makes you want to scream. Scream at the bosses, the companies, the institutions who don't seem to care about the pain you are witnessing, and people are experiencing, only the money, the tabulated increasing numbers, the fools fixation with the number of zeros in their ledgers? All that pain!

I guess that is what death feels like? Saying no to the lie.

It is only now that I live:

It is funny to think that I have treated people for going on now nearly thirty-five years, thousands of them, and for the first twenty-five of these years pretty much the same way, day in and day out, another small dose of the same old treatment for the same old issue, another what had become a sort of fast-food burger for another person who rushes by the window.

And never in that whole time had any of these people credited me with saving their lives, oh sure, they thank you, even praise you for helping them, but did I, did I really? Yet now I seem to hear that statement more and more frequently; "You saved my life" they feel better, no, they are better, their life, their real and blessed life had been saved! When nothing seemed to help, suddenly now they are better, when they had no hope, now they do. When they used to trust the lie, now they believe the truth. They have their life back, I guess maybe their life and my own really had been saved!

Now, this is a reward! This became my life, maybe for the first time in so many years', I am really living, doing something Good?

Who cares about losing the job, or a boss denying pay? Who cares about the institutions saying you are crazy or slandering you to their friends. Who cares about Cabalists taking you to court over and over again, lying, slandering, stealing, not caring what it will cost them only interested in hurting you, why because they can't stand what you stand for, no, more than that, because they can!

What greater reward could a man or woman feel than the realization they had helped another, maybe put their own life, their reputation, their pay, their field, at risk to help another, save another person their life? I don't think I could think of a greater compliment?

Didn't God Himself say; *"For there is no better gift a man can give than to lay down his life for another? For sure! Because I can truly say to you, if you do it for even one, even the smallest or most insignificant of one, you do it for Me!"*

I have no choice! I must tell everything to them. I am dying too!

No, I am living too!

Oh and one last thing:

Now that I have already died, I realize there is nothing anymore to fear!

In a world where fear seems to be everywhere, people staring through masks fearing the Bogyman which might be behind the mask, the realization that it is all just a lie, seems to drive fear away like a candle being lit in a dark room, darkness flees instantly!

"For I was once afraid, I now realize there is nothing more to fear!" Corona Virus? Why fear? It is really just a shadow on a wall.

Maybe that's why He said and continued to say so many times in the first place; *"Fear Not..."*

"Dear Lord; give me the strength to pass on the wisdom and share the experiences you have so graciously given me, without fear."

THE WHIRLWIND OF OUR LIVES

Subtle surprises of long gone horizons, the fleeting heartbeats of lovers sing by, their sonnets do sing, with scented melodies they bring, filling hearts that fly through the skies.

The whirlwind comes by and with it, a kaleidoscope of seeming ascension takes place for so many unwitting seemingly blessed, but in reality, cursed caterpillars as they are lifted skyward with what no doubt appears to be a treasure trove of leaves and other delectable spectaculars. What a majestic view this elevated status has suddenly provided so far above everyone else an almost godlike manifestation must occur as they know they are flying seemingly higher, loftier, and freer than those still anchored to the ground.

That might be true, but these caterpillars can't see, and little do they realize, but as they slowly make their descent back to the ground in which they came, the great winds that brought them there long gone unto other lands have left them to slowly drift down now clear targets for the more sinister predators of the heavenly realm. They would be Kings and Queens of the skies, but unless God Himself proclaims them so, they will really never truly be. Foolish caterpillars who dared think they could fly before God gave them wings to do so.

"We are all but whirlwinds in these but fleeting moments in time."

I have written in previous writings regarding the image of our soul (our entire life), being compared to a cork floating on an ocean, whereby the spiritual aspects of our life are not merely a drop in the ocean but the ocean entirely. For the sake of discussion regarding the topic of ascension, especially when it comes to health and wellness, another image may be more appropriate.

As we try to imagine how it may appear physically to ascend whether it be in the physicality of health, wellness, or our overall healthcare status, we must first examine what exactly we are ascending to? Ascension of any kind in this life must represent an act of physically looking up, and whether people want to believe it or not, looking up is, in essence, a quantum reflecting physical and metaphorical gesture to looking up to God.

There are plenty of examples in the Bible where people are being healed by Jesus, the Apostles, even profits of old, in every case these people had to look up, reach out, lift their heads away from their problems, or at least call out for something hoped for, even when exactly what was still in question.

For what were they looking for?

In most cases, these people had no idea what they were hoping to receive, as a matter of fact, for the many they had been told their entire lives that they had an affliction, permanent disabilities or otherwise, diseases being incurable, born with or acquired by misfortune, either way, there was nothing that could be done? The overall conscious perspective among the afflicted, then and today is, for the most part, they feel they had either done something to deserve it, or they were being cursed because of something that happened with them or in their family in the past. I cannot tell you how many times I heard people say, even when they about to receive therapeutic advice, "You have no idea what I have done, but it is for these reasons I have this affliction."

But the truth of the matter with the "Healing" experience there is in each case a physical shift of awareness from the earthly, or in the case of the examples stated, from the affliction they were suffering from to upward-directed attention, to a more spiritual belief-based expectation of hope. Hope only found in something that cannot be seen, sometimes heard, occasionally understood, but most definitely believed in.

In the Biblical case of the father of an afflicted boy who throws himself to the ground or in the fire, with fits of what seems to be epilepsy, the poor man had the humble honesty to not only ask our Lord for the healing of his son but when Jesus responded; *"You merely have to believe,"* the man re-responded with his own doubting truth *"I believe, now help me with my unbelief?"* This is by far one of my favorite statements written in the Bible, I have on numerous occasions mumbled it in my own prayers.

Faith is not always the physical manifestation of belief, but often the hope for the ability to believe.

Belief is not the only prerequisite for healing or health, even though standing alone more can be accomplished with good old fashion belief than any other emotion, yet love, faith, trust, forgiveness, and wisdom are all healing instruments. Pretty much anything that is created by God can be used as an instrument of healing, and since all healing comes from God, and the matter on a quantum level is basically composed of the same base energies, then one must conclude that it is irrelevant what physical form the delivery system might find itself manifested if God desires a person receive "Healing energies" then those forces will manifest into the child receiving them regardless of the shapes or forms base energies find themselves along the way. All physical energies are merely the conduits for the transfer of healing energies from God to us?

Now in the case of the father of the son suffering from the seizures, he already was looking up, looking forward or towards something greater than himself, and certainly greater than the affliction that which plagued his son. It is for this reason, merely the statement of faith along with his own humble admission of his doubts, not only opened God's heart to heal the boy but also has inscribed the man story forever in the annals of Jesus's greatest works of the New

Testament.

But back to our example; looking up, at what? Well, Ascension is more of a looking up in attention or concentration onto more spiritual observations.

In my previous books, I described the comparison of the body, mind, and spirit to images that we have been presented our whole lives true and untrue. Making comparisons to the pyramid on the one-dollar bill, and in reality to an upside-down pyramid where the body is the smallest most insignificant point that touches the physical earth.

If we continue with a similar illustration, the mind in the many layers above the ground level the earth represents the infinite layers of memories of every physical stimulus this body has experienced in the past, present, and imagined or dreamed of in the future. Rising higher in visual awareness as the memories take on a more actual dreamy, creative, or visionary remembrance so do the expanding qualities of the visual vortex as it becomes an ever-expanding larger diameter of view, growing with the expanding size of this tornado-like image the person is experiencing in the whirlwind of his or hers life.

As the conscious awareness climbs into the spirit realm, it now possible with our widening conscious observation to take on a more infinite nature expanding upward and outward without limit like trying to fill the expanses of the sky into the infinite expanses of the stars.

As I stated above, in a different example I made a reference of our life is like that of a cork bobbing in an ocean; the cork being the physical body, and likewise every wave motion, day passing, water caressing its surface, fish nibbling on it or birds picking at it, every possible experience represent the mind and memories of this physical life.

The spirit on the other hand, how we feel about life, God, love, hate, what attracts us, or repels us, what we actually emotionally feel, every awareness that is the infinite spirit of or existence; this is the ocean. Now combine these all three and stretch it out to the end of time to create our everlasting soul.

While our spirit we may exist in the ocean, a drop spread out throughout the entire recesses of the ocean, being a part of the ocean, as we are part of God, we are not the whole ocean, we are only the smallest portion of the whole, and we certainly did not create the ocean, we merely have the pleasure of dwelling in it and our own splendor. We did not create it any more than we can control it, but we do reside in it.

For the purpose of this book, and to illustrate the actual aspects of ascension in health, I am going to use an illustration of mind, body, and spirit as a great whirl-wind or tornado.

Imagine a whirlwind of immense intensity defined by the spinning motions of its wind vortexes, expanding upwards at first narrow and clearly defined, like witnessing a slender but powerful tornado far off in the countryside. One can almost make out the ribs of wind as they spin around climbing ever so higher finally widening as they reach high into the sky. Once they reach the clouds they widen out almost to infinity across the clouds and sky.

The point in which the whirlwind tornado touches the ground, this is the point of greatest physical effect on the earth itself, where the most damage on the physical ground can occur. From a distance it seems like a small sharp point but the greater the pressure of the twirling motions, the greater the force being inflicted by the whirlwind itself and the greater the impact on the surroundings. A great deal of stress and tension has the most destructive effect its presence has on the immediate surroundings especially on other living things.

When people are busy with their lives, jobs, busy acquiring the sand in the sandbox they happen to be playing in, when they cannot take their eyes or attention off the issue in their life even if it is a simple sore little toe, their whole life becomes that little toe, defined, fixated and extremely narrow-minded. This concentration on the ground coupled with intense mental activity and emotional velocity usually has a destructive or at least damaging effect on the matter they concentrating on.

I have a great deal of experience with this ill-placed focus anomaly, especially in the affliction arena, people who are suffering from issues that have them grounded to the world, and as a result, they cannot hear anything except talk about their issue. They only see the smallest of issues they are suffering from, and are almost oblivious to what is happening around them. Any discussion or concern except their issue is completely out of their awareness, they have no life except their issue, their issue encompasses everything they are busy with day in and day out. They become completely enslaved by their affliction.

A person doesn't have to be suffering from an injury to be a slave to the smallest of worldly concerns, of course, pain issues have their own influences on our attention, and I will talk about the symptom of pain later in this book, but almost any earthly concern when fixated on or even idolized not only has a destructive effect on us physically but on all of our surroundings. I have known more than one fanatic business person that due to greed and the narrow-minded fixation on money, has literally watch their entire life pass them by, including families, significant moments, and all possible good things God has blessed them with only because they couldn't take their eye off of zeros in a bank account.

Again, what happens when in nature concentration of the vortex is a sharp, powerful, and high-pressured place, it is like taking a simple garden hose volume of water and spraying it through a very small and sharp opening, the resulting increase of concentrated force can cut paint right off the surface of the house. Nothing good results when people get this way in their life, they are so focused on earthly things that literally the sky of blessing can float by and they see nothing but their little toe. Even the smallest most insignificant injuries become great fearful giants that dominate their lives.

"Yesterday's plowed gardens are tomorrow's forgotten grassy fields." Many a man has wasted years of good work and faithful planting just to lose all to the weeds of neglect all because he had his eye fixed on a single little thing in his life.

When we are concentrating down into our bodies at one single thing, vexed, controlled by it, enslaved to it, fearful to take our eyes off, almost idolizing it as a controlling deity in our lives, it really does at that point take control of us. Our attention is so fixated on the earthly speck we hardly notice what is going on around us, through the day that pass by like leaves in a flooded flowing river.

Ascension in Health, Wellness, and Healthcare is lifting the attention away from the ground and moving it up the vortex into the sky.

Moving up the ascension vortex has a resulting effect of opening up one's mind to greater realizations; this can be accomplished simply by meditating, creating with art or writing, cooking, praying, relaxing while watching a child play, or as simple as gardening, even raising chickens, any wholesome activity can all have a Godly inspirational effect on a person's health and wellbeing opening the individual mind to a download of healing.

But to have an almost miraculous effect on the healing process a person has to delve into the spiritual realm in order to open up one's mind and focus enough to download the wisdom God provides everyone who asks.

"We have not because we ask not." This statement stands out throughout the whole Bible as a challenge placed to us by God to merely ask and we can receive. Since one of the promises of God is that He keeps all of His promises it can be assumed this one is also definite. So is it in health and wellness?

Since belief reigns in the realm of the spiritual, when we place our beliefs into the venue of spiritual heavenly places, the resulting manifestations especially in the health arena comes to be. We, in essence, get out of the way and allow our God-created bodies to heal themselves.

In the spiritual community these days, there is a great deal of talk regarding the activation of presently unused DNA within us. Whether a person believes an activation is accomplished on a purely spiritual level or a physical reaction to some kind of physical stimulant such as light rays emanating from the center of the universe to activate our dormant DNA, the result is the same; God created this physical universe, and likewise has in His infinite mercy seen fit to provide a means in which we all can rise to a higher state of conscious awareness if we are willing to lookup?

"If you but believe as small a mustard seed, you can command this mountain to pick up and be tossed into the sea..." Jesus Himself said this. If having belief as real as the smallest of physical seeds can do such massive physical potentials, imagine still the incredible effects in the spiritual infinite sky such belief can have?

Belief is necessary for people to understand that the majority of the things they have been told their whole life regarding their health or healthcare, much of which was based on control, manipulations for monetary gains, and lies. Our whole society especially from the standpoint of health "assurance" seems to be shrouded in mystery, confusion, and a need-to-know basis, basically they let us know when they decide we need-to-know. This separation of understanding has really only one effect and that is too illicit fear?

Belief in the standpoint of Ascension of Health is necessary for people to understand that the cause of the issues they suffer comes not from within them, but comes from outside and attacks them. If they are willing to just consider this concept it makes it possible to consider a posture of resistance, they are willing to believe they can

49

fight, and maybe even drive the darkness away merely by turning on the light.

I don't believe it is a coincidence that the media, over the recent ten or so years, has been drilling us increasingly with propaganda statements and images that speak of the permanent nature of illnesses, how they are somehow in us, waiting like time bombs to attack from within, or genetic imperfections we all have somehow as if we were created with these flaws? Seems to fall right into the narrative that we are really not loved by God but merely forgotten, discarded, and alone. Ascension is the realization of truths and the revelation of the lies we have been fed.

Belief is necessary for people to understand they are not doomed because man has told them it is so, God has control of life and death, not men. God is in control of every aspect of life and death from the climate in the case of storms, or droughts, to plagues and whether people shall suffer or not. Over the course of centuries nations and peoples who followed God flourished and had happy lives, and while they may have been oppressed by evil men they still experienced love, and light, and health even in the direst of situations. On the contrary when nations chose evil and worshiped demonic spirits plagues, droughts, and worse would befall them.

Belief is necessary for people to understand they have much more control over their own wellbeing and health than they have been brainwashed to believe. Miracle and cures are all around us, but we must believe in the promises of God and not the dark lack of chances we have been given by doubters or worse evil men who would merely wish to control us and enslave us.

And lastly, belief is the gateway to true Ascension whereby revelations in many dimensions reside. Like the stars in the sky of the infinite images in the clouds, it is in the vast discovery of the unknowns of that which God has created and we have only yet to realize can we turn imagination into something we can view "Real" with our "Eyes" and "Realize!"

By Peter Colla

SOCIAL ASCENSION

In the life of a blind caterpillar sometimes the grade of ascension, or descending for that matter, when at first appearance seems to be a dramatic change in elevation, such whimsical notions are often dismissed by the other caterpillars as merely whimsical even fantastical thinking, one can't help but wonder if soft reported secrets or legends of vast spirit-filled kingdoms in the sky may actually be true.

To suddenly have enough money where a person would not have to worry about bills or the need to slave for it day in and day out, as they progress ever closer to that inevitable day where they don't need it any longer, most would say this might represent retiring, others hitting the lottery, for a more dreaming few "contentment" with what they have, some call it "arriving," and probably for most "Heaven?"

As strange as it may seem, every person I have ever known who appeared to have "arrived" financially, seemed to share one common issue; they were afraid they would lose what they have to others who lacked.

But if everyone all over the world would suddenly and spontaneously receive a large sum of money, or let us say unlimited free energy, or even their fair portion of the gold that has been stolen and hoarded from all of us, from our parents for centuries, by the self-proclaimed ruling class, the idea of money or at least the dire need to scratch it together out of nothing would cease to exist.

It has recently come into public awareness over the course of the last twenty or thirty years, especially after the broad access of the internet and the sharing of information, the control a few elite families have not only over the finances of America but literally over all the major companies, banks, more sinisterly the syndicated crime over the entire world. The words; Deep State, Illuminati, Pizza Gate, adrenochrome, even witchcraft, have become more of a fact verified realities than media-driven conspiracy theories regarding many of these topics, leading many simple researchers to believe that these allocations may actually be true regarding the desire of these parties to enslave all of us, siphon off the produced wealth, and perhaps reduce the population to a fraction of what it is today, creating, in essence, a smaller more manageable working society that they can control, and use to sustain them.

A simple example recently surfaced out of the courts of Africa demonstrating that these families have managed to withdrawal 99.99% of all the wealth the continent produced only allowing the remaining .01% to circulate thus causing the entire continent to linger in poverty while being fleeced of its produced wealth for the past few centuries.

It is easy to imagine this scenario if we were to imagine the entire US and Africa merely as a large farming states and then yearly out of America 80% is removed from the crops leaving the remaining 20% for the rest of the people to survive on. So in America, there is still enough crops re-circulated so at least some people can prosper, the majority must work their entire lives to just survive, but of course in Africa that number is only .01% so those poor unfortunates live in poverty pretty much over the entire continent, even though they have by far the greatest natural resources and have produced the largest quantities of exported precious metals dwarfing the rest of the world combined.

If this wealth was merely removed, sold, and re-circulated, products would be purchased, social structures would develop ultimately providing jobs, success, and benefit for all, much like in the early annals of our own history, when a town or community discovered and harvested resources everyone seemed to prosper. But that is no longer the case. Since the industrial age, the amount of production, mining, farming, and harvesting has all steadily increased yet the costs of merely living have steadily increased as well. Taxes, insurance, energy costs, interest upon interests, medical, communications, everything while becoming easier technologically, has reduced the entire population into what appears at least in the US and other so-called developed countries into slave state that works their entire life merely to pay for their home, education and the vehicle they transport themselves in. Ever running like a gerbils on a wheel until they either wear themselves out or fall off sick, in both cases to be shelved away and labeled "No longer useful to society."

Did God put us on this earth merely to produce wealth for the few banker and gangsters who think because they print the money we use they somehow own everything?

We are taught our whole lives "Dog Eat Dog", "Only the Strong Survive", go to school, strive to accomplish, push for that ultimate goal that never quite seems to come within our grasp, ever running down the race track of desire, accumulate, and envy. Little do we know it is merely the prison, my prisoner patient so eloquently described, mentioned in the earlier chapter, where we are placed almost from the moment of our first thought in the "system," onto the wheel when we are barely old enough to understand, already running like the poor gerbil where the only way to finally stop is either fall off the wheel or wear out and die. Any attempts to stop or look for a different direction other than the wheel is met with fierce opposition from all the other gerbils running in the matrix wheels next to you.

Isn't a better system "Help Each Other" in the best way we are each created to, each with our own God-given talents and desires?

While school used to only be places of higher learning, since about the onset of the industrial age they too began to push the competing against each other agenda, always strive to be the best, "The Top." Sure, you can help others, this is even encouraged but always along with precise and directed guidelines that agree with the established system in place, sharing and brotherhood in sports was encapsulated even in the educational programs, military, or simple friendly competition. But again we are always brainwashed to not share too much, you don't want to give your advantage away.

If we suddenly all of us had everything we needed; "monetarily speaking" there would no longer be any need for this endless "gerbil in a wheel" run we all seem to be pursuing day in and day out throughout our whole life. Maybe instead of chasing what we seem to feel is our "job," the social assignment we have been given, whether by our parents, the educational society, or the system regardless of who we may be, we might pursue something we are called to, designed by a higher calling by, or Heaven forbid love to?

The ascending realization we would suddenly choose to do perform, create or assist others in the way we have been designed specifically by God, whereby we could find all of us our own specific callings, unique to us, our own specific gifts to everyone around us, the very thing we love to do, does sound quite Heavenly. I was always philosophically told if people did what they loved, they would always do their absolute best, regardless of the pay, because the reward of knowing they are doing what they love is life satisfying reward in itself.

What would that look like? Maybe an "Ascension of Sorts"? Maybe this NESARA/GESARA thing they have been talking about for so many decades?

Critics might call this communism? Everyone has all the money they need why would anyone need to work? Who would drive the busses, plow the farms, or do the dirty work?

Communism is not everybody seeking to contribute, each in the best capacity or specific talents as they can, no, it is an un-Godly system that denies individuality and places everyone into a serf-like service ideology. Since everyone is considered the same, there is no individuality, people are merely placed into their slots to fulfill their functions to serve the whole. That whole being the few that rule the system, the few chosen ones who tell the many others how they must perform, think, and act. Kind of like what they are trying to do today.

That's why the Masks are used in witchcraft? They are used to block or restrict any verbal contamination from individuals participants in the spells or rituals they are performing.

Unlike Communism, unilateral freedom from monetary enslavement would mean people would have now the opportunity to seek out functions that they feel they truly are called to do, instead of being forced to do through social pressures or fear they can't pay their bills, feed, or house their children.

There will still be people who love to farm, fish, build things, or take pleasure in recycling things, create things, helping others, teaching others. There will be people who enjoy flying, and driving, wishing to do it because it what they love. But the difference is in such a society the majority of the wealth will not be siphoned off and hoarded away by the extremely evil few.

I had a run-in with a Cabalist earlier in my life, a man who had more money than he could spend in many lifetimes. When I found him openly trying to steal my precious lamb from me, what seemed ridiculous since he could buy thousand without a blink of an eye, it was a shock? His desire to take from me the most ridiculous small thing and for him the most inexpensive item, I asked him one day; "Why do you want my lamb when you already have so many and could buy as many as you want."

With the smile of a devil, he looked at me and said; "It's not that I want your lamb, I just don't want you to have it!" "Oh, by the way, I am going to take it from you because I can!"

These people don't hoard the world's mountains gold, hidden artworks, gems, or money because they want to spend them or even sit and look at them, they steal them and bury them in a jar so the other people of the world won't have them.

This is exactly the same greed and evil Satan has for all of us, it makes no difference God the father gave this blessed world for all of us to enjoy, some truly evil spirits would take everything that is good or a blessing from us because they don't want the rest of us to have it.

In small personal relationships, Ascended Relationships, like Godly marriages when two people allow each other to really seek out what they truly desire to do, be who they wish to be, or aspire to accomplish what they feel they were called to do, and they help each other accomplish this; this by most peoples observation results in perfect partnerships. These relationships, though few and far between, are often extremely successful, full of happiness, love, and joy, such individuals "Ascending Pairs" in their relationship to the for-betterment of each other, and thus the resulting improvement of their partnership as a whole. We see this example naturally with soul-mates or best friends, where both would much rather see the other succeed than themselves.

When this cooperating desire to see each other succeed translates to an entire group such as close relatives or groups of cooperating friends this becomes a whole Ascending Family.

Groups of families or small cooperating entities, shops, like business entities such as health care providers, or fishing boat communities, can work together for each other's growth, this is a "Small Ascending Village." In days of old small villages, people all helped each other, each in their own capacity as they blossomed through life and overcame whatever hardships happen to present itself together. They even came together and built homes for the newlyweds perhaps in a single weekend, giving them a blessed beginning along a path that painted a picture of prosperity, love, cooperation, and unity.

Various Villages help each other and these become towns or "Ascended Townships". Towns combine into entire communities whether they became cities or counties, which they themselves Ascended into Larger Ascended Communities.

Finally resulting in entire States that help each other in their own States, multiple States, and even Countries each striving to lift every member of its own community to the capacity of each of its member's abilities.

How wonderful would that be if countries could suddenly cooperate with each other as best as could be, each in their own capacity to grow? I think we would finally have harmony, like a concert of musical instruments of an entire planet's Ascending melody, as we all strive to the next crescendo level of awareness.

By Peter Colla

PEACE, ASCENSION, & THE PLANDEMIC

As with all things these days seem to be evolving into pictures, no scratch that, masterpieces of creative beauty only possible through the direct hand strokes of God Himself, I find myself seeing more and more the absolute creative nature of God in every single day unfolding.

What does the very act of Ascension look like, or more importantly can we feel it? Perhaps not much different then a grand root of a seemingly large and ageless tree drawing up into the heavens as if preordained into some almost Godly destination or pre-destined appointment, brings with it a sudden and hopeful mere physical ascension, an unfolding that there may be more to this world than the basic three dimensions presented before us?

Now how could anyone in their right mind possibly make that statement in light of the COVID-19 or Coronavirus attack, with its resulting worldwide pandemic effect, or in other words, how could anyone possibly look at this and apply the single simple Biblical truth that; "God can turn all storms to good if we but look to Him?"

Well, I can sight at least one example my beautiful wife noticed almost from the very first day the shutdown took place in our home in Phoenix.

In Phoenix, almost exactly to the day our great President Donald Trump ordered the flight restrictions from Europe and other places known to be afflicted with the virus, as well as advised people simply to begin to stay at home from schools or start "self quarantining measures" it began to rain in Phoenix. This too, seemed for us to be a miracle considering she had returned merely the day before the shutdown from overseas caring for her father, only just one of the many people suffering from the medical system's withdrawal from care based purely on the lies being spread regarding COVID, infection rates, busy hospitals, and false images of people dying in the streets?

Peace, just as life and death, healing, or any of the infinite gifts that only come from God, seemed to be increasingly clear to anybody looking, where exactly it originates and more importantly by Who?

The rain itself, is not by most people considered a blessing, but for us dessert dwellers in Phoenix, rains are usually looked upon as blessings from God being we sit in a dry arid climate, most of the time doing without if for the majority of the days of the year. This particular year we have, although, had quite a nice share of consistent rainfall that has as a result turned the normal late winter desert into an "early spring" of blossoming green.

One might call that a blessing, and I am sure it is, but that is not the

"Blessing" I am talking about in connection with the Corona Pandemic, "Plandemic" or "Scamdemic," as many are already beginning to refer to it.

What I am talking about, and what my wife noticed almost the first day of the shutdown was a sort of "Quietness" that has suddenly and most distinctively touched the Earth. A sort of stillness or even a degree of "Peace" which has suddenly, yet most distinguishably, been added to the mix.

As we looked around our garden, we noticed almost overnight an immediate blooming of almost all of the plants, many of which we had no idea they might even begin to blossom, and certainly not this early in the year. Plants suddenly growing adding inches in only days, buds, or leaves, where dryness or dormant plants reside merely days before.

"When did all these butterflies suddenly appear, and where did they come from, flying too and near,"

"A dance of vivid ballerinas flowing shades of daffodils, peace and joy the beats they drum, kiss whispered hearts so still."

Now to be honest we do have a particularly unique garden for Phoenix Arizona, my wife being of European origin, and us both loving Tuscany Italy, have to a degree mimicked our own garden more towards the "Tuscan look," creating an image one would hardly ever expect possible in the rural neighborhoods of the Phoenix desert. Our yard is grass, with trees not exactly indicative of the region; Oak, Elm, Olive Trees, Nuts, and Fruits, even Papaya and Guava, some of which usually don't weather well the cold and when they do come back have to sprout nearly from the root to return, but that's not the case this year?

Many people have told us we have a bit of a "Magical Garden" or what I like to "God's Garden of Healing," but that too is mostly due to the fact that my wife would pray for the water when she watered the trees, and even at times quietly speaks to the vegetables and plants as she cares for them. She even sliced up one of her favorite tomato's last year and planted it in the flower bed next to our pool, from that single tomato we had the whole flower bed full of tomato vines along the side, even dangling into the salted waters of the pool. The kids would pick and eat them while they swam, many people said they were the most delicious tomatoes they had ever tasted. I believe that it was God's simple answer to my wife's prayers when she blessed the water, a subject we will go into depth later.

Like I said, we almost immediately began to see a rapid and complete blossoming of our garden from the very moment that first the days rain of the shutdown came, even the tomato plant started blooming again! Is it possible the very prayers she spoke somehow assimilated into the energies of the garden on a quantum level precipitating a much more fertile gardening result?

The fact of the matter was the world seemed almost immediately to have become "Quieter," the air seemed fresher, cleaner, and yes that always the case after the rain, but this was different, there was an undeniable fresher smell in the air, and a cleaner quieter feeling to everything around? Perhaps on the quantum level, a message of God's peace was also resonating throughout all the land?

The very next day my wife looking around the garden in the now clearing sky, as the rain subsided, noticed there seemed to be less traffic noise and no sounds of airplane rumbling at all in the skies? And while I knew that the President had ordered restrictions from Europe, I was not aware that reductions of any domestic flights had taken place yet. I looked up myself and couldn't see any signs of flights of any kind in the air.

She was right the world had seemed to be cleaner and quieter? Or maybe we had just stopped, looked around, and quietly noticed the "Peace" for the first time?

We, like others, began to find things to do at home, now that we would be spending more time here? For us, thinking about what to do meant deciding what we would have to get today at the store for dinner or perhaps call our family back in Europe to see how they were doing in these newfound restrictions?

For me, this means having a quiet call with my Mentor in Pagosa Springs Peter Laue, the godliest man I know and a man who has intimate experience in Godly Ascension, plus, who happens to live in one of the Godliest places on Earth. Seeing how things are going there, possibly report what we have seen here, especially the newfound quietness that we seem to have suddenly seen, these reports seem to take on so much more relevance as the attention was taken off of the Earth and lifted towards the skies into the heavenly places of Awareness.

I was amazed to hear he too had seen the almost exact experience there in Colorado and was curiously aware of almost to the moment we were. Now granted Pagosa Springs is high up in the Colorado mountain's and Peter's house on the lake is always peaceful, but he too had to admit something had seemed to have changed, and God has, certainly, ushered in a most undeniable portion of "Peacefulness" into the world, and with all the reported turmoil, how could this be?

Even as we spoke, Peter notices something moving just outside his window? He gets up and looks, he sees what looks like an ear moving, sitting there right next to his house was a deer, just laying there, resting looking at him. I asked him; "have you ever had one lay so close to the house?"

"Never, in all the years has one laid so close to the house, or laid down for that matter in his yard." He said with such excitement. I asked him to take a picture, but unfortunately not having a cell phone he couldn't take a picture. "That's ok, we would just have to enjoy the moment together over the phone." Luckily, a woman came to the house after our call, who had a cell phone, and was able to take a picture that I later posted on my blog describing this event.

Luckily for all of us the friend came over a couple hours later and was able to take a picture, which he sent me because just like in all miracles of God, there were still layers of the onion that could be pealed. When I showed it to my wife Anna, she immediately reacted; "That's a miracle, look there are no signs of tracks to where the deer is laying? It looks like it just appeared there when you were talking. I believe it's a miracle. God's Peace!" I later verified the tracks should have been there finding out from Peter it hadn't snowed since the day before, and there was no way the animal would have gotten there without leaving tracks.

Later that same day I went to the store and I must say I was shocked to see the immediate result at the stores, as people began to clear the shelves from what they clearly seemed to be necessities such as toilet paper, hand sanitizers, and bread, but nothing else?

I remember thinking to myself how stupid could people be? I don't know how much bread a person can store in their freezer, but I certainly could not keep more than a couple loaves for a few days without it getting stale? But hotdog and hamburger buns being suddenly gone, that is just crazy! And toilet paper; how much of a life necessity is wiping your butt if and when food suddenly disappears from the shelves?

But God is always faithful to provide.

An almost Godly occurrence; our good friends Karen and Lukasz only just visited us a few weeks earlier, and Lukasz presented us a homemade bread he had baked himself at home. My wife being from Europe has on more than one occasion sent me on a quest to find a truly good loaf of sourdough locally that can come close to the ones she would get daily from local small bakers in Amsterdam. This for me meant at times I needed to make that thirty-plus mile round trip drive to one of the few remaining private Bakeries to get something decent.

But when we got to taste Lukasz's bread, and he told us the recipe was simple, something you can make the same day in your own home with simple ingredients, I asked him to send me the instructions. So why not try it now in light of the great American hamburger and hotdog bun shortage, gather the necessary ingredients to try myself?

Needless to say, I wasn't the first to think of it, because flour and more importantly yeast seemed to be in short supply, but luckily there was still a few sacks of flour and a couple of packets of yeast still on the shelf amid the great toilet paper crisis day!

I was amazed, not that I could make bread at home, but at my wife's reaction as she stated that my bread actually tasted better than any bread she had thus far tried here in the States, including our corporate private bakery. This merely prompted me to make another loaf every day, trying slightly different strategies, each on the quest for the "perfect loaf?" Seeking for myself how long to let the dough rise, or whether to try my own starter instead of dry yeast, refrigeration time, whether or not to knead the dough, even down to the size, shape, and metal of the pan to cook it in?

All those years of practicing medicine, college, studying physical therapy overseas, needing to learn a foreign language that I, at the time, could not speak, treating so many people in my own private practice, like everyone else that really practices learning as I go, yet when my wife looked at me with that smile and said; "You've become a baker," I have to admit I had a real sense of accomplishment that overwhelmed me in ways I have rarely felt perhaps for years?

A feeling of "Peace!"

Maybe it is the finding of simpler joys, one may find now that a person has to spend more time at home, gardening, or making their own bread? The blessing of cleaning your own pool, cutting your own grass, making your own bread?

Maybe it's not just noticing everybody is suddenly looking at you in the stores as you walk by, wondering perhaps if you have flu symptoms, but taking a moment to actually notice each other as we walk by?

I made bread from a two-dollar sack of flour and a little yeast? One sack makes at least five loaves, fifty cents, and my wife has stated they taste better than any she has ever had. Almost makes me want to make a few and give them away? I guess that's why the Amish call it "Friendship Bread?" One thing is for sure, I will be making my own from now on!

Sure there are fewer people driving to school, to work, or flying, but enough that immediately the air seems cleaner, the Papaya suddenly blossoms, or deer suddenly start laying next to houses? Green New Deal? God can do in an instant what politicians would pay billions to try and never come close to.

We even decided to get a few chicks and try the chicken coop thing, my wife does love her eggs each day. Our nine-year-old daughter already seems to be having so much fun with the whole chicken, eggs, and feeding regiment. When did 4-H stop being a course or club you could take at school, I think it used to be offered, I can't remember that far back?

I think people, in general, are getting a taste of slowing down, simplifying their lives, stepping away from the "Rat Race," and at least this guy is wondering do I really miss any of it? Do I even want to go back?

This Coronavirus, many people believe it was a biological weapon, some believed it is maybe a plague, one thing was clear it already had a devastating effect on our economy, affected and even killed many, perhaps many thousands all over the world, people who perhaps wouldn't have died if they had been treated differently or perhaps would not have been locked down, locked away. Plus how is it possible that nobody is dying of the flu anymore, old age, or other issues that seem to take the same amount of people worldwide? Everyone is dying only of COVID? But if statistics are right and there are fewer deaths worldwide, then maybe COVID cured the rest?

How could God possibly turn such a devastating occurrence, attack, whether constructed by our own hands or not, into something good?

Maybe by slowing down the world, injecting Peace, we actually are finding simpler more significant creative moments in each day of our lives. We wanted climate change, maybe God said; "Let me show you who really is in charge of the climate," and with a simple stroke of

His majestic brush and a little help from our truly inspirational President, He cleaned everything up, quieted everything down, and brought people all over the world into a more illuminated light of pure godly truth. At least they started noticing each other.

They wanted epidemic, panic, and fear, but all they got was more and more people seeing the lies and beginning to ask why; the result, the Ascension to the truth. Ascending thought equals slowing down and seeing life, instead of looking at the dirt and watching it pass you by.

A SINGLE STEP IN ASCENSION

Considering the need for ascending especially when it is in conjunction with health or healthcare, one must realize a change of a person's perspective, or at least their concentrated attention, must move towards the spiritual end of the spectrum if they wish to receive a spiritual effect from the heavenly realm. In other words, they must turn their attention towards the heavens from the problems of our daily lives.

What I mean by this is; as a person concentrates on more basic things such as the needs of the world, especially health care concerns, little or nothing that takes place around them is registered in any way? We will continue to use for the purpose of this illustration their own "sore little toe." I have seen this particular issue manifest itself in patients especially when they are having acute symptoms and/or are under direct spiritual attack. They have one small physical problem in size compared to their own total body size, which may or may not have a devastating effect on their whole life, yet they seem to concentrate on this small lump of rebellious tissue allowing those oh-so small and few cells to dominate their entire being.

As a person concentrates continuously on the "sore little toe" it is difficult if not impossible for the same person to place their eyes, let alone their attention, on anything else. No need to talk to the same person about anything even remotely spiritual, they will absolutely not hear you. Any conversations, happening, or good report that has anything to say other than regarding the absolute mind-boggling importance of the "little toe" flies right over their head completely unnoticed like some orbiting satellite up in the bright day sky.

With these people, it is of utmost importance to remove their attention, even if it is for a moment, from the all-encompassing "little toe" that has dominated their whole life or soul (the same thing, by the way). But of course taking steps in spiritual ascension is the most important, and absolute if there is any chance for the person to obtain spiritual healing. We see this manifested in real-time these days as the social, pandemic, electoral, and just about every other kind of concern is bombarded at us repeatedly through the media. Hollywood, social media, even our educational system, all regurgitate horror stories and doom that seem to have only one purpose and that is to place us all in fear and lock our eyes firmly to the ground, which by the way is being repeatedly displayed by the TV.

Two thousand years ago, prophesies foretold of salvation from our sins those we ourselves facilitated and many others perpetrated against us, how many people knew the signs of the times, yet ignored the same signs when deliverance showed up. A man appeared and it was reported that if all the miracles he did in only the three and a half year time span he brought the healings were documented, they would have filled every book that had even been written. Yet how many people didn't bother to even lift their heads as Our Lord walked by, missing out on the very healing only steps from their grasp?

Today in this time of reported worldwide turmoil, fear, and persecution, especially towards the helpless and innocent children, one would think people would gladly lift their heads from their daily concerns of trivial contemplations and at least inquisitively consider the afflictions of so many fewer fortunate.

But I am seeing that for the most, a consideration that any of the issues or atrocities being realized, especially in the recesses of non-mainstream reporting when it goes against the flow of the murky river full of garbage they are being constantly fed from all directions, it is just easier for most to keep their heads down, or worse yet, buried in the sand, locked up in the box, at least turn a deaf ear to distant cries of the suffering?

Recently my wife who also has had such frustrations with a few friends who even refused to open articles and read for themselves documented proof of the issues being dealt with behind the reported scenes of the mainstream media puppet news. In her frustration, she asked; "How do we get these friends to see, when they even refuse to open their eyes?"

So I posed that question in my prayer meditations I make in the closing or opening moments of any particular day. And as clear as if someone was speaking next to me I hear this sweet voice say;

"You want help someone to start Ascending you don't start by showing them the whole stairway up the mountain, but merely present them with the first step, a single step only, and if they take it they will themselves come to the realization that everything they have been told around that step is a lie. This is the first step of Ascension."

"Start with a simple single fact, especially something they can identify with, a single small seed, they can plant in their thoughts, water by wrapping their arms around and blossom into realization. Let the true flowers of creation become real in their eyes."

When people start to truly realize they have been lied to about practically everything they have come to know to be true about media, government, financing, education, even religion, it is not the lie that lifts their consciousness but the quest behind the lie to discover the "Whose," "Whys," and finally "What Else?"

Why did these people lie to us for so long about these small seemingly insignificant things, but just as important, who is behind the lie and why? When people start asking this for themselves it is then a small light is lit in that so dark cave they are living in. But again what happens when light enters a dark place; darkness must flee!

It is not our job to show people the whole picture at once, they can't take it. No, show them one small piece, a piece that relates to them, maybe that relates to their little toe? Once the light comes on, off they go into a world of investigation for themselves realizing more and more the great spiritual battle out there, how long it has going on, and how much, the oh so many things we have been deceived about?

Our President Donald Trump is not only the greatest president this world has ever seen, due for no other reason than the fact he has actually taken on evil itself and is trying, with God's help, to irradiate it from this world, or at least a large portion of its leaders and the vast superstructure evil has built on the backs of all of our family members for centuries. He is also an incredible genius, he sees himself that he cannot tell everyone everything he is doing all at once, for the same reason you never wake a sleepwalker, the shock and panic would be devastating to the many people asleep?

Sure for the people who have already ascended in their realization, we would love to see all the proof right away, arrests, warrants, picture, and even executions, but what about the so many people who have their heads stuck in the sand, or worse, the many millions or billions that are also good people but have been so deceived by these Deep State systems that lead and have infiltrated almost every aspect of our lives? The many people who really believe they are right even if they are being told to do something stupid like riot or hate for no reason?

They too are children of God, but merely misguided and deceived. If President Trump told them everything at once they would look at the mountain in front of them and would run the other direction or maybe want to die? No, God loves them too, and they need to convinced slowly and methodically, one step at a time.

The wonderful thing is with each in their own way light gets turned on, and in another small part of the universe it is as lighting a candle in a dark mine shape, the whole cave is lit up, darkness flees and there is a realization; there is no Boogie man merely a bunch of foolish lies, deception, and shadows that run like wet cats as soon as the light appears.

One other thing, just like any major reaction, there is plenty of kindling out there! After a while, enough people over the whole world will light up and at a critical moment when the mass exceeds the "threshold for combustion," an explosion of awakening will occur all occur the world? I talk about the "Threshold for Ascension Combustion" in my book Quantum Levels of Ascension in Healthcare, soon to be released.

I believe this threshold is actually happening as we speak! When this worldwide combustion occurs there will be no place for darkness to flee and it will have to leave the planet for good.

So for all of you people out there who have already taken the "Red-

Pill," don't worry about telling others about the whole enchilada, concentrate on one single fact, one that may touch them personally, help your brothers and sisters realize the truth hidden within one lie, embrace it and when they ask "why," tell them with a smile; "Why don't you go out and find that out for yourself?"

For the caterpillar who cant see the signs, barely has time between meals to investigate a truth or consider a development that might be right in front of his face, all she has is that subtle soft voice, not command her but gently nudging him, the chirping of a bird, or the warm sweet voice of another speaking encouragement instead of gloom, for we all know in this world of free will, and infinite choices, truth and the tender persuasions of a soul calling to touch our senses like the gentle breeze of a passing butterflies wing.

By Peter Colla

CRITICAL MASS REACTION

Why is it so important to get the message out there?

Not for monetary gain, or fame, hits, or simple "likes" on your channel, these are all vanity, it is important to get the message out for those who are looking. There is really only one reason why it is important to get the message out there and that is because that is how God wants it.

Why does God want us to spread the message, and why doesn't He just reveal it supernaturally himself? Anyone who has experienced the migration of caterpillars either from direct participation or by casual observation will attest that seemingly ordained by Glorious edict suddenly the entire massive migration takes place where the entire multi-pedal fuzzy-headed leaf eaters almost spontaneously decide almost in uncanny unison to venture upon a noble quest. Directions of said adventure at first seem to the casual observer haphazardly directed in every possible direction except together or with purpose.

But it is after repeated laying down of information, or casual bumping into and interacting with other adventurous companions that finally a seemingly victorious destination is determined first by few and yet later by the many, as the cross country and sometimes cross busy road pilgrimage changes from one of a moving ground-cover image to one that actually resembles the need to go in one direction and ultimately climb. Somewhere along the line enough of our illustrious ground-based carpet crawlers make the decision, take the step, lift tiny heads, and instead of just being satisfied with the flat steady ground, decide up into the heavenly realms an adventurous and heavenly bound quest is the only choice.

The reason for Ascension and healing for that matter is for us human's always; a result of free will. We are all participants in this world He has created for each and every one of us, we are all important, all of us those who need to hear what is going on, and every single person who has to make the decision to share the message of truth are all significant voices in our own private universes. We will see as we move forward that on a Quantum level the very energies we experience are influenced by the intentions of the mere words each of us speaks not only in our own limited local environments such as our bodies but absolutely throughout the entire known physical universe. This makes each of us, regardless of our station in life, significant.

The Rabi's, ancient Meester's of old who derived their knowledge not from certificates of paper, or a few moments in a classroom, but through experiences bought on the shoulders of long hours of study, combined with, most importantly, solitary reflection whereby they would describe each and every person in the world as a universe within themselves.

It is written in the Bible that God the Father cherishes each and every person's soul more than the combined total of the entire physical universe. Perhaps it is because on a quantum level the vast expanse of a single spirit or the soul of which it fractionally embodies is greater than the combined physical particles of the rest of the known universe? But that too is for another discussion later in the book.

The world, or the natural, demonstrates everything in the supernatural, this is how it has been throughout creation, this fact governs the natural laws that everyone can rest upon regardless of their sex, religion, or race. Scientists have continued to be baffled at the systematic and physical similarities microscopic structures have to vast galactic counterparts high up in the heavens, and how when the seemingly most unrelated structures are analyzed patterns emerge that defy any logical assumption of spontaneous formation. Basically, everything seems to have a perfect order to it, giving credence to the concept of God's creation and not a merely accidental occurrence.

Such universal laws such as light driving out darkness, or love always prevailing, or another one; God is always in control, there are so many and people have come to know them as truths in their hearts whether they want to believe them or not.

Let us for a moment examine one of these laws of nature and how it may apply to the geopolitical environment we find ourselves in today.

I often write about the applications of spiritualism or Godly belief in relation to health or healthcare, of which this text is specifically oriented to. Yet as with everything, compositions of all matter basically being formulated from the same rudimentary parts, and those structures merely variations of sound, lends the most credence to the statement; *"There will come a day when we are held accountable for our every word."*

For the sake of the more scientific observation, I am going to chair a discussion regarding what appears to be a slow revealing of facts regarding the many discrepancies we seem to be seeing, throughout our entire society whether it be in healthcare (my field), or politics, media, finance, even the foods we eat?

The question on the table; "Why, if they know there were falsehoods regarding any of these issues is it so slow for the whole story to get out?"

I believe the answer to this important question can be observed in nature and is clearly demonstrated by God with a simple explanation.

Answer;

The Natural Laws that govern Equilibrium, Catalysts, and Reactions.

For anyone who has studied chemistry or perhaps stayed awake in high school long enough to remember, in simple terms; when two reactants are brought together, they mix or blend together separate yet together, slowly combining until a threshold of reaction potential is reached. The chemist then introduces a catalyst, a small facilitator that when added will induce a reaction of the contents of the whole, this causes a chain reaction of activity and often then results in a total transformation of the whole into a new and more energetic product or result.

Basically, it is like mixing the basic parts of gunpowder; potassium nitrate, charcoal, and sulfur, all potentially flammable products but increase the heat in any part even slowly and eventually enough "boom," or when a threshold of heat is added to facilitate the reaction of the whole, a chain reaction occurs that cannot stop until all the reactants are exploded or ejected from the mass by the sheer force of the reaction. As a matter of fact, people have to even be careful when mixing it because aggressive movements can produce enough energy to facilitate the reaction aka the explosion before the spark is ever introduced.

In chemistry, the chemist will often bring the two reagents into close proximity mixing or in contact, then drop by drop the catalyst is added in order to get a uniform and complete reaction. Adding the catalyst too fast could cause a massive explosion, resulting in so much force that results in some of the products being ejected without having an opportunity to react.

Now let's look at what is going on today.

I think most people would agree that worldwide there seems to be a sort of polarization of thinking that seemed to start around the time President Trump took office. A strange phenomenon where it seemed while people in the past demonstrated more "on the fence" type attitude about things, then and now, more than ever, a sort of pressure was placed on everyone all over the world forcing them to choose which camp they wish to belong to. I believe this pressure was pressed upon people by God, forcing them off the fence, placing them into active reaction potential.

Sure, four years ago this seemed to be a simple choice whether you were a Trump supporter or not, but today it seems to be even more concentrating on a decision of; "Are you interested in truth or have you bought into the lies they the system have been feeding us for a millennium?"

We have without even knowing it created a volatile environment full of kindling where only the smallest amount of catalyst can be added and it results in a spontaneous reaction. Too much, too fast and the explosion could eject by the mere force of the reaction a great deal of unnecessary loss.

Lies, evil, and darkness as they become ever so much more evident, literally, everyone throughout the world has become aware that a not-so-secret evil faction is set on controlling and perhaps destroying us. If not, they are at least aware that these dark ruling classes are there and have reared their ugly heads from the recesses of their hiding like some black mold that suddenly may have appeared in the shower cracks.

The good news is the product or result of the reaction is "Awareness," call it "Ascension," 5D, growth, truth, it doesn't matter what you label it. When people get enough input of catalyst which is Truth, God, or goodness, the reaction worldwide is inevitable.

Every person in the world is important, and likewise so are all the souls that may have been deceived by all the lies throughout our entire society that are too important. Of course, there are truly evil people who have gone down a road of no return entering into practices that feed upon our very children, but like black holes of which I have written earlier, there is no hope for those.

Our genius President Trump knows this, and if he was to tell the masses too much, too fast, it could cause an explosion that while many already ascending individuals could react the right way, many others could burn up or be expelled out of their minds by the vast power of such revelations.

So the catalyst, the truths have to be added slowly, methodically, one drop at a time, allowing them to mix throughout the entire compound, taking time to assimilate into the whole, to guarantee we have a uniform and eventual critical reaction allowing for total ascension or reaction, leaving no parts behind.

President Trump, under the guiding Hands of God, some "Q"uantum-like wisdom, is dealing with an entire world, and End Times war not between men or countries but between good and evil.

Because the fight today is no longer between countries, religions, sexes, or even rich and poor but between good and evil our president is fighting for the souls of every single human being out there. Every soul is important, every soul significant.

As I said above; God the Father speaks clearly in the Bible about the fact that every single soul is precious to Him, as a matter of fact, He clearly says; He considers a single soul more important than the entire physical universe, so why would this be any different today?

I believe that our President is not only being led by God, inspired by God, and protected by God, but I also believe he is being enlightened by God with knowledge and Wisdom to bring about victory in this world to the point where so much evil will be reduced or illuminated for all to see, as well as so much goodness and the truth will be injected, that a catalytic reaction will occur throughout the entire world in which the entire human race will Ascend. When Darkness is Illuminated with light we already know what happens; "Adios Muchachos!" poof darkness runs like a scared white rabbit.

The fact of the matter is; we are also, each of us in our own small universes a part of the whole, like drops of water in the vast ocean, each of us has a responsibility to share what we have learned, spread the truths as they are revealed to us, be the light in our own private rooms. We are all called to be messengers of truth to our brothers and sisters. We are either dark places where shadows can hide, or we ourselves are illuminated beings that each in our own corners of the created universe light up our spaces giving darkness one less place to hide.

You never know when the "Critical Mass" will be reached, and just one final person will be enlightened, then a total worldwide awareness reaction will spontaneously occur and all of us will suddenly explode into "Ascended Awareness," "Upper Dimensional Thought," "Heavenly Existence," NESARA/GESARA, Total DNA switching on, carbon crystal transformation, call it what you will, it is all the same, they may all happen at once, the world will suddenly become a brighter place, and everything will become so Godly Good and clear.

By Peter Colla

WHY MASKS

Why masks one might say?

When you are born without eyes like the caterpillar is, and your whole world around you is based on perceptions without a clear image but merely sensed by the interactions of a list of unending seemingly similar bland meals, repeated time frames of warm and cold experiences, and the occasional scare as suddenly something out of nowhere picks at you, attacks you, or tries to destroy you. Even having such a small mouth dictates itself the uselessness of such a tiny voice, so why even bother to speak out even when injustice is so evident?

But voices do matter, otherwise, why would God give you one in the first place, and they certainly matter when speaking to other caterpillars who pass by of at least the few new revelations a young adventurer may have already witnessed.

We cannot fully understand the treachery and danger our society faces by submitting to wearing masks without first understanding the significance and history masks play in our society as a whole?

The wearing of masks until recently had not been implemented into the medical profession for the prevention of transmission of diseases, but merely to protect the operational participants from the splattering of blood. As a matter of fact, it has only found its way into the procedural apparel of medical treatments the last few years (pre-COVID), when dealing with diseases of unknown origin and or working in close proximity with the persons infected.

I myself know this fact because engaging as a provider of healthcare in the recent prior decades and literally only seeing the use of masks implemented when dealing with severe transmittable diseases where body fluids may be a possible contaminant such as Hepatitis or MRSA, left me puzzled at what has suddenly changed with disease transmission to warrant such widespread action? Prior to this recent anomaly, I worked in a medical testing lab handling some of the most dangerous pathogens in history including the Black Death, never having to wear a mask even though many were available, nobody ever caught anything or got sick.

While we are on the subject of viruses, we were taught in my earliest years of medical training that viruses are the smallest of organic compounds, so small they can barely be seen with the most powerful electron microscopes. And while I am not going to get into a discussion of theoretical virology, I will say we were taught for years viruses were unable to move, completely dependent on their infested host for temperature regulation, replication, and life itself, that is if you could qualify a simple organic compound an actually alive? These smallest of organic life-forms, if you can even call them that, are so susceptible to even the slightest change in temperature, that the fevers our own body produces, are the best naturally God-given mechanism to thwart infection, and is usually enough to rid us of these pests.

These small strains of merely replicable groups of molecules of proteins (viruses) are nothing more than small contaminants from the outside, brought into our cells either accidentally or with a purpose to initiate a reaction. For the most part, contaminant or if you will potentially attacking agents result in our bodies first trying to eradicate them by raising our temperature to a level that destroys them, and if this doesn't work, the body adapts further to improve its own resistance to fight them and others like them in the future, that is when the bodies resistance hasn't been compromised itself.

Television, our educational system, and more diabolical the entities that own and control the Big-Pharma, our insurance industries, even some of the governmental agencies who we pay supposedly to protect us, would paint a "giant" picture of fear surrounding the smallest and most insignificant of these biological structures known to man. Magnifying these small portion chains into an image that if we don't give up our freedoms, lock ourselves and our children away, deny ourselves even the most rudimentary social functions, basically all forms of interactions that generally make people happy such as smiling to each other, oh, and let's not forget to wear the mask, we are doomed to a horrible death. Yet the death counts didn't match the predictions, the contamination didn't even raise to the worldwide levels of the normal flue, and the preventions proved to be useless, yet the masks persist?

So again why the mask?

Perhaps we need to examine where the wearing of masks originated? While it is not exactly clear how far back the masks first appeared, it is clear that the earliest recorded applications of produced masks seem to have ties to both witchcraft rituals and the ancient slaves, perhaps both simultaneously.

In ancient Rome and before, slaves were a common household commodity, and it has been discovered through recorded depictions as well as physical excavated evidence that slaves were often masked especially when used in ritualistic sexual, entertainment, or sacrificial rites. What is interesting is that the masks do not inhibit the slaves' ability to see or hear, but the mouth is closed or non-existent basically restricting the slave's ability to express themselves in spoken words?

Slaves of the more recent American Pre-Emancipation Era were often masked again to restrict their ability to speak, and in severe cases, metal masks were used as a means of punishment pressing their tongues up against the roof of their mouths. And while the slaves of North America have the most historical accounts, slavery was in fact practiced uniformly around the world and perpetrated against almost all of the races.

That being said, there seemed to be an almost universal obsession with restricting a person's ability to speak. Why is this? Perhaps, could it be for the same reason the masks are being pushed on us today, to limit our ability to express ourselves?

One of the most famous masks ever used in conjunction with the practice of medicine is the famous "Beak Mask" which finds its origins as early as the 17th century where the mask was used by the physicians of the times in conjunction with treating "The Plague." While the mask was used when the doctors would visit the sick it was not for protection or even warding off spiritual darkness, but merely in the beak, the doctor would place herbs and scented ointments to mask the foul stench of rotting dead people who littered the areas the plague hit worst. This Beak mask then and forever was associated with evil medical spirits that searched for victims.

When we examine witchcraft, it would appear there are two main types of masks used, one; where the leader of the demonic rituals would wear a more ornate mask often in the image or depicting the demon entity the conjurer wished to invoke, this one seemed to have an open mouth? The spells, chants, incantations, or sacrificial rites all are accompanied by some kind of verbal chant often in what appears to be Latin or some other forgotten archaic language.

The second; one that seems to resemble the masks being pushed on us worldwide these days are the masks being worn by the other witches and warlocks around the incantation, they can watch and hear but for some seemingly dark rooted reason of control, they are forbidden to express anything verbally themselves. When a person checks out a site online to purchase witches masks, we find literally hundreds to choose from each being touted to be used in a particular incantation. They are either black or have various symbols printed on them as they seem to express the participants' silent, passive, and cooperative participation in the act they are trying to induce. So, while the mouths of people are being covered the intention behind the spells or the evil forces driving them can be proclaimed uninterrupted.

Could this possibly be the deeply hidden intention of the masks being pressed upon the whole world today? As I discussed in earlier writings the power in the spiritual is infinitely greater than the physical universe we see, feel, can hear, taste, or are aware of. The verbal expression has not only a dramatic effect on the quantum energy environment but may have through the intention or meaning of words added vibrational attributions people who wish to stifle or control may not wish manifested?

Is it possible the "powers to be" have a plan to bring the whole world under submission, enslave us, nullify our vote, stifle our ability to express ourselves especially with the spoken word, only to let their own media mouthpieces spew out the curses and programming they desire? In order to do this effectively, they must invoke worldwide spiritual incantations, and all of us must through our own unknowing participation wear a mask, quiet, and reject any spoken opinion to the contrary? Is this not exactly what has happened?

There is another part of wearing the mask that should be stated as to at least examine all aspects of such an act may have an effect on us, and that is the fear component.

Masks have for centuries also been tied to acts of terror. Worn by thieves, yes to hide facial features seems obvious, yet also in most cases to incite an immediate response of fear. Terrorists worldwide have been documented wearing masks even when they are training. Is it possible that fear may also be a factor in the plan?

But why would they want to incite fear worldwide? Could it be tied again to some worldwide spell of evil that means to have an effect likewise throughout the entire population? And if the world could Ascend by the mutual or critical mass reaction, then perhaps the mask may represent a world-wide buffer?

A buffer is simply an agent when brought into a solution facilitates a stifling effect on the potential reaction, so even when the catalyst is added no reaction is possible. In simple terms it's the pail of water thrown on the campfire wood, then try to light it; good luck!

It is the belief of this author that the majority of everything that happens to us throughout our lives, regardless if it has to do with our health, happiness, or state of being, has a momentary small physical aspect, a larger more permanent memory with its mind based aspect, and most importantly an almost infinite spiritual component.

If we align this same principle to the wearing of masks then it is important to examine the spiritual effect as being the most important one to consider.

Godly good spiritual emotions such as love, peace, compassion, healing, health, even light in a spiritual sense all have a positive effect on our wellbeing and have been scientifically proven to even improve our immune system and thus our resistance to diseases.

Yet on the other hand; depression, hate, chronic anger, and most importantly fear have a counter effect not only on us, our emotions, our very resistance, but on the world around us.

It has been proven scientifically the water has the ability to absorb, conduct and transfer emotions whether these be good or evil, I have written of this finding in earlier writings and will not delve into it here yet, except to say since we are ourselves the majority consisting of water, then as well such spiritual effects must have a likewise effect on us.

Acts of kindness, love, grace, a compliment, a good deed, a smile, not only have a positive effect on the person we are doing it to but have an equally positive effect on the equilibrium of the whole universe around us.

If, in contrast, the wearing of masks not only has an effect physically on the people wearing them but has the effect of radiating fear and terror into the entire world around us, we can then multiply it by the total number of people in the world wearing them, this has a potentially devastating global effect? I would say that it would have an almost satanic effect on the world as a whole.

But luckily we are also finding more and more individuals both in the medical community, as well as the communities of the world at large, awakening to the lies of such a masked proposal, the false reporting of the so-called pandemic numbers, the lies behind them, the dark agenda of potentially toxic vaccinations from certain evil individuals or agendas, and the overall evil of the people behind the profits that seem to benefit by this deep state this hoax brings.

The voice has always been the most powerful tool we have that has a direct effect on the spiritual world and thus on the world as a whole we live in. It is no different in the arena of Ascension of health and wellness.

One of the most effective mechanisms we have is speaking, or commanding our desires into space regarding our health. The realization that this is possible coupled with the knowledge that this concept has not only been created by God but established in the accounts of the Bible, of which I have written extensively in my past writings, demonstrates the effectiveness of commanding negative attacking spirits with specific statements that will have a positive effect on the body but more importantly the spiritual realm. Let us merely say for the sake of this Ascension process that speaking positively is essential for manifesting in the physical that which we desire. It is more than just positive attraction but manifesting reality through positive belief. It is "Belief" as a mustard seed that can move mountains.

Simple positive thinking, "Positive Attraction," while being promoted and heralded lately as advanced thinking mechanisms to produce in the real universe the desires being spoken, lack the connection and ascended focus into the realm of God, necessary for the creative manifestation for actuality to occur. What I mean to say is if a person doesn't consider God in their desires or spoken words they remove the most infinite portion of existence in our lives, if one wishes to create a better world, one much consider the Creator of the world to do so.

People have often asked; do I have to believe or honor God to receive His healings. I would simply answer by saying; if you receive His Truths, and Believe them True, then you Honor the giver.

We know all Truths come from God, recognizing any truths as true leads to the recognition of he who creates Truth.

One might say; where do unanswered prayers fit into this, or why does it appear that patience is needed to receive the positives we are asking for? The answer lies in the same supposition that I just spoke of above; God has a plan, and we must realize that sometimes with our limited minds we may not see the best path forward merely based on the desires of the present. In other words, some of the greatest opportunities in life are on the backs of prayers those of which were seemingly unanswered by God.

No amount of positive thinking alone can change or facilitate the removal of darkness, it is only by turning on the Light (God) to those areas of darkness that illumination and revelation can occur, and thus darkness ceases. Unfortunately, we must acknowledge the darkness, many people (so-called positive thinkers) would close their eyes or bury their heads in the sand thinking this is all they need to do to ascend into a higher vibrational state, ignore darkness or even deny its existence, yet they are frustrated that darkness continues in and around their lives. Sweeping the dirt under the carpet or locking the dirty secrets away in closets might seem like a temporary solution but have the long-lasting negative effect of dirtying our house and keeping our feet grounded firmly to the dirt.

With each person that awakens there is in their own small universe a light that is turned on to the truth. This light has the effect of driving the darkness away, leaving only the truth for each of these awakened people to exist, to then further investigate themselves and tell this truth to others is not only an opportunity, or pleasure, it is a responsibility. Light tips the scales of a world's equilibrium of dark places and islands of light combine to form many bright candles all around us streaming glorious colors and light energies illuminating the entire human race into its designed and planned Godly paradise of brilliant cascading symphonies.

Soon everyone in the world will be aware of the many lies that have been perpetrated against us for no other reason than to enslave us, devour or destroy us, more than we already are, and muffle us into submission. Lights will simultaneously turn on and darkness will have no place any longer to hide.

I guess underground darkness must go, or perhaps off-planet, but our home will no longer tolerate its lies.

QUANTUM DESCENSION

So as it is in the human experience, the same patterns of creation repeat themselves not only within the universe of our own existence but also in the greater cosmic universe. Micro, Meso, and Macro; extremely small those too small to see, our size visible to us in proportions, or infinitely large size those too large to be seen. All these structures seem to reflect within their base building parts patterns and similarities that appear to reflect a common matrix and certainly give credence to a common Creator demonstrating a uniform base structure, one that has universal rudimentary physical laws that govern them all.

Atoms in the micro resemble solar systems in the macro, clusters, and galaxies could be clusters of atoms which in their own associations form only recently discovered systems between stars perhaps throughout the entire known universe. Hurricanes resemble galaxies, sun rays are warming while the light of the moon cools, babies when first created smell perfect, and butterflies can flap their wings on this side of the planet while causing a hurricane thousands of miles away. The perplexities of this majestic creation are nearly as unfathomable as it is remarkable.

Nowhere is this ever so evident as in the hypothesis and description of the anomaly of a Black Hole. As we have discussed in earlier

105

writings the distances between the actual physical particles, at least those we can physically detect and measure are vast compared to their relative size, leaving science with the realization that the majority of space even within our own physical bodies is for the most part empty space.

Without getting into too much of the actual astrophysical description of a stellar black hole, it is commonly believed and taught that when a star of much greater density than our own sun burns up a key part of its available fuel, a resulting collapse upon itself can occur when by its own sheer gravitational density the sheer weight of this accumulation surpasses the ability of the star to explode in what most stars find as their fate into supernovas, and the result is a crashing into itself rupturing the very barriers of creation and the atomic structure itself resulting into the ultimate formation of a black hole.

Without getting into too much astrophysics we will bring to the attention into the Macro sighting simple differences between supernovas and black holes being; supernovas at the end of a stars life explode outward into vast newly formed gasses and elements (the products of their life as a star) that then go on to form other more complex systems, many more stars, and possible life. The black hole on the other hand is a product of a life of a star that held onto too much material perhaps stolen from other stars, either way, hoarded vast amounts of physical energetic materials, and when its life finally comes to an end a collapse upon itself into a selfish constriction to the absolute void of nonexistence, death, and timelessness occurs.

The process or the mathematics of this theoretical anomaly, and I do say theoretically because while the presence of a black hole can be observed, it is not the actual black hole that is being seen, but the effect the anomaly has on the surrounding environment that has led scientists to believe they not only observe them but also study them. It is these effects that the black hole has on the surroundings that I am correlating to the study we are discussing here.

A black hole is an ever-hungry pit of darkness that only sucks everything in and rarely generates anything except possible destruction in return. Everything that falls within its grasp is sucked down to what has been called the Continuum, whereby nothing of reality can exist. All physical matter is so compressed by the sheer force of the gravity this glutinous entity emits that matter itself is compressed into such a small insignificant point that it is theorized that there may be absolutely no distance even between the singular pieces of raw energy, capturing and then suffocating any and all physical energy even light into a single infinitely small space, the waves of sound like energy literally cease to move and thus die.

A sort of depression of energy plays out in an ever-spinning to an absolute dark lifeless center point which could only be described in the most philosophical manner as the opposite of ascension or as we have coined descension.

For the purpose of our discussion, I would like to make a correlation between the anomaly of a black hole and pure evil that can occur in the hearts of some truly evil people.

It is the belief of this author that when God banished the enemy "satan" or "Lucifer" from his presence he stripped him of everything that would be considered Godly; Light, Love, Peace, Joy, Mercy, anything good. If we assume as God created the physical universe and called all of His creation in their turn; "Good," then likewise everything physical was removed from evil leaving only the spiritual essence of it to dwell in darkness.

The positive emotions or actions such as Truth, Kindness, Compassion, Wisdom, all come from God and thus fall outside the access of spiritually dark creatures who by nature must flee from anything Godly especially light when it is engaged. As for the creatures who dwell the closest to this absolute darkness all essences of these spirit anomalies as well become physically nonexistent, within their own individual universes, their souls home God gave them envelope ever-darkening shades accumulations until the resulting death collapse occurs.

Thus, also the necessity to articulate in negative Anti-God emotional or energetic endeavors such as fear, torture, slander, lies or deceit, because if these poor creatures with their very existence are doomed to flee from God it is only within these remaining shadows that any kind of existence can be realized. Falling prey to these emotions does a sort of Quantum descending or "Descension" occur? In the world of our direct view, we see similar patterns play out in the relationships and interactions of the souls who are privileged to observe.

As the bird or any number of other unseen assailants suddenly attack from the unrealized sky, seemingly touch out of nowhere, scare or startle our young caterpillar, the initials response is to coil up in a ball, a desperate attempt to hold and protect any and all private parts from attack, and play dead. The only problem is we all know that snowballs always roll downhill, any upward momentum is suddenly and drastically lost as the grip on the present level of ascension is lost and a sudden and possible painful fall to the hard unyielding ground awaits.

This sudden, and often repeated fall due to an unexpected and unseen attacking flying spirits from the sky, have a drastic and possible permanent negative effect on our young adventurer's soul. The soul being different than the spirit is the accumulation of the entire life experience in this crawling life and the next one of flight. This repeated face planting, the unmistakable injection of negative energies, malevolent energy that seems to counters any positive long term progression that might be remembered, results in such a slow and gradual slope of reality one can almost forget they are supposed to be climbing in the first place.

But now back to the black hole; as I have stated earlier it is my supposition that we are all universes in ourselves, entire galaxies and trillions of star systems that harmoniously cooperate in this wonderful creation our dear Lord has seen fit to create into each and every one our singular lives, good and evil must be demonstrated clearly each as pigments presented in the painting to give the observer a clear depiction of the painting before them. For he did say Himself; *"For I knew you, even before the first star was in the sky, or drop of water appeared in the sea."* This in itself would support the fact that we have always been here and we are, in the likeness of our Creator immortal beings. This fact I too will touch upon a little later in the book.

So as entities of the like of trillions of star systems there is a part of us that represents the very heart of our living soul. In the physical universe, it has been stipulated that at the center of the largest galaxies reside in its center a black hole. I myself have not seen evidence that this is true, and since these same scientists can merely hypothesize about it, without actually basing it on observed data, I will assume that in some cases, this may be true, and perhaps in other cases it may not be. Perhaps in some cases, a large cluster of stars so bright and correspondingly massive, their combined accumulated forces drive the engines of large galaxies, yet in others, these driving factors are in fact dark and ominous.

Even in our own larger social and national structures, it is easy to see when governments are controlled by good leaders, their people and the land thrives, yet when it is clear that evil reins destruction and death soon prevail. I believe when we cross-correlate what occurs in human beings the same can be said in the Meso; some people have brightness inside them that is so evident that it radiates literally out of their eyes. He also said; "The eyes are a lamp to the soul."

Likewise, people who have chosen darker paths for their lives also demonstrate more sinister and dark eyes, the worse of these even seem to lose the whiteness that surrounds as the physical begins to mimic the spiritual resulting in the eyes revealing an almost spiritual snake-like slit of darkness where their eyes should be.

I have known people who have willingly taken on with what appears to be darkness in their hearts. As we look upon them with "Ascending Vision" it is apparent they almost have a small dark spot that seems to reside right in the middle of where their heart is. At first, this is the most insignificant of small spots, leaving the observer with the notion; "Is it there, do I actually see something or am I just imagining it, that shutter, or small crevasse that seems to be forming where their heart is supposed to be?"

But as more and more evil is poured into the black hole that resides in the center of their chest the larger and more profound it becomes and likewise, the hungrier this ever consuming, never satisfied lust is, always wanting more, increasingly depressed, never happy with what it has, falling, descending and headed for death!

One example, I can only imagine is that if it is fact, which all of the hidden evidence out there seems to state about the subject Adrenochrome; a substance derived from the torture and killing of innocent children among others. That when people start ingesting this substance they receive such an incredible "high" and seemingly physical benefits, that their desire to replicate that initial high immediately becomes so strong they cannot control themselves but must feed the dark black hole they have now invited into their being. Ever growing in the dosage, an ultimate and uncontrollably dark addiction, drives them to continue to lay at the feet of the dark spirit everything and anything it may desire.

The evil these people who engage in this ritual, who have freely sold their soul too, that dark spot that resides there now, is absolute, utter darkness and Anti-Christ; they must obey, they must sacrifice their very children or others they may have within their grasp, throw their brothers and sisters into the fire, sacrifice any innocent, even betray humanity itself, or die, irrelevant at what they believe is right, what it will cost, or who they must kill to do it.

I think feeding any kind of spirit that has control over a soul has the potential to manifest itself into a dark hole like entity, but truly sinister deeds perpetrated against the most innocent among us must risk crossing the line of "Sins against the Holy Spirit?" What purer spirits exist than those of newborn small children? Obviously, no light can reside in a person who would choose to partake in any fashion in such a ritualistic activity as drinking the blood of a traumatized child merely for whatever physical satisfaction or personal gain they may receive.

I heard a lecture back in college from a converted ex-high priest of the satanic church who said when witches or warlocks, high priests, would engage in these ritual sacrifices, thereby the most coveted persons they would seek to acquire as victims would be the purest of heart. Of course innocent elderly, afterward children, eventually babies, and ultimately young virgin girls were among the most desirable because the pure essence of these spirits is that which these creatures wished to capture. But in cases of lack of supply; animals, rabbits, rats, even insects would be used if only to have something when better and more potent choices could not be found.

It was this high priest that said when they would capture and torture these poor victims, the essence of their purity could only be held for a short time in the compound or elemental structures they coveted, sold, traded, or desired, and thus they would have to continually search out more victims to feed the darkness they themselves served.

Again everything under the sun is an example or tries to mimic that of another of God's creations. Within the great power of the black hole with its almost infinite strength of greedy gravitational power, light is regularly ejected from its polls. As a matter of fact, the intensity of the light that is ejected from the polls regularly out of back holes is so intense that it is equal in strength at that moment to the combined output of all the stars in a galaxy or more. It is these ejections that scientists have used to at least demonstrate the existence of black holes at all.

Isn't that true though; greedy selfish people, after they die are soon forgotten, but the lives of the good are often spoken of long after they have left leaving embellishing honor unto even their Descendents' for many generations to follow? Many people would be proud, and even lift up a descendent of George Washington or John F. Kennedy, but few would even admit to being the descendent of a John Wilkes Booth or Manson.

Even the great power of the greedy black hole cannot hold onto the light, and after holding it for even a moment in time must release it into the vastness of space, pure light must leave the grasp of the dark foe and illuminate back into the vast heavens of God's entire universe. Hawkins, Einstein, and many others who have the mathematical calculating capacity to work out the calculations of a black hole state undeniably that in this singularity even time ceases to exist? If on the Quantum level all energy is sound, if even the most rudimentary sound in the black hole is compressed to the slowest and ultimately single still moment the wavelength becomes zero, then the sound must cease to exist.

If time ceases to exist, and energy stops moving, and all space between the halted moving energy disappears, then is it is not hard to fathom on a quantum level that when death occurs and this black hole effect likewise occurs, this vast world of evil compression down into nothing perpetuates a vanishing into the world of non-existence.

Ascension must win? If darkness only embodies the smallest most insignificant point of space, completely void of movement, remember physical energy on a quantum level is sound wave movements and time itself is the movement and measurement of these waves, then this negative energy can only reside in the shadows of walls of our homes God created us? This must be the case-in-point by the small remaining essences of dirt or darkness we bring in ourselves and veils the light to cast shadows of our own homes.

As we ascend in our consciousness collectively and more and more individual universes of people brighten their reflections, shadows disappear from their own existence, and darkness fees leaving only the bright colored hues of the magnificent masterpiece God's creation for all of us in the first place. Healing is from God within the same spectrum of light, love, peace, and joy, filter out the darkness, clean the filth off the walls and floors of our mansions leaving only the light to shine through as Ascension Truths are discovered, healing must occur.

RIOTS, WHAT IS GOING ON?

It has become evidentially clear to me that as we press further along the wars waging out in the streets and in the hearts of people who look from the sidelines deciding for themselves exactly what is going on, that this has digressed into a clear and worldwide struggle for "control." The powers that would control us merely by financial oppression through a corrupt banking system, or physical discomfort via the toxic and manipulative medical system, have now progressed into the venues of isolation, repeated propaganda, and fear.

The controlling factions, the ruling classes, it's puppet subclasses, hidden societies, and cliques of Olé Guards that have been placing their own knees on the necks of more and more people have enjoyed for years ever increasing-control, riches, and power. But with the recent changes of political movement and a deeper desire by the majority of the American voters to usher in "Change" even "Make America Great" again, these cults worshiping ruling factions' as well as the realization of having control slip out of their fingers, and possibly have it stripped from them completely, has led these Satan driven control freaks to desperate measures, they have decided they must gain back control at any measure!

They don't care if they must develop a plague in a lab, or fabricate one from a lie, train and facilitate riots and looting throughout the world to kill and burn down all of society, "chip" everyone first to control and later eliminate them, it would seem they will stop at nothing, hold back no lie, accuse or even kill any innocent, even the little babies, as long as they get what they want and regain control!

My wife and I as we learned pretty much the hard way, in our own experiences, the only way to true healing and health was to FREE people of the "Control" the health care system seemed to place not only on their bodies but on their very beliefs, but as we increasingly perfected these freeing ideals so also where the attacks pressed and intensified against us by those who would desire to hold control of our medical practicing methods, our businesses, finances, children, or even our beliefs.

Control, or the Jezebel spirit that inhabits people who long for this controlling power, like some blood potion to drink, especially over other children of God, are the true enemy that in their own servitude knowingly or unknowingly feed dark demonic powers. They actually believe they are in service of their own desires but have fallen victim to the greatest of fraud, the power and control they so desire is merely given them as long as they serve darkness, but when their service expires, anything and everything they have been given is taken back. These foolish Cabalists needs to be flushed out of every aspect of society, and I pray that this flushing out of those who wish to control is being done today.

Once flushed to the light, it is only then that the spirits that control them flees, leaving these poor foolish misguided children standing naked without support to face the severity of God's Judgement-Light in their own lives. It is at this point they too can repent and come to the light, the only other choice turns a rebellious face against this light and parish.

But the good news; more and more people are watching from the sidelines, they are observing the real struggle that is playing out in front of them as well. Truths are being told. They are elevating in their own understanding and realization; they are ascending in spiritual growth and knowledge. People are asking the questions to the "Why the lies" and finding the answers.

People are realizing this is not some random pestilence but manufactured attacks against innocent people, these are not peaceful protests for change, but riots and destruction that has one purpose to illicit chaos, fear, anarchy, and hatred. They are seeing the revealed lies by the many popular people who we have ourselves lifted up in society, seeing even these who would claim to be leaders, doctors, idols, "Saviors," offer solutions to the fear pestilence, the concocted fairytale, that we know is rooted in lies, are these same problem-solvers perhaps the same who play a roll in it's creation!

It was a common practice in recent wars and conflicts for men in power to create an issue, merely to then bring the solution, requiring us, the general public to give up some gifts to them whether it be riches, faith, or liberties in order to game peace from the fear they established in the first place.

I have written in previous articles how the insurance industry high-jacked the healthcare industry, merely to then purchase almost all of the hospitals, at which time they jacked up the costs of care, placing us in fear to the point where people had no choice but to purchase health insurance. Under Obama Care, the same industries wrote the Affordable Care Act, Obama Care, and mandated every American must purchase their insurance. Now they not only have full mandated sacrifices to the dark spirit, but the same have full control over all the care that would be given.

These are the same powers that are forcing doctors to diagnose COVID to everyone who comes in the door, bribing the entire healthcare industry to close hospitals only to keep them open for nonexistent plague numbers, or sentence people to isolation into nursing homes whether they have active symptoms or not.

When many of the medical private medical facilities closed due to the shutdown, and the majority of my colleagues refused to treat home health patients because of virus fear, I volunteered to treat these patients for anyone who needed me. I was amazed to find that out of the many so-called COVID patients, none of them had active symptoms at all. At least half never had symptoms of any respiratory kind, and a few were diagnosed and placed into lockdown even after testing negative repeatedly.

One poor man not much older than myself was being treated for cancer regularly with chemo. One day his doctor had him committed to a nursing home where he was placed in a room with a cot, a plastic chair, and a TV, nothing else. He could not leave, return home, and since he had nobody to call for help he suffered there. On his door was a sign that said COVID-19 positive; full garment, masks, and gloves required. Yet his chart clearly said he was COVID negative and tested more than once. When I asked the charge nurse if this was right, she said it was, but she had to follow orders. That poor man feared he already lost what little possessions he owned when he didn't return to his apartment now going on a few months.

This will stop, it must stop, the real cause of the sickness must be rooted out; I pray it is! And like black mold that has perpetuated itself throughout a home, we must eliminate all the darkness, first by exposing and putting the light on it, then identify where it originated, and finally remove it. It is only then that real freedom from infirmity can be realized. Who are these dark spirits that perpetuate these lies in the health care system, if it is true, then they are truly guilty of crimes against humanity. It must be discovered, and the perpetrators brought to justice!

Funny as I think back and the slope of the roots ventured with the partners or those who directed my path when it became obvious as to no blessed real increase in height seemed to be obtained or the many difficulties that seemed to manifest along the way, one might have at this particular juncture in the journey determine that the wrong tree was being climbed and perhaps even one that was already dead and lying on its side basically perpetuating a lifetime of wasted time with the ultimate goal of being as low as I started if not lower still.

I believe our great President under the promptings of our Great Lord Jesus is doing this very thing right now.

And I believe society as a whole is seeing it as well. They know the real reason the riots, the false pandemic numbers, the lockdown, the fear, the economic devastation, the anarchy is to put a ripple in our Great Presidents term, the cheating in the 2020 election, and possibly inhibit his chance for re-election. But all of their dark plans will turn against, for God himself said; *"I turn all things too good."*

There are many more good people than there are evil! With each person who realizes but a single lie, one more places a step up that path of Enlightenment, and this wonderful world illuminates with Godly light as another soul Ascends.

TOWER OF BABYLON

The caterpillar stands below the great tree with only a mere nudging of ascension in her mind, as she glances towards the instrument of her own deliverance. The vast nature and ageless wonder of this mountainous creation suddenly seem to take root throughout the earth and seemingly stretching forth vast arms into the imagination of her dreams. This great tower of promise and revelation before her opens up a natural spring he only dreamed before, creating with it opportunities before her which seem to beckon to him as she lifts his face ever so slightly and considers the truth that suddenly seems to miraculously manifest itself before her path.

What did so many of those naysayers say, their never-ending banter of repeated doom and gloom, the denial any ascension physical or otherwise was possible, constantly touting the need to deny the very existence of the heavens, perhaps God Himself, and just keep a face-planted in the dirt and firmly covered with the fading green leaves of the ground? But how does a little caterpillar deny it when the truth presents itself right in front of her. Oh well, I guess one has no choice but to climb up and see for themselves?

The Tower of Babylon may have stood for centuries as a reminder of what happens when humankind not only strives to ascend to God through our own foolish ventures but does so through the communicative cooperation of everyone on the planet in unison. For didn't God the Father Himself say; *"Is there nothing they cannot do if they all speak the same language?"*

Historians have told us, in-regards-to various conquerors throughout our world, that had it not been for the great distances as well as the difficulties to communicate with intercontinental peoples, the world may have been conquered long ago. A "One World Government" would have been established and darkness would rule the world. This has been the agenda of the controlling factions known to control the highest aspects of our financial systems for centuries, a dark desire to reduce the population, placing the rest of the controlled working classes into servant slavery greater than what is already present today, is only a fraction of the many plans they have had for the rest of us.

Let us for a moment suppose the idea that the powers to be have given us the internet as a means to try to control, censor, and manipulate the world's entire population by thinking they control the information narrative, is in any way presented as a gift to actually help us? Now granted that is to assume that the idea actually came from them, when we know all wisdom including creative intuition comes from God, it is only downloaded into the random society with His intent to be shared for the betterment of all peoples, an act rarely instituted by the recipients of these gifts, but it is also through the free will of those who receive these gifts that they then turn them to use for their own dark agendas.

The earliest internet was by initial setup primarily a place for a sharing of clerical information, gambling and porn, its basic information could be accessed, videos freely seen, written or researched information could be shared, and basic information could be transferred, at least that is what it seemed to be purposed in the earlier years. In my own field of medicine, there was a systematic almost threatening push to have all records, billing, and information processed first electronically, but ultimately through the internet. This mandate came right from the top of medical system institutions long before initiated by our government.

One would think that this push would be dangerous for increasing controlling interests considering the ease of hacking, the negative effect of energy outages, the fear of viruses, or the seemingly simple presence of counterfeiting claims, all risking waste of money or potential losses with a mere keystroke? Yet these now ruling entities pressed for greater and greater electronic participation from every aspect of the medical treatment arena, revealing a furthering of their complete control and stranglehold on every possible aspect of the healthcare of individuals always pressing us as medical providers further into the swamp of internet participation.

But back to the internet, as usual, the weapons that the enemy would use to destroy the Children of the King have indeed been turned against them. What has in-fact occurred; the internet at least in the earlier years, had provided a platform whereby people could publish and pretty much share unadulterated information even about the most seemingly ridiculous topics, suppositions, or theories those even being considered conspiracy, be it truths, fantasies, facts or whimsical fabrications, they could freely be shared with everyone? Plus as time went on, documentation, video footage, whistleblowers, leaks, and classified material dumps seemed to become a common thing.

This single miscalculation by itself would not have led to the demise of the Dark State alone, since the "powers to be" do control, at least from an administrative perspective, the internet, or at least they think they do by owning the companies that facilitate it.

No, their miscalculation is not learning from history when it was right in front of them all along!

About fifteen years ago when the internet was in its infancy I noticed an anomaly while playing online chess on one of the earlier browsers; when I would talk to someone, specifically chat, a new and very basic concept then, they would chat back in English no matter where they lived in the world. I remember remarking to a person from Mongolia; "It is amazing how good your English is?" He promptly responded; "I'm not writing English but typing Chinese and your responses are showing up in Chinese."

I was instantly amazed to think at the time just like the days of the

Tower of Babylon, today we are all able to speak to each other perhaps even in the same language, and as God, the Father did say; *"If they can communicate all of them everywhere with the same language there is nothing they cannot do."*

What an interesting development of the most recent years; now that we are all speaking the same language over the whole world, there is a worldwide sharing of information, wisdom, and the good gifts God has given all of us which may also include revelations of truths that can lead to Ascension. I believe the world is awakening to the fact that we are all Children of God, there is literally no difference between races, colors, locations on the globe, or even basic religious belief, and the only real enemy out there is the true enemy of evil, darkness, or the Satanic minority that would only control, enslave or destroy us.

We had to go full circle with God and now that we are all talking, we can finally now all stand up together against evil, there is nothing they can do about it except cry. As the light is turning on everywhere in the world the darkness is fleeing, guess what; they are running out of places to flee!

Could the Revelation John spoke of in the Bible actually be revelations as to the truths of what is going on around us is revealed? Even the word apocalypse derived from the Greek word "Apocalypto" means to reveal, uncover, or disclose, and that seems to be exactly what is going on these days. It is only recently that even the majority of internet companies seem to desperately be engaged in the illegal act of censoring content especially when it doesn't agree with the political narrative they seem to be touting. But like idiots with every censor, they merely place an emphasis on the person or subject being censored and stimulating even more people to look.

The powers-to-be may have given us the Tower of Babylon with the internet, but they had no idea what kind of Pandora's box they were released, and just like genius my wife Anna so often says; "It's impossible to un-cream the coffee once the milk has been poured in."

With every lie that is revealed another person can take that critical first step of Ascension.

ASCENSION & EVIL ELIMINATED

Over the course of the last few months of 2020 with the COVID, there has been sporadic talk about NASARA, debt forgiveness, Ascension through various venues, whether they be real within the perspectives of our own physical universe or more of a supernatural origin stemming from Godly more spiritual aspects one would only have to wait and see. When it comes to Ascension it really matters little the basis, spiritual or purely physical from its origin, the result is the same; an increase in Godly awareness from people in regards to Mind, Body, or Spirit resulting in a direct and absolute increased spiritual awakening.

This spiritual awakening is important to say the least, especially when it comes to the entire human existence on our planet. This spiritual awakening, or the gifts that seem to come with it especially health, wellness even economics, the release of the slavery mentality tension from the people, freedom from lies, and its overall happiness associated with it releases the hidden truths of health knowledge actually out there. These personal benefits are insignificant in comparison to the other battles that are waging, speaking to the fact that the world is in an end-times' war between good and evil.

If what they say is true and our world has been held captive for a very long time by a very few people who not only rule the top of all the power pyramid of political control but are unthinkably evil in their plans for the majority of us, their manipulation of media, the false indoctrination of the royalty, obsession with oil, the witchcraft associated with medicine, as well as the financial control of the worlds monetary systems all bent on one purpose and that is to enslave. This might account for the overall image that many of these industries portray and that is one which has little interest in the people's wellbeing at heart, merely their own selfish interests and gains.

Up until recently many of these sinister atrocities perpetrated among the most affluent among us have gone on behind dark locked doors, being hidden in the shadows unaware to the greater majority of the public, they have infiltrated and perpetrated control of every major industry in the world including all of the healthcare system, but now having these evils come into the light is a necessary step in dismissing their power as the darkness spawned energy the controls them flees. This same power-mongering group would seem to have lost their grip on the withholding of the narrative as their secrets seem to be leaking out like water through a strainer. This fact might place quite a Godly and literally prophetic meaning to the Biblical statement; *"For nothing is secret that will not be revealed, nor anything hidden that will not be known and come to light…"*

Much worse than all of this control is their reported devotion to Satan along with its' deep addiction to perpetuate absolute evil selfish interests, these acts seem to be reported repeatedly throughout the world especially towards the most vulnerable and innocent in our societies, the most vulnerable extremely young children. This represents deep-rooted attacks against all of us, against humanity itself, a physical onslaught of either direct and indirect warfare, the worst war crimes. They are using unending waves of media, verbal, and visual degradation to hide these secrets in plain view, not to mention the literal dumping down of our physical senses, seeding poisons into the foods and waters that hold off our ability to spiritually grow. These direct negative actions all lend direct therapeutic consideration to the answer of the question; if so, why and by whom?

Just from the perspective of healthcare application, I have found myself as we began publicly to integrate God into the treatment model, even in the most rudimentary way, an immediate counter negative response began being pressed on us in an ever greater aggressive degree. First, this negative response was casual and subtle, the systems withdrawing from using of our services to later blatant spoken rejection, and finally, even progressively aggressive action against us, all when the mere idea to place God even in the most fractional manner in the healthcare regiment was attempted. These threats had a counter effect on us as I found with the degree they seemed to fight against the spiritual notion, the more obvious we must have been onto something good?

It was, in this same manner that we actually began to follow Donald Trump long before he was nominated for President, and then increasing more after; if the ruling systems are so aggressively against him for no clear and obvious reason but merely what appears to be hate, then is it possible he actually represents a possible answer they seem so desperate to attempt to keep from us? Same lies, seemingly different subjects?

This end-time war, if it indeed has traversed into a battle between light and dark, and I pray that is true, what a wonderful fact that would represent. With the understanding, our illustrious President Donald Trump has first "Cut off the head of the Snake," as has been reported, and he is now after others, the second tier and their cronies that participate or profit from the same reported atrocities, could this possibly amount to a monumental reduction of evil in the world?

It is unfathomable to think of the network of support and the reciprocal mopping up it would take to likewise take down the entire corrupt spider web that must exist to abduct a reported 22,000 missing or abducted children worldwide a day. It is equally inconceivable to think how much control they must have over the money, governments, all aspects of society including communications, education, transportation, even the medical fields, processed food production and distribution, drugs, etc., to keep such a large scale human trafficking ring running to the point of such numbers silenced for so long, and moreover keep it almost completely under wraps from the general public for perhaps generations.

Of course, such a spider web of deceit, cruelty, and horror of such a Machiavellian level would have to encompass the entire world and would most likely have to be in place for such a long time in order to grow to that volume. It says in the Bible that the followers of Baal, a demonic powerful spirit, resembling a three-headed spider; one head which could only represent an old fool who wishes to be king wearing a crown or "Corona," the second head, one of a cat crafty looking away, probably representing a witch or witchcraft, while the last head that being of the toad, another witchcraft representation, more in line to the foolish servant that starry-eyed looks out into space, docilely following orders right into the hot boiling water, unaware of the death it will lead.

Many researchers, investigators, whistleblowers, and insiders who have been captured or turned throughout the world, have reported with increasing supporting evidence these atrocities making it increasingly impossible to keep such diabolical secrets under wraps, especially for the perpetrators of torture and participate in human sacrifice of children. Within this information sharing environment of today, with its increased cooperation throughout the world has made it impossible for such evils to go unnoticed any longer. We seem, now that we are all talking to each other to be indeed in a time of enlightenment, or should we say; "Revelation?"

As I have already said the actual word Apocalypse comes from the Greek word "*Apocalypto*" which means to be revealed or enlightened, something not spoke of or even inferred in the church, yet often spoken of in many religious arenas. If we are truly in the end times as spoken of by John in The Book of Revelations of the Bible, it would certainly look like for the first time in history things are truly being revealed worldwide, especially when it comes to the horrors perpetrated against the most innocent of our children. But also on that fact, there are many places throughout the old and new testaments where significant warnings are specifically made against harming children.

"It would better a person have a millstone wrapped around their neck and be cast into the abyss than to harm one of these little ones," Jesus himself said that.

That's another thing, our God-led President did sign into law almost immediately an Executive Order; that anyone partaking in human trafficking against children received a mandatory death sentence. Such an act could only mean that enough intelligence has surfaced, enough information had come into the light to warrant such a drastic and definitive response.

I don't think it takes a great deal of contemplation, nor do people have to have children themselves, to realize that acts of cruelty towards little children, especially torture, rape, or sacrificing them to

Satan, constitutes a deep-set evil inside of a person, and itself demonstrates a grievous act against humanity itself. Children on even the most basic levels represent our future, anyone cruel enough to participate in such atrocities in any capacity has no good whatsoever inside them.

I recently contemplated with my lovely wife the difference between people who maybe act bad, or possibly have bad behavioral tendencies, compared to people who are truly evil, and we came to the conclusion that people who act bad, while often they know what they are doing, there always remains an opportunity to repent, make up for it, or turn it around for good. But for people who have crossed the line into the baby blood-drinking, human sacrifice, child trafficking, cannibalism arena there seems to be no going back, these people by the way of partaking in such horrible acts, actually freely invite evil into themselves. It has been scientifically proven that participating in cannibalism facilitates permanent physiological changes on a cellular level in the individuals whereby many become insane.

But back to the Ascension, if truly the most horrid evil is concentrated in the highest echelons of the rulers of the world, then first identifying the evil, bringing it into the light must be the first step to eliminating it altogether. If by only the means of eliminating all, or a large portion of the evil in the world that is responsible for the perpetuation of child trafficking, as well as profiteers in the human trafficking system, the world as a whole could with one stroke of elimination seemingly filter away the largest portion of darkness from the surface of our planet. The remaining people's world would find themselves in a much cleaner, and as the result, much more enlightened spiritual universe in which to reside?

I guess in a simple example; take a dirty glass of water, foul-smelling, even harmful for a person, then filter out all or the majority of the toxic components, the resulting glass becomes clear, life-giving and refreshed; "Enlightened." These few dark components may appear to darken the whole, but on a quantum level, their energies are so fractional compared to the masses of good light energies that once removed a crystal clear more illuminated result occurs.

I believe when the largest portion of these "Luciferian" bloodsuckers is eliminated from the world, the amount of evil eliminated will have such a global effect on the whole, that people all over the world will spontaneously begin to ascend merely by the clarity of the environment they suddenly find themselves residing in. Many of the deceived people who might have found themselves doing bad, will suddenly see the uselessness of it for themselves and others around them, maybe no longer wishing to do it, a sudden ceasing of hostilities.

The remaining whole world may begin to ascend spiritually, mentally, and finally physically.

THE DAM HAS BROKEN

Coming to a sudden end in a time-dimension reality is as surprising as being suddenly and unexpectedly plucked from the branch by an unseen and completely unexpected villain from the air.

Sometimes a shadow is cast upon me, perhaps by myself by my own misconception of beliefs I have cloaked my lonely heart within the many lies taught, bought, or placed upon me one spoon at a time throughout my entire life. The result; a blocking out the light only moments before the ravaging claws seize innocent flesh, villainous greed descends from above to set upon and steal the few precious gifts of one child for the indulgence of a thief who will never gain a grain of appreciation or satisfaction from its theft. So is the hunger to capture, torment, and devour all young caterpillars.

I had a dream, and in my vision, within the dream, I saw a great build-up of debris holding back the waters of a clear beautiful creek. Clay and dead timbers and all sorts of discarded objects were used to form up an ever-increasing barrier, higher and thicker until it took the shape and form a large dam.

It was clear the dam was being built up by the enemy, for it was grey and cold, its rough surface in no way demonstrated anything but harsh resilience against the waters that were behind. The sky was churning with darkened greys swirling ominousness of white towering clouds, not dark because of the enemy, but because of the anger that was brewing in the spirit of God.

God's blessings of a very long time were sitting behind that dam, denied to the people down in the valley below! Gods waters were being built up, held back, denied from the people downriver who have been thirsty, almost choking for its few drops. The enemy could not take the waters for itself but could hold it back, denying the children its existence. Yet the flow continued and up the dam rose, it had to grow, higher along the canyon walls, the dams' claw-like talons holding tightly to the rock walls as the accumulating reservoir continued to swell every day, year after year, perhaps even for centuries now.

I looked at the grey rough now rock-hard face of the dam and suddenly I noticed small cracks and droplets of water forming on its vast cold now concrete-like surface. These watery appearances were becoming more and more frequent, a few even began spraying forth with popping sounds as small rumbles of greater pressures hidden within suddenly erupted sending with it small pieces of debris hurtling into the now vast chasm down the canyon valley below.

I saw more and more cracks, and in the darkened sky I suddenly heard the ominous sound of the alarm, a great siren warning the people below of some impending danger.

My eye immediately goes to the valley where I see the people down in the deepest recesses of the city, some of them looking up at the sound, a few more casually dismissing the siren as "just another warning test, nothing to be alarmed about, they are just testing the system again."

Many go right back to the business they continued with before, busy in the muck and mire of their daily lives, right in the very middle of the valley streets. The deeper within the valley the more prominently crowded as well, the darkness that sits at the center of the streets, the sewer filth that flows down the middle of these streets seems almost reflect the expressionless faces of the many men and women standing over them in enslaved obedience.

Especially the people in the lowest part of the city, the sewer filth is the strongest, they play and wash their clothes in the refuse, wiping their faces, scratching their mouths, rubbing their eyes with the filth stained hands unaware of the poisons they feed themselves. The high walled buildings and busy roadways make it hard for the people here to even see the fact that they are deep in the valley, from their perspective they are on flat ground. Many of these people are too busy to even take the time to look up from the sound of the sirens but ignore it altogether.

A few of these individuals, although, try to move out away from this deep center, the panic of the distant sirens having at least some small effect on these. All these people seem to frantically ask each other if they should at least try to make it to higher ground? Pushing and pulling each other to listen as they engage in a panic gathering of the useless items they were busy with, trying desperately to carry the soiled cloths, heavy chairs they were sitting on, and argue with others pulling at them to just sit still.

Further away from the center, the people can hear the sirens more clearly, they are not as muffled by the crowded buildings and constant noise of the center, most of these at least look up. These people seem more aware as well, being a bit alarmed by the loud sounds, many more of them actually start moving towards the edge of town, discarding the labors of their hands and taking the hands of their children or elderly, offering each other even confused gestures of help, as little as they can, quickly trying to get to the foothills of the mountains that line the valley.

As we look at the foothills we see people who were slowly walking up now running up the mountains. Some frantic almost pulling their friends out of the way or stepping over others to get up. A few foolish doubting people are almost fighting holding people from climbing the paths, arguing and screaming trying to turn them back to the valley, calling them fools, reacting with such hate and anger as they desperately push their former friends, family even brothers and sisters to the ground rather than let them pass.

Then there are those already at the top, some of these are actually coming back down trying to help the others up to the top yelling out their own warnings of the dam which is about to break. So many people just laugh as they casually head back into the valley seeming unable to comprehend the dangers that lie waiting for them.

I look back at the dam which is now squirting out water from many fishers simultaneously like many dozen high-powered fire hoses, a thick blanket of water is already pouring down the cold dark surface of the great manmade structure. The many attendants of the dam are now frantically leaving the facilities trying themselves to escape, they appear from the distance to scatter like cockroaches when the light is turned on, rats jumping ship only moments before the imminent sinking occurs. Many of these have no idea which way to go, turning one way then the other, only to run into each other, even throw one another off the road as they mouth their silent screams, which have no chance to be heard over the loud sirens and the deep rumbling coming from within sounding more like thunder than anything else.

I then hear even a greater rumble like the crashing of a thousand waves or the deep echo of an underground atomic bomb and with a great cracking noise like seconds long strike of lightning, the mad roar of some long-forgotten demon, or a thousand explosions all at once. The ground shakes with a sudden movement as what clearly feels like an earthquake erupting underfoot and inside the center of the dam, large slabs of stone start immediately to shift with a now deafening devils screech of low pitched grind. A great wall of water over a thousand feet tall presses through all at once and falls through the dam, crashing into the open dark space below. All the water of the huge reservoir that had been held behind for a millennium flows through like a gigantic tidal wave a thousand feet tall, just flowing in one solid block, tearing the cement, walls, buildings, all the remaining structures of the dam with them, as it crashes forward down the chasm of the canyon into the valley below.

All the people feel the huge sound and even feel the ground shudder as the sound reverberates through their very being like thunder striking deep under their feet well before the sound reaches their ears. All are frozen in awestruck fear as they look up the valley into the canyon to witness the origin of the sound they already fear as some dreaded dooms-day beast of nightmares returning.

There is a ghostly silence for but a moment right after the initial shock turns to uncontrollable shaking as people just stare in still confused realization what their eyes are registering yet in their minds only moments later suddenly takes shape. The huge wall of water tumbling down the face of the mountain upon the canyon in front of them turning and plowing buildings trees and electric poles, churning them in the distance like toothpicks, this image suddenly manifests itself like some sleeping elephant that suddenly appears charging right at them, yet this one is tumbling and rolling down the canyon towards them.

Panic is now apparent, screams and startled chaos like bats in a cave as the people of the center move in every direction, hitting each other, pulling and clawing almost hindering each other from any chance of escape. Everyone is crying, doors slam closed with the sounds of bolts locking, widow shutters slamming shut, the rich staring in silent disbelief as their cries for help are ignored. The leaders, and judges, and men of power fall first as the people strike them down mercilessly for lying to them for so long.

The people in the top of the valley the rich and powerful are first hit, they always believed their position above the filth of the city would keep them safe, for them the initial wall of water, the fury of God's wrath hits so suddenly like a baseball bat to the back of the head on a dark moonless night. Is it the power of the blast or the sudden realization they were so wrong that kills them, or the shame of being such fools, only God knows?

The deepest in the valley, those who wallow among the most filth are the next to be swallowed up by the churning debris which looks more like a sideways rolling tornado than any water wall now. Constructs of tumbling buildings and all manners of churning materials form a juggernaut of power and destruction as the front wall slams into more waiting buildings, these are the many businesses and homes of the workers of the city, safe they thought they were inside the construct of monetary idols, their walls of wood and brick are no match for the power of the water coming.

The crashing sound is quickly followed by a thundering roar almost like hearing an enormous lions' roar with your ear right next to his mouth, the water only flows past the highest on the sides of the valley, the most sturdy brick-built buildings clearly built on solid rock. Its cascading waters filling the streets in the center of the valley to the brim with the earlier destroyed materials, all forms of debris, walls, wood, fine furnishings, plants, soil, all cascading movement blending into a dark grey soup of muddy mass, creating a scene of almost solid movement. In the deepest center of town, the whole dark muddy gulley in the middle seems to now be sliding itself down the valley as if pushed up into one massive heap of muck dissolving as it goes under the churning waters and white frothy foam.

All the people running towards the foothills, while some seem to be pushed downstream a bit, others were close enough to the high edges, or firm foundations, to lift themselves out of the danger even as they soon realized how far they actually were in, sudden illumination to what manner they could lift themselves out manifested itself. Some even attempted to help others close to them to safety risking their own lives in the process, especially the weak or young these seem of the most paramount to aid from the angry ravaging waters.

The very young seem almost instinctively to know how to climb trees or other structures to just get out of the reaches of the raging torrents. Some of these very young on the contrary, even jumped into the more calm waters on the edges playing in their crystal blue and white spray, satisfying weeks even years of thirst as their fears are suddenly turned for them into blessings of joy.

As the rumbling torrent quickly passes downstream people slowly begin to walk out of the hidden refuges of their homes just to look with amazement at the now clear stream that has replaced the filthy sewer down the center of their town. They walk up to its edge with smiling amazement and reach down with expected hands as they cup for themselves cool fresh waters lifting it with eager anticipation to their thirsty lips.

The clouds part and the angry sky is replaced by light beams shining down along the glistening shores of diamond sparkled drops of heavenly waters, resting softly on the fingertips of leaves, grasses, the soft edges of peoples homes, reflecting the colors only moments away from the same soft touches of their own sweet smiles. Amazing everything seems cleaner now, fresher, healthier, clearer.

By Peter Colla

VACCINATION TO LIGHT

A question was posed to me by a new friend who was curious how the principles of Health and Wellness, specifically addressing sickness or injuries using techniques of Body, Mind, and Spirit could be applied to the area of corporate business, and not just Healthcare business, considering he was in the business radio talk program owner-developer.

The very next day a very prominent local International Business Owner and Manufacturer posed almost the exact question to me but related to advising the Queen of a foreign government; "How could the concepts for improving the Health and Wellness of an individual be of any help to a Queen who wishes to develop the resources of her country and lead her people into prosperity?"

I thought about what each of them said or wrote for a great while after reading the last email, perplexed at the similar questions being posed to me within that twenty-four-hour time frame.

Interestingly enough I was posed a similar question by a man who interviewed my wife Anna and me on the radio only the previous week, just a day after we were on the radio with a friend, speaking about our new book Heal Yourself; "For God's Sake" in which we brought up methods and correlation of healing while using techniques that encompass Body, Mind, and Spirit concerns, treating and evaluating to the causes of infirmities and not just symptoms. Again the subject was placed more into the physical aspects of positive change and not merely healthcare of which I had written.

An yet again in a phone call, the question came up basically; "How could these principles you write about in healthcare and the treatment of afflictions using spiritual, mind, and body techniques be translated into the business environment, and be useful for businessmen or the corporate sector?" This was an interest of his since his platform primarily addresses business or at least is a business talk radio show, in this case, young business entrepreneurs?

After receiving the question from three completely unrelated directions nearly simultaneously in the same week, I figured it must be something that needed to be on the front-burner. The preponderance of this thought especially after reading my friend's email about the Queen and my wondering how such information could possibly affect business, what possible good could it be for King or in this case a Queen, to be used as a positive effect for an entire country? Seemed to me to place an even more daunting weight into the question already swimming in my mind.

So like I often do when I don't understand something or find myself contemplating a riddle-like I did in the above-mentioned book; "Why do some people heal and others don't?" I decided to take the question to God.

There immediately followed four days of silence, and then I heard something.

He answered! As I wrote the Queen, I will write to you in the following texts the answer to my question exactly, and in the same manner, how it was delivered to me. Whatever you do with it, it is totally up to you.

The question in my mind was;

How hard would it be to apply the concepts of healing I have already been given into the corporate or business or even an entire country model?

The answer was a shock to me, so I will just give it to you as I heard it.

"It is not hard at all, as a matter of fact, it is much more difficult to heal an individual than any group of people, whether that be a family, company, city, or country for that matter."

"Actually the larger the group the easier it is."

"All attacks regardless of what you see as the size or circumstance are all mostly

spiritual in nature."

"Attacks on individual persons are done at the cellular even molecular level and performed against a soul in the smallest and most insignificant places compared to the whole effect on a person's life. These attacks of entities being the smallest and most insignificant of physical essences are the easiest to manipulate, and it is only through dark spiritual "intent" that their actions turn perfectly created children into slaves."

"There are trillions of cells in the body but changing the belief of the person or spirit as a whole, in essence, has the effect of changing the social structure of the entire body. It allows for the initiation of genomes, in the smallest of places, that have the ability to elicit goodness in the cells. This same principle is a constant regardless of what size group of molecules, cells, people, or an entire nation of people you are dealing with."

"Belief is the key to health, wellness and healing."

I recognized this principle displayed out in information given to me in the past by my wife Anna describing the discovery of Epigenetic's and the fact that we could change our very genes, initiating firing of positive actions and illicit hidden and almost miraculous functions with our very thoughts, but even more importantly initiating healing in ourselves and in others with merely our beliefs. If we feel we are sick or more importantly told we are doomed, we become what we believe and thus begin to manifest it. More importantly likewise, if we just feel we can heal, it is a great first step in manifesting it in our life.

This is in essence the Ascension of Health and Wellness.

While bodies are made up of trillions of cells, companies or cities at the most are made up of hundreds or thousands of individuals, and countries likewise are a mere fraction compared to the independent numbers spoken of in the human body. The voice continued…

"Inject the same principles into the individuals of a community regardless of the size; a single cell, a corporation, or an entire country and the effect is an increase in light, healing occurs, and darkness must flee."

"In the case of Kingdoms, the principles are even easier to realize than in the cell. It is because countries are led by their leaders, and reflect the heart of their leadership good or bad."

The Old Testament is full of examples where Kings come into power, some good, some evil. Under the reign of the good Kings, the people flourish, under the bad ones they suffer. While God may decide who gets to be born a King and who doesn't, it is up to the individual King to decide to become a good one or not, and even in some cases a great one or truly evil one?

"With great gifts come great responsibilities, leaders are always indirectly responsible for the prosperity of those they rule. You on an individual basis are

responsible for your temples given to you. Parents are responsible for the children until children come to the age of accountability and begin to make the choices for themselves. People choose to heal as easily as they choose to believe, and it is the same way a kingdom can prosper, it is through the active choice to heal by its leaders themselves, that prosperity prevails."

Like a King or Queen, as an Owner of a multinational company, or even President of society regardless of size, the facts remain as constant as set in place by God for us all good leads to life, evil leads to death. Rain or God's blessings fall upon all heads equally. With great responsibility comes great accountability. We can believe in our own sovereignty, health, and happiness, but we can also believe in our own doom, this is why words whether spoken by us or at us are so powerful.

The consequential understanding of this principle then dictates an ideology one may need to embrace as a precipitator to facilitate Goodness in their life, especially when it comes to leadership. A person merely needs to *"pick up their mat and walk,"* a distinct movement towards light must be made.

Corporate structures, countries, or cells in the body all have the same basic portals in which blessings or curses can enter; through their eyes in the form of light, through sound in the form of sounds or speech, fed to them through the products of their labors, and last through the experiential structure of the body as a whole, through the good or bad experiences on the skin. It is simple mathematics in the matrix comparison of Health, Wellness, and Healthcare Production.

Let us continue our assumption that all physical structures in the real universe are made up of the same electromagnetic energy oscillations, then the only difference between energies that bump up against us reside not in the difference in structure, but "Intent." Some energies are intended for nurturing, goodness, light, and love, while others have the intent for destruction, hate, darkness, and evil. Positive energies build, and negative ones diminish, steal, kill, or destroy.

In my own medical field, I have come increasingly confronted with the realization that prescribed, required, or injected therapies that are stated to be for healing or health have included in these components that are toxic, depressing, deadly, and can kill. Nowhere is this anomaly more evident than in vaccinations. If these components such as Mercury or Formaldehyde are known to be harmful and serve absolutely no purpose to be included, then the only conclusion one could make is their inclusion is of malicious intent; they are put there with the intent to harm, a curse!

While I will not get into an expose about all the negative revelation regarding vaccinations, one thing is truly troubling and that is the push of the medical system to vaccinate babies supposedly against all sorts of diseases almost immediately upon birth, knowing full well the child's immune system has not yet developed at all, one would wonder what the intent is in those so-called vaccinations. I know one thing as a therapist I have treated dozens of children reduced to vegetables because of the negative effects of vaccines as well as seen a significant increase in autism the last two decades, another subject for later.

Injecting any factors of goodness into any system thus has the effect of increasing all good things in that system merely if by only pure quantity. But the retrospective conclusion would also be said to exist; injecting any darkness, whether it be any of the four windows into the mansion we call our physical life would result in a decrease of these structures. But since darkness is the absence of light it cannot be a quantitative element, it adds nothing to the equation as a whole merely has the effect of diminishing by its increasing presence.

A conclusion could be made that any positive factors or intentional energies can be placed on the line of positive real factors, and any negative factors can only be replaced in the line of divisional elements, thus having the effects of reducing the whole numbers as their presence increases.

Example;   500   Portions of Love, Light, Healing
divided by   25   Portions of Hate, Darkness, Sickness

The resulting atmosphere of experience is 20 remaining positive productive components, the darkness cannot reduce the initial 500 inputted Godly portions merely has a "reducing" effect on their potential strength. Regardless of what is created in the physical universe the least amount of shadows a single object can cast is one.

Thus if no additional darkness is added to the factored equation of any gift by God then the sum of the whole;

$$500/1 = 500$$

But when a structure, or the sum of the whole, in essence, increases through the increase of light that shines within it has the effect of causing the darkness to flee and thus diminish even the single shadow that exists in the physical.

In essence, we could be "Vaccinating" light into the structure whether it be an individual or a group, this would be much better than injecting the person with mercury, of a COVID vaccine for a disease that doesn't even exist, but that's for another day.

The resulting blessed bread and fishes reaction basically has the physical effect of allowing the given shadow to be diminished as a factor below, resulting in the sum of a single or a mere fraction of its original;

$$500 / 1/100 = 50,000$$

Injecting Godliness into any structure causes the structure to glow with its own inner radiating light thus not only has the effect of causing the darkness to diminish, or flee but also has the indirect proportional effect of increasing the original gift from God through the multiplying effect of additional light.

A basic equation for production could be extrapolated from the above-mentioned factors as; Production of a system, equals the combined components of Happiness, being an additional input of Godly energy, realizing happy corporate members will not only produce a more energetic work environment but add to the overall physical reality of the community by adding real goodness to an already constant ever-fluctuating universe.

All Good things come from God, so Happiness must, by logical conclusion, also come from God.

Health/sick X Wellness/slavery =

Happiness/depression X Gratification/worry =

Creativity/boredom X Fulfilled-Life/uselessness =

Production/waste

People who are healthy, do not call in sick, they not only come to the workplace but come with life-giving and Godly creative enthusiasm. When people have an expectation of wellness in their lives, they release themselves of the lies and slavery the media brings in the dogma of doom these afflictions attempt in their Big-Pharma-driven lies. These are nothing more than dark attempts to enslave innocent people in endless medicated lies, surrounded by curses, filled with poisons, and if one would examine the same scenario merely a few centuries ago, they would see it as sorcery or witchcraft.

Happiness is given in the same proportions to health in people's lives and with it a gratification that what they are present within their labors of the day is exactly what God would have them participate with today, a working knowledge that they are receiving gladness as a wage to produce hope. There is no need to worry about tomorrow for the same God who gave them the gladness of today takes the responsibility to create the new day that is full of blessings tomorrow. This is ascended through in the workplace.

Productiveness is increased if merely by the addition of Goodness, Light, Happiness, or any other positive factor in each member of these social communities' immediate environment. Increases if even a fraction is an increase none-the-less, the increase is growth, with growth comes experiential wisdom, another gift from God, and this can effectively translate into a fulfillment that transcends a life of a particular soul. The Ascension begins and up the stair-step, we go into enlightenment.

Ultimately all of these factors when Growth is achieved in any way, on a cellular, personal, community, business member, corporate entity, or even country level the increase has the effect of increased creative production on an individual scale. We are all created in the image of God; creators ourselves. We create good and bad with our every word.

Decreasing any of the negative factors to the minimum of a single shadow, cast by the individual objects of participation has the effect of reducing waste to its most minimal singularity, it completely disappears!

Increasing Godliness into any of these structure has the affect of increasing the Godly light in the structure and causes the darkness to flee thus fractionalizing it to the point where it will increase the positive factor at hand and increase the overall gift already present by astronomical proportions, as seen in the case of 500 becoming 50,000. Illumination!

When it comes to leadership the reason it is so easy to effect the overall outcomes is because of the multiplying results leadership grants.

The Leader whether it be a President, King, Queen, Director, Coach, Father or Mother of a family, or friend, has granted to them by God the responsibility and grace of the leading multiplayer;

Leader (Health/sickness X Wellness/slavery of their peoples) = Production/waist of their communities as a whole.

Adding any positive number has a positive effect on the whole, but adding a negative number which has a likewise negative effect.

If the leader increases Godliness, Health, and Wellness into their own life, they must increase the effects throughout their entire social environment of their people. This is a Godly constant and a promise.

It is impossible for a company to prosper that is being led by someone who is afflicted by greed, vice, or sickness, but at the same time as healing comes in so does the countries health proportionally increase. Ascension into the light is the revelation of prosperity.

By Peter Colla

BRICKLAYER

I had an image appear in the early morning whispers that awaken from the dreams of my mind. One of a bricklayer sitting on a small stool and laying bricks along a cobblestone road in some remote village street perhaps in the European countryside of some not so distant land or past. He is casually sitting on the simplest of wooden stools humming to himself and smiling at the passers-by. He hardly seems to be concentrating on the rapid motions of both of his hands as he places brick after brick into their perfect place, repeatedly, and I may add, meticulously forming patterns in the road in such perfectly flat and uniform manner it seems like it could only be done by some sophisticated machine.

He speedily moves up the path scooting his wooden stool over the now recently finished part of the road he had just completed, moving the stool so often it appears that he hardly sits for a few seconds and then he has to hop the stool again a few feet further. Other workers are all around him, some in front of him preparing the sand, raking and smoothing the section he is moving towards, others bringing and stacking bricks in front of his hands. All of these men move in almost frenzied worry trying to stay ahead of the bricklayer as he just smiles and continues. These men and their nervousness to prepare the path sufficiently with adequate speed to keep just ahead of the bricklayer do nothing to diminish his mood as the casual smile or occasional greeting to a passer-by, always remaining at what seems to be the most peaceful casualness. He continues to move up the road at what seems an almost impossible pace.

So many bricks are being placed so fast his hands are almost a blur as he places one with his right hand, then another with his left; back and forth while he only sways with the most insignificant motion, like the gentle sway of a tree in the afternoon breeze. Less experienced younger men are straining, hurrying to dump wheelbarrows full of bricks right next to and in the path of each of his hands so all the bricklayer needs to do is reach out and take the next brick needing to be placed. The motion involved, and all around the bricklayer seems to suggest that he is delivering exactly what he needs to do in the task he has been given, doing it is a way that is exceedingly appreciated.

Even his boss who watches from a casual distance has a smile of satisfaction watching him, a clear pride for having such a valued worker on his team. For why would the boss of the road construction company give this bricklayer so many helpers if he didn't think the man was valuable? Other bricklayers at other places along the road seem to be moving much slower and have to go get their own bricks or only have one or two persons helping them.

I think I know this man of my dream, like someone out of my past life's experience, perhaps a friend I knew years ago, long before I began doing the work I am doing today. When I think of the man of my own memory, in any context, I always see him in my mind with a smile on his face, a cigarette dangling from his mouth, even while running or playing sport. His full-bearded face embracing the smile that seems to always be on his lips, that and the obvious fortitude, his back clearly demonstrating muscular strength only usually seen on the most accomplished power-lifters, yet I know he probably never lifted a single barbell in his life or spent even a minute in the gym. He didn't need to, he lifted two-pound bricks at least a hundred times a minute all day, every day, his whole adult life.

If someone was to ask me what the bricklayer looks like, I might describe long blond hair, stocky looking like a cross between a short, smoking, bricklaying version of Thor, and maybe what Santa Claus might have looked like when he was in his late twenties? That and the fact he was wearing wooden shoes to his workplace did seem to make him look more like a village farmer in Eastern Europe than anyone a person might expect to see in their normal life today.

Not everybody needed to use the roads he worked on, but for the people who did happen to use these roads, they seemed to be cleaner roads, good roads, roads that were designed to bring destination and protection from the surrounding irregularities of the forests of the countryside and weed lined road edges. These forests that were just a short distance from the road, they are thick growth, touching the autumn skies, giving the layered green canopy a mysterious dark undertone, not frightening, just a tint of unknowing that leaves people with calm reassurance, they receive at least a feeling granted them by walking on the road, the safety of not having to venture forward through the darker unknown forest.

The many people who passed by the bricklayer greet him, and if they didn't first, he greeted them, that was when they lifted their heads for a moment from the road to look up at him as they walked by or when he greeted them. Everyone he met he seemed to like and they seemed to like him. The many that even smiled back with a greeting often bordered on genuine appreciation when they came to the place where he was working. For he was a skilled bricklayer, a seasoned road worker, and it has always been an honorable job with what seemed a noble cause; helping the many people who would come by. Maybe not directly helping them, but indirectly for through his obvious talents, the road seemed so smooth and perfectly created? Plus, it was because of his efforts they could travel down this particular part of the road he was working on. Smiles of appreciation for the work he did maintaining the road, laying the bricks on the road they needed to use.

He was not always so good at what he did, it was a skill he had to learn, but his own God-given talents allowed him to hone the skill into something that others seemed to see as truly mystical, almost artistic, even at times miraculous. Yet, he was the first to remind them; "He was only a bricklayer, he just happens to be given some unique skills by God that allowed him to move in a way that a bit faster than most."

The basic education of bricklaying was taught to all of them the same way, and in that, his own early development which was not much different than any of the other workers around him, everyone learns the same methods, works along the same way, does the same job. But it was not long, perhaps only a single year before he and everyone else around him began to see the talent that laid in wait within, and he became quite fast and methodical at what he did, so much so, even getting a bit of a reputation for being one of the best bricklayers in the region. Maybe this is why his own body took on an image of the sort of strength mimicking the intended security and stability the road was purposed to perform. For let's not forget, it was a road that brought the people where they thought not only they wanted to go, but needed to go in this junction of their life, in this corner of their soul, was it not? The bricks were merely the individual stepping stones along with a much more complex and calculated system of transportation.

Maybe it was this added strength, the abilities that seemed to come naturally, maybe it was his desire not to just stare down at the ground, or look around at not only the people that came by but anything; the trees, the birds, the children, that prompted him to look at everyone who passed by while also smiling and even enjoying the gifts of each day? An inquisitive spirit to observe rather than just stare at the ground and place brick after brick into its intended spot?

On this particular day, he was working, he suddenly heard a faint cry in the weeds along the road, realizing there must be a poor unfortunate laying crying, maybe even dying in the high grasses of the ditch next to the road? While others kept busy or just kept meandering down the road, his attention was fixed on the sound coming from the ditch. Other workers made gestures with their faces, some demonstrating that they seemed to know of the sad sound, but kept at their road work, all walking by, most never even bothering to as much as turn their heads to even glanced this poor soul's way. Some, many of which were co-workers of his own group, would venture the person in the ditch a quick glance, but quickly return their attention back to the task of the road, for nobody would help this person in the ditch. He decided to take a break and step off the road and look at what was going on.

He reached down and pulled the poor person out of the muck, brushed off the dirt, and lifted him back up to his feet, it was quite easy for a man with such strength. To the bricklayer's amazement, the injured person felt immediately relieved and went his way without even needing to get back on the road. Dashing into the forest with hardly a glance back, a thank you, or even a casual goodbye. Many of his co-workers saw the interaction and stood there in amazement at what transpired, all of them "dumbfounded," even as much as he himself seemed to be. Were we all really "Founded So Dumb" the bricklayer thought to himself with a chuckle?

Suddenly while even still standing in the muck, our good bricklayer noticed another up along the road who also had fallen also into the muck, in the overgrown gulley that he hardly ever noticed was even along the edge next to the road. A great deal many people lying there, most face down struggling to even draw breath, many trying to push themselves with weak arms out of wet mud, or kicking in a slippery black tar-like stench trying to crawl out, all were in pain, all were crying and suffering. But also, he saw from this vantage point, the most subtle irregularities that were in the road, what seemed like the many slight flaws that were there, especially along the edge that may have caused these poor people to stumble and then fall into the ditch in the first place?

His first thoughts were to help some more of these poor people up ahead who had fallen, but there seemed to be so many, and with each step forward more and more came into his awareness as he looked up along the edge of the road. A few even tumbled into the ditch even in the place he just exited another. In front and behind him the gulley hidden in the weeds along the road stretched before him like some dark sewer hidden in the recesses of a weed-infested swamp.

The first few he came to, he tried to help them in the same way he had helped the first one. Some of these individuals would get up and walk away happy, content in the same way the first guy did. Many others would quickly climb back onto the road and continue down the same path often with hardly a glance back. A few of the people who did get back on the road, he noticed, would immediately hit another flaw in the road and tumble right back into the ditch again. There were a very few who even refused his help altogether, demanding he leaves them alone, even pushing his hands away from any help he might offer, only wishing to lie in the ditch, to cry and suffer. It became immediately obvious that many of these particular few seemed to be in the ditch by their own choosing, not wishing to leave, seemingly feeling a liking to the attention they received from their aching cries or complaints. They complained about being covered in mud while taking the same black filth and wiping it on themselves?

After a while of attending to the first people he helped out of the ditch, he went back to his bricklaying job but also started to fix a few of the flaws he had witnessed in his direct vicinity, and at the end of his shift reported back to his boss about what he found. The first reaction of the boss was positive, but quickly changed, and soon it became evident, if not directly, but eventually in writing; "That he wasn't getting paid to help people out of the ditch, he was getting paid to lay bricks, at least to concern himself with the people using the road, and that's all."

But how could he ignore all the people in the ditch, in his heart, he couldn't just leave them there, so he helped them anyway, explaining each in their turn how to avoid the flaws the road seemed to have. It became evident to everyone, including the boss, if he spent so much time helping the people out of the ditch, he couldn't lay as many bricks as efficiently as before, at first his pay suffered, but soon he was called back again into the office with the boss.

The boss expressed concern he wasn't working as efficiently as he had been before, it seemed the result was there were fewer people needing to use the road as often? But the bricklayer explained, while that may be true, his primary work was helping the people on the road, wasn't that why he was there in the first place? Plus, he was still able to lay more bricks than his colleagues, he was, in truth, laying a much more positive road now without the flaws, safer for the people to continue down without as much risk to fall along the way. Fewer people falling off the road, meant a better road, and ultimately a better reputation for the boss and the company? Perhaps this may ultimately lead to more people wishing to use their road?

One thing was for sure, this explained why everyone who used the road seemed to stare at the ground, maybe it was perhaps they sensed the flaws or at least were fearful of them, either way, the flaws seemed everywhere, in the middle, in the beginning, at every turn, but especially along the edges. Maybe that is why everyone who used the road seemed depressed, their eyes were being digressively focused into the ground!

Before the conversation was over, as an added bonus, the bricklayer presented the boss with a written report of the various flaws he found in the road, a quick note of the few he had already helped, even a few letters from some of them, along with simple techniques and cost-effective changes that could eliminate the flaws forever throughout the company so others would not fall into the ditch. The boss thanked him for the list, then fired him on the spot and told him if he said anything about what was said regarding his time working on the road, any of the people he helped in the ditches or the flaws, he would sue him and do everything in his power to ruin or destroy the bricklayer as well as his family. The boss threw his papers in the trash and said with a smirk; "If you don't like it take me to court."

The bricklayer went to work for other companies, for he was a bricklayer, and he needed to feed his family. But he quickly found many of the same flaws and likewise people in the ditches along the roads, some with terrible issues, sicknesses even cancers often caused by again the faults or the black tar-like toxins of the road. How could he ignore them, especially the crying pleas of the suffering children? All of them he helped, he even begged not to tell anyone, especially the bosses, of the help they received, because he knew it would mean his job, but they always seemed too, or someone standing off to the side would see and report him, and of course, within moments of these reports, he would find himself sacked again? He lost job after job, position after position, and even found out one day his original boss was calling ahead and slandering the bricklayer with lies to convince the new bosses to fire him immediately.

He then decided he wouldn't work for a company unless they had a policy in place to help the people in the ditches and or correct the flaws in the roads. In some cases, he was even specifically hired by the owners of these companies to eliminate the very flaws that they themselves had already realized existed. But here again, the minute he either helped someone out of a ditch, even sometimes through instructing other co-workers how they might or actively fixed any flaws themselves, even a single brick, a sort of attack dog; an almost Rottweiler looking person showed its vicious teeth and eliminated him with a hateful smile. Usually, this one appeared in the form of a supervisor, or assistant executive of the company, one would rise up and command him first to stop helping others, later slander and ultimately try to destroy him as well. One or more of these Rottweiler looking individuals even went so far as to dismantle entire companies and destroy departments of major multi-state organizations rather than let any of the road fixing processes take hold. They seemed willing to cut their own throats rather than let any procedure take hold that could help the roads become better.

All the major and most of the successful companies quickly began to ignore his pleas, the smaller ones didn't seem to dare to contemplate such a seemingly radical thought or willing to go against the wishes of his first boss. When it came to even admit the flaws were there, even though many of the larger companies, frankly the entire industry, reluctantly did admit it already existed. Many of the bosses and other bricklayers for that matter were reluctant to use the roads themselves, knowing in their hearts the flaws that existed.

Soon they even turned away from his offer for service in any way, not being interested in his bricklaying skills at any price, often telling him he was overqualified to lay the bricks and they needed a younger person, someone in their words; "They could mold into the model and beliefs of their company!" It became evident to the bricklayer that the big bosses not only wanted but may have intentionally designed the roads to cause people to fall into the ditches in the first place, seemingly wanting the people to lie in the ditch and suffer. Those poor souls became, as it were, prisoners of the road! Somebody did design the flaws and dug those ditches that were along the road, didn't they?

Quickly and finally the bricklayer realized the only way he could have any hope of really helping anyone avoid the traps that seemed to be lurking in the ditches along the roads, was to start his own road making company. No need to have a ditch if the people didn't fall off the road, and if the flaws were gone, no stumbling, people could look up when they used his road, faithful that no flaws were there. But here too, all the contracts for the roads were being sponsored by the big contracting companies, any payments for the bricklaying needed to go through them, and they would not pay him unless he held to the strict designs of the roads; they wanted their constructs to include everything they expected from the other companies which clearly included the ditches and especially flaws.

The bricklayer went on and started just helping the people out of the ditches, preparing the roads where he could, often on his own or even in secret. And while the many people in the ditches were pleasantly thankful for what he did for each of them individually, nobody ever offered him any supportive thanks for his help, not even a bite to eat or a drink of a cup to help feed his children. They all seemed to look at him with confused looks; "doesn't or shouldn't your boss pay you to help us since we all fell while using the road, are you not a bricklayer, isn't it your job to fix the road?"

The big bosses seemed to not pay him any attention anymore, yet they did actually the opposite and paid close attention to his every move, secretly scheming and coordinating slander all around him, attempting to destroy him and his family any chance they had, remaining true on their promise; "To destroy him and his family if the bricklayer didn't do exactly what they said." Without putting his finger on exactly what or when the bricklayer himself seemed to have increasingly bad financial luck and suffer setbacks all around. People stealing from him, even the little he had, doors closing for no apparent reason, promises made for business or help, and then suddenly nothing as these good people just vanished. It was as if a carpet would be placed under him to give him hope and then suddenly be yanked out from under him for no other reason than to watch him fall.

The old boss kept making up reasons to pull him into court, all along laughing because he didn't care win or lose, breaking the bricklayer was his goal. Could it be possible the big bosses are trying to destroy his family like some jealous beast only wanting to take that few peddles, his meager garden of land, that single blooming flower, or some precious lamb he happens to have, just because they happen to want it, rather than use one of the many they had, or rather than looking at the vast forest they possess, the great abundances they have their own yards? It didn't make sense.

One day as he worked secretly fixing the ditches along the road a great leader of the land came by, a truly good man who not only loved the land and its people in word and promise but expressed it in every thought and deed he performed. He had been gone for a while and now it was time for him to return. He spots the bricklayer digging along the ditches, sweating hot in the sun, straining on the shovel, dirty, worn, and tired. "When did you become a ditch digger?" the great man asks as he looks on to the bricklayer leaning tired and heavy against the shovel?

"I'm not a ditch digger, I pulled a person out of this ditch and now I'm repairing the land here because these ditches catch people in the muck and mire." "Maybe if I fix a little of the land here, get rid of the mud, when the people fall in they won't get so stuck?" "That's my thought, anyway?"

"Does it work?" the rich man says.

"I don't know I just got started."

"Who's paying you to do that?" the man asks with a confused look on his face.

"Nobody, as a matter of fact, if the people who make the roads knew I was doing it they would probably call the police to stop me."

"Well, I'm not trying to stop you, but I have come here to try to help you." "I'm giving you some solid gold bricks so you can go build a road the right way, one that will get people to their destinations without fear or flaws, so they don't have to look down while they walk but can venture down this path with their heads held high and see all the wonders God has given each of them on every glorious day of their journey."

"I tried that before," the bricklayer said, "but my old boss and his powerful friends shut me down like a spider with a great web, every turn I make, try to destroy my very family, I fear for them."

"Yes, I know," the Good and powerful leader says, "but you need not worry about your old boss, I am very aware of what he has done. For that man thinks this is his land, and he can do what he wants, but it is My land, and I will deal with him directly."

"Why are you doing this?" the bricklayer asks, almost not hardly believing what he was hearing?

"Two reasons; one, because the very first person you helped out of the ditch, I don't know if you remember, but it was me, you saved my life." The man says with a smile that doesn't border on any pride but mere fact as if the bricklayer should have realized it all along.

"I do remember the first person and while it was a while ago, I don't remember him looking like you, but again it was a while ago. But even with that, how could I save anyone's life I am only a bricklayer?" the bricklayer asks with a little confusion.

"Lifting people out of ditches is a life saving calling upon itself."

"When you do it for any of my subjects, especially the least of these, you do it for me." "For, I am the King of these lands."

"But the second reason I am giving you these golden bricks is simple; because you are a bricklayer." He smiled and reached into his coat and pulled out the first solid gold brick. Handed it to the bricklayer and took the shovel from the bricklayer's hands and turned to walk away.

"Wait, what road and where do you want me to lay this brick?"

The King turned back and with the sweetest most loving smile a good Father ever gave his son as he said; "I will let you know."

...

Many people ask me why I don't open back up my own medical office, or just go back to working on patients, especially considering I have seen so many people healed in such miraculous ways. And they always wonder why I don't just bill the insurance companies for the care I give people?

But the answer like the dream is simple; I am the bricklayer, and the care had literally become as laying bricks, the flaw and the traps are in the road and the organizations that profit from their participation. Try as I might, I couldn't get the bosses to agree to change the flaws in the road, and when I fixed them anyway, I was cast aside, on more than a dozen occasions. I am persecuted even today.

The threats are real, the attacks are as well, and while I do not mention names, or companies, or even industries, it is not to protect the innocent but to protect the identities of my loved ones and the people who happen to experience freedom from this tyranny. For the system has created a temple or in this case, a road, where people may come and travel down, intending to experience healing, but all they receive is deceit, suffering, and imprisonment.

Despair and Hopelessness; these seem to be the promptings this road propagates and certainly the ditches the people find themselves in.

THE MARK OF THE BEAST

I would have to say that the consideration of what exactly was the "Mark of the Beast" as spoken of in The Apocalypse of John or commonly known as The Book of Revelation in the Bible, has been for me a pondered question for at least the last nearly thirty-five years. Precise interpretations of exactly what it would look like have been presented, especially from the more evangelical churches of Christianity, to be anything from a simple tattoo on the wrist or forehead, to a sinister chip being implanted into us. This could be done either by means of a surgical implant or even through vaccinations as is being proposed today, and everything in between, including even the cell phones we hold, or the bar codes that have shown up on every food product that must be transferred from hand to mouth are all only a few of the dozens if not hundreds of possible explanations to the images John spoke of?

I vaguely remember back around the time of our countries Bicentennial, there was an increased Revelations interpretation of the then signs of the times, speaking of the many facts and the deciphering of prophecies spoken of in Revelations. This manifested itself into exactly what the various symbolic representations of John's visions meant, how they were demonstrated in that particular time, even how various technological advances could only be interpreted to mean the return of Christ, along with the exact meaning the dread of the evil mark of the beast signified within itself was unquestionable.

The unanimous thought was the ultimate acceptance of this mark more importantly resulted in a voluntary relinquishing of God and a sort of bowing down to Satan that was unmistakable as well as irrevocable, of this fact nobody seemed to dispute.

That being said, the actual need to, in the process, with the free will choice of participation requires some sort of ritual bowing and acceptance of Satan into themselves, must be fulfilled through active and responsible acceptance. This has discarded the more innocent theories of involuntary participants such as cell phones or vaccinations nano-chips to be discarded as not feasible because they eliminate an active acceptance on the part of the person accepting the mark.

This is not to say the dark entities that would plan such things would hate nothing else but to corral a large portion of mankind especially the innocent, that they might try to develop such programs for those specific purposes. But God in His infinite wisdom has placed fail-safes into the physical universe that protects innocent people especially from plots and plans evil-doer may design to remove from His children their options of free will. In such cases their plans would never work, God is always in control.

Maybe it is for these reasons that recently I have seen various aspects of what is being shown in the furthest hidden recesses of hell on earth, the revelations of human trafficking, the trafficking of small children, the vast as well as unbelievable dark reasons why such acts could occur? I have to admit to myself, as much as I have researched in the past the darkness that hides behind human trafficking and its connection to satanism or sex trafficking, I could not fathom that it could be of such numbers worldwide to warrant the then-candidate Donald Trump mentioning combating human trafficking, needing it to be on the forefront of his Presidential docket. Nor after his election the need to actually send in multiple warships into the Caribbean to battle drug and human trafficking?

But how do the observations of such atrocities in fact aid in the ascension of people? It would most certainly lend credence to the statement by our Lord; *"I turn all things to good..."* As we have already discussed seeing and thus shining the light on the Truth that is hidden in the lies of the world are the first step in ascension.

As for now, at least recently, information has been revealed of the true nature and the actual product of which could be acquired through a massive network of child trafficking and child abduction, and that is the production of the chemical compound known as Adrenochrome. Adrenochrome is the chemical compound that forms in the blood by the flooding of adrenaline into the bloodstream as a result of the victim being literally scared nearly to death. And of course what are the easiest people in the world to scare in such a way but the innocent and youngest, most defenseless among us; our littlest children?

Apparently, this chemical compound not only has life-improving qualities such as making women appear younger more womanly, men more masculine, muscular, and young, but apparently along with its many age reducing and disease halting attributes it renders upon the user an intense almost uncontrollable "high" which is immediately and completely addictive, many thousand times higher than the strongest heroine. Making it as well the most sought after, expensive and addictive drug in history, and thus making it only accessible to the richest and most affluent on earth.

Now back to the "Mark," right about the time the COVID "Scamdemic" broke information regarding the wide usages of Adrenochrome, as well other facts regarding this chemicals vast network necessary to facilitate such a market, let alone keep it secret, began to leak into the internets back alleys of research and truth seekers investigations from so many different sources all over the world, whistleblowers, and even scientific researchers, that denying its existence could no longer hold any water. Mainly regarding only the excessive usage especially among Hollywood elites, but also many of the ruling class politicians, royals, and even athletes throughout the world were enough to demonstrate that this problem was not only true but vast and diabolical from nature.

Another interesting fact was the information that it was being reported whereby there was supposedly a lab in China which accounted for the world's synthesized supply of Adrenochrome processed from the blood as it was harvested from children and then distributed. In the same lab apparently, the COVID-19 virus was developed in Wuhan. It was also reported at this time that the supply was cut off, but shortly before, the last few months of supply of Adrenochrome were allowed to be shipped out but were "Marked" with a specific, non-transmittable, and particular strain of COVID whereby if anyone used this substance their body would be forever "Marked" by this virus, and all the authorities would have to do is test the blood and a person would be revealed if they were an Adrenochrome user or not?

The other factor is when people are reported to use Adrenochrome even if in the most minimal sense when they are suddenly denied the substance apparently the physiological changes that apparently surface are so distinct and horrifying usage cannot be mistaken, visible markings on their hands and face gives them away, most distinctively.

Immediately when I heard this and the fact that it was referred to as being "Marked," I had an "Amen" thought in my spirit about the Mark of the Beast. Perhaps this was what John was referring to when he said anyone who took the Mark, would be damned. It certainly would be Godly justice for Him to create such a mechanism hidden within the elemental sciences of the usage of this atrocity.

Ritualistic drinking of human blood and eating of human flesh is nothing new to this world, and while Hollywood may desire to somehow shirk it off as artistic or hip, there is no doubt the connection to the darkest aspects of devil worshiping or satanism that seems to be the driving force behind these activities. This in itself speaks to the spiritual nature of such endeavors, a fact that I find quite remarkable considering the almost fanatic anti-God or more so Anti-Christ ideology portrayed in movies, especially when it comes to a possible life after death.

Science has also proven recently the correlation of Cannibalism and the physiological changes that take place within cellular physiology as a result of people who ingest human blood or human flesh, the result is metabolic changes occur that are not only permanent but are certainly deadly. They have also proven a correlation of people who practice cannibalism with direct neurological changes in the brain resulting in the person going insane.

I think a person would already have to be insane to even think about drinking the blood or eating the flesh of a traumatized child.

There are also references in Revelations about the mark would be clearly visible on their hand/wrist or their forehead/face, and at first, this only seemed like some kind of coincidence, I also began to realize that people who commonly use this drug clearly show signs of it on their hands, but especially that it causes them to develop black eyes about the time when the drug's effect is wearing off.

The atrocities that seem to be insinuated in reference to what these beasts must do in order to facilitate the production of Adrenochrome in abducted children are almost too unthinkable to imagine let alone speak of. I believe it is in reference to these acts though that Jesus himself stated; "All sins could be forgiven, except those against the holy spirit." What if he is referring to holy spirits as those that reside in children?

He also said; "It would be better a millstone was tied around your neck and you were cast in the abyss, then to hurt one of these little ones."

The President did sign into executive order a mandatory death sentence to anyone involved in or benefiting from the abduction and trafficking of children.

Children are among the purest of spirits, I believe the enemy knows this and has spent centuries trying to brainwash us into believing that we are all born into sin. While that might be so, I also believe these children we are speaking of are all innocent, and if our Good and Noble President has truly waged a war against trafficking and satanic ritual abuse worldwide then I believe God must be on his side in order for him to make any marked advancement on ridding the earth of this evil once and for all.

I believe that anyone who places Adrenochrome to their lips must know in advance not only what they are doing and the demonic severity of their choices as well as knows full well where it comes from. They must in essence be willing to bow down and sell their souls to Satan in order to partake.

Those children that were abducted, raped, and even killed for their blood, for the innocence of their blood, the only good news is that try as they might, evil cannot hold onto the light. While these demon-possessed animals that hunt our children may benefit for a short time from the physical essence of such pure spirits as little children, the essence that is spirit cannot be held by darkness thus resulting in an immediate return to God the Father.

The souls of the innocent are Martyrs for Christ, and we who are believers, who have lost family, loved ones, friends through the greed of a few blood drinkers, we will have our vengeance, we will see our loved ones again in the next life, but rest assured the perpetrators of these atrocities now that the truth is being revealed will be paraded through the street naked for all their sins to be revealed, God Himself has promised this because our vengeance rests with Him.

God has created the very mechanism that was their lust, and the very mechanisms of their vice have become the Mark of their death.

"I believe ascension will show the involvement in ritual child abuse is The Mark of the Beast."

By Peter Colla

LIGHT SEED

The caterpillar seems like a helpless victim of an imminent attack, but ultimately when realization is made that God has already equipped him with everything she might need to overcome, all she has to do is relax and stand confident, demonstrating the true colors and special markings God Himself has adorned the caterpillar with; the mere sight of these realizations send the attacking villain's of the air to wide-eyed flight.

But that too means one must recognize such an attack only moments before it lands and thus react, not making oneself constricted and protracted merely taking it for another asset later, but posturing in defiance with the confidence and conviction that resides in the embrace of wisdom, a relaxation that comes with peace.

People moving towards spiritual in such a manner as could be described as ascension are as bundles of impulses that flow out in every direction yet with a perfect organized motion following synchronized harmonies seemingly predetermined like the paint strokes of a masterpiece, these beautiful pigments are altered only by our own individual choices, intent, or emotions. Realized in sparkling arrays of exploding lights illuminated off into various yet perfected directions as they too aid in the oscillations of the life particles they come in contact with.

What exactly is a "Light Seed," the "Remnant," God appointed King's or Queens, Angelic apparitions, Prophets', a Seer, Juan O' Savin, Oracles, Healers or a "Palladian," these Supermen and Wonder Women all blessed with gifts due to their higher ascension facilitations seem to the rest of us ground dwellers to have almost supernatural qualities to them? There have been many names given to these five-dimensional Ascended souls throughout the ages, and may all very well be of the same construct? One thing is certain, as we have already ascertained, they are made up of the same base energies on a quantum level, merely vibrating in a higher frequency than the normal majority of the rest of us around the world today.

Let us for the sake of this discussion consider the name Light Seeds. I must say from experience that it has been truly my pleasure to meet a couple of them in my lifetime, but truth be told, I had to search almost the entire world to find one. They are the purest of people, kind, filled with unfathomable love for everyone even strangers, animals, children, as a matter of fact, I can say when witnessing their behavior towards others they never exhibit even the least fraction of negativity, jealousy, or lies, except when it comes to coming in contact with evil, then their reactions have almost lion-like veracity in them. The youngest of children recognize them without hesitation often smiling or reaching out to greet them without any fear. Animals even ferocious ones often pause to consider them almost bowing in submission to their presence.

They are easy to recognize for those who are looking, having attractive qualities about them that defy explanation, soft yet indistinguishable beauties male or female, movements that rest within the nuances of almost musical notes, voices that resonate in reflection to the good words so often spoken by them, even their eyes seem to sparkle with lights that emanate from within. I have only known a few of these people in my long/short life and must admit in every case they possess an uncanny ability to facilitate happiness, gladness, joy, as well as peace into almost every being they come in contact with, regardless of the disposition, background, or affliction the surrounding finds itself in.

These light like radiated explosions that these people undoubtedly resonate with are not destructive in nature but creative, ever reverberating into continuous and reigniting crescendos of new and brighter colored waves mostly whites yet tinted ever so softly by the light colors of the subject and individuals they contact. They are completely encircled by the reflection of the elemental energies that they happen to consider, and the whole world around them, in loving reaction, transform and add to the colors they exhibit. The whole world is thus their canvas and pigments they have no need to own or possess, they merely use them while others take care of them for us. They seem to have one single goal and that is to make the world better for those around them. They truly seem to seed light!

The dark ones, on the other hand, those of descending destinies, may seem to be rich in the material earthly product yet they ignore pretty much the majority of the world around them in their quests keep in their perceived grips the fluctuating energies lusted with their eyes, concentrating on an ever decreasing and singular points of physical energy, often focusing on what they don't have, greedy to hold God-given energies for themselves, hoarding what they have within their grasp rather than sharing any of them with others around them. They seem to concentrate on such a singular and small point in their life that the entire rest of their surroundings begins to at first blur and eventually results to dim to the point where it darkens and eventually blackens completely, and the only point of any light entering is the small ever-narrowing hole they are looking towards which itself is but a shadow because it is something they do not have rather than what they desire. This has the effect within these of turning any aura energies radiating outward to be inwardly directed, ever concentrating, shrinking, condensing dying shell until an almost black hole effect is manifested.

The world around these dark spirits eventually darkens to a walled cell seemingly cold concrete in form, reinforced with bars of the jail they have themselves constructed with their lusts thought out their lives. They exist in this self-constructed dark cell ever peering out towards the one small speck of light they imagine they want in their life, the small idol of desire they cannot take their eyes off of no matter what happens to them physically. The rest of the world seems so scary because, in their world, it is dark and cold. Fear drives them, for everyone must want what they desire because this little speck of concentrated energy; it has become their entire world.

The ultimate hypocrisy of it all is the deep bunker existence of this dark construct, the great assembly of negativism they have built around themselves through continued lust for power. Their fear is the ultimate creation of emotional "Destruction" within what they feel or believe they have already built, the dreaded fear of loss becomes the driving force pushing them towards an ultimate goal that they must ultimately know is not good for them. It is all but an illusion, they have built nothing except a concentrated fixation on the single thing they continue to stare at, trying to hold energies they cannot hope to grasp, like clutching onto winds, vainly giving their devotions, their very lives to other spiritual constructs that care nothing for them, merely playing the fool in someone else's grand game.

"It is easier for a camel to go through the eye of a needle than a rich man to enter the kingdom of God"

The man who is rich in material things because he has spent his life accumulating now lives in a cage of materialistic darkness ever fearing others, someone, something will take it away, until finally, the small candle he calls his body given him by God shrivels up into a dark useless husk and parishes. This descending of spirit has a clear negative effect on the body, pulling on the skin, hardening the features, placing stresses and strains on various bodily functions until those systems either rebel or fail altogether, a diminishing functional development takes place, which can be patched but never heals ultimately leading to death. Wars wage within him, cancer like fighting gangs each pulling to at least re-immerge from the dark muck they have fallen in, trying desperately to find some semblance of the function they may have been created to fulfill in the first place?

The lighted person on other hand continues to take in the same portions of light given anyone else, yet shines out all the light that comes in from every direction, sharing with those around them, blessing, and even healing as God's life-giving energies are redirected, amplified, and even concentrated into useful, love and life-giving creations of positivity. They give because they have been given, re-gift every portion of love they have received, the ledger is balanced, one might say balance is evident in them.

It is commonly said of a light seed; "The whole world surrounds her and belongs to him, others merely take care of it, so why be concerned with owning anything, we will just share with people everything we have and they can share with us as well." Giving out as much that goes in is the essence of true riches.

"Riches stored up in heaven where no rust, or moth, or thief can steal. For where your riches are there your heart is also."

Science has told us that we have physically so much untapped potential using one a fraction of the capacity we were already created with. One example is our brains, using only 10% or so, and if we could somehow increase merely the functional usage there is literally nothing we couldn't do, even live or exist outside the restrictive capacity of our own bodies.

I have also read that science long ago realized that on a functional cellular level there is really no reason why the body ages, or cells finally age and die, having the capacity to replicate themselves nearly forever, yet for some yet unknown reason cells all begin at a seemingly predetermined date to breakdown almost as if on cue.

One amazing fact that has recently leaked out into the awareness is that out of the twenty-three pairs of DNA strands in a human body only two are actively being used thus leaving the other twenty-one dormant to be later activated, used, or potentially created but seemingly inaccessible until later?

It is my contention that the awareness process or an increase in the spiritual expanding consciousness in effect activates unused or dormant strains of our own DNA and thus illicit functions spoken about in the research mentioned above along with any or many other possible functions we can only imagine. We can all potentially become light seeds after ascending the right amount of steps, yet with our own individual Godly created specific talents, I believe that with ascension consciousness it is possible to fully activate the already created treasures of our perfect initial creation, bringing us back to the enlightened pure illuminated state we were initially designed to be.

THE HUNTED BECOME THE HUNTERS

In the continuation of our discussion regarding the Ascended Star Seeds, it must be realized that while we all can spiritually ascend, yet for the very few, they are born it. This fact has for its own revelations an understanding that swims deep within the murky waters of reality as we know it. Those who know full-well the hidden illuminations these higher spiritual beings represent also understand the rewards turning them over to darker rulers of the shadows brings, for darkness seeks them out not out of understanding, a longing to grow or enlighten themselves, but out of a desire to either solicit them into their own dark purposes or destroy them in the process?

The powers of darkness understand all too well the potential of the Star Seed, knowing many of the hidden secrets the young ascended themselves may not yet fathom. It is for the darkness lurking in the shadows, perceiving the light from afar even from the moment of his or her births, that possessing them becomes a quest even an undeniable obsession, for they seek not what they wish to become, but to have or destroy what they deep down know they will never be. It is as with everything in this world that is a gift from God, if the darkest of hearts cannot possess it they would rather destroy it than let others around them share.

The Star Seed's birth is literally written on the stars, yet it also those who understand and study these prophecies only for their own selfish gains that then use them to first seek out the gifted births, even following them throughout their lives, ever watching for the moment they may strike from the shadows and take them. It becomes apparent as the Star Seed comes to age that certain people seem to appear out of nowhere with promises of fame, wealth, or power, but for the true Star Seed already ascended none of this is desired, for they seek not gold, popularity, or even to rule over others but travel to discover the ultimate reward that only can be found yet not paid for, and that's God's love.

While the darkness craves fear almost feeds on it even as the driest parched lips crave mere water drops in the hottest sandy desert, so does the ascended realize that only out of light and love, which by the way are the same things, does life arise. The ascended are drawn even at the earliest age to leave the comfort of the nest, seeking the horizon to discover throughout the entire world the many faces of love God has created, and while the Star Seed emulates love, so does she need it in return. The enemy knows this full well, and often can only approach such a Star Seed as a wolf under a cloak of a lamb promising love, family, or comfort, but when the veil is removed it becomes clearly apparent the demonic lies hidden under sheep clothing and the betrayal and greed that awaits. Many of the Star Seeds have fallen betrayed the most by those closest to them, by the very people they have loved.

It is the gifts of God that the Star Seeds possess that the darkness wishes so desperately to obtain. Male Star Seeds are hunted and lured by the enemy to elicit the talents and individual leadership powers they may have hidden within the undiscovered recesses of their yet un-ascended genomes, if they cannot be turned to darkness every attempt is made to emasculate them. The Women Star Seeds, while they too can possess personally talents the enemy would love to illicit to their team, it is for their birthing abilities, and their offspring potential, even those already birthed, that they are often hunted, it is for this reason sexuality almost in every case is used in the seduction as well as rituals surrounding their abuse and capture.

This is the dichotomy in which we have found ourselves increasingly in these end times, making it more perilous for a person to strive or perhaps even decides to venture down that path God has placed them on, ascending up out of the valley, climbing the mountainside of truth and revelation can be not only physically and even mentally dangerous but often test the spiritual perseverance of the climber.

These people being pure at heart cannot help but share the truths they discover with everyone who might need them, in essence, stick their necks out for others. They help everyone and anyone along the way they come in contact with, whether it be truth, purpose, or even just by being. But they too are then watched, isolated, and even hunted as it were while they seemingly meander down the path of this life garden.

The dark creature lies waiting in the shadows of the bush, often hidden among the flowers of the Star seeds own garden. But ascension grants with it its own rewards, allowing those who climb clarity of vision as they look back upon the valley they have ascended from, seeing now clearly not only the darkness the lingers below, but clearly, all that may have tried to hide in the shadows. From a higher advantage point, any movements even in the shadows are so clearly seen. As one ascends even the restrictions of the physical universe dispense fading away as the boundaries of time, space, gravity even death seems to be less a wall, but merely appear as a semipermeable membrane one learns to step through at will.

With each step higher so does the desire for the ascending to discover more truths, with it comes more questions; not only what was the truth hidden in the lie, but why and by whom were these lies formulated in the first place. Puzzle pieces of seemingly unrelated facts from ages past suddenly assemble and depict an ever-increasingly clear picture of truths hidden in the past.

One could say a clear saddening though is the fact that as they ascend higher the seemingly lonelier they begin to feel, for there are increasingly fewer people the higher one climbs. They say it is lonely at the top, and even hearing God himself warn; *"They will hate you, because they have already hated me,"* itself does present a saddening thought.

An ever-increasing hunger for more truths propels the Star Seed higher up the mountain until they have climbed so high they are no longer vulnerable to any attacks from the valley. Wisdom becomes itself almost more desirable than food, and truth be said, wisdom is the most valuable of the gifts from God.

The Star Seeds that sits high up on the mountain can look back and clearly see the movements of the villains slithering below, a more distinct view is granted allowing them to deduce the traps and would-be victims as well as the plots they are attempting to ensnare. Downloads from God, the collective, from Heaven, even Angels, all being the same whisper softly into their ears as the songs of morning birds whisper softly in their dreams. Their visions can be clearly examined and interpreted from above as they then look back down to aid others still in the valley. It becomes easy, almost child's play, to formulate plans to deliver the truths, and issue out warnings with much clearer and audible voices granted them from the higher state of existence that inevitably thwart the attacks.

These counterattacks are not done out of hatred for the snakes and wolves hiding in the shadows but out of love for the people still sitting on the valley floor unaware of the death lingering but a short distance from them in the shadows. Subtle warnings are delivered in pure unadulterated truths and while the creatures of the shadows might overhear the warnings they understand not the trap being set for them that catches them like a bear trap that they so foolishly step in.

When an ascended soul climbs high enough a transformation takes place; the hunted becomes the hunter, the lamb becomes the lion. A realization becomes clear to anyone watching the lion and the lamb was always there, merely two sides of the same coin.

Probably one of the only disadvantages of ascending the mountain in any social structure such as government, education, media, the arts, family, business, or even the medical environment that both my wife and I practiced for years was as truths are discovered and then shared with others the very structures that we believe we are helping are actually the now aggressors immediately springing to the attack to silence these truths from surfacing or spreading. They say one should never stick their head out, darkness will most assuredly cut it off if it has the chance. Unfortunately speaking truths to those who need them results most directly in a neck revealing posture.

The old saying; "It's lonely at the top," while they are talking about usually ruling or leading in earthly social structures, I can say with most assuredness that as you begin to climb higher along the ascension path two things become clearly evident, both spoken in the Bible at length;

One, as you begin to learn more of the truths of God, increasingly dwelling in the spirit and not in the world you become less and less of the earth and become more and more of the spirit thus lending credence to the statement by God; *"You are no longer of this world, even as I am not of the world."*

And Two; Earthly, physical, or carnal possessive desires lose their glimmer and ascended individuals find themselves seeking more spiritual fulfillment than only mere physical endeavors. *"Lay not your treasures on earth, where moths can eat, or rust can corrupt, or where thieves can break in and steal, but lay up your treasures in heaven, where there is neither moth, nor rust, nor thieves to steal. For where your treasure is, there will your heart be also."*

When do enough of the caterpillars relax and enough dark spirits from the sky realize the frivolousness of even attacking any longer, for evident as it is to all that God has equipped all his little children with everything they need to overcome any and all attacks in the supernatural realms of the heavens? There must be a critical moment when the villain runs out of shadows to hide, a tipping point when the light of wisdom reverberates throughout the entire community and the ascended collective merely continues the ascension no longer concerned with invisible comings and goings of winged creatures above.

God would that we are all ascending, it is unfortunate that while he loves us all, He also loves us so much to allow each and every one of us the free will to choose to go up, down, or just lay in the middle with our heads in the sand, free will is always our choice, at least from the point we come to the age of accountability, a topic for later.

For those of us who believe that God Himself sent His son to dwell among us and later He ascended back to the Father, so are we also called to Ascend up into the spiritual heavens, adding to our vibrational frequencies, opening with its understanding of resonances these newfound colors depict, and thus join in the spirit with Our Father on earth as it is in heaven.

THE DESCENDED

A father, a brother, a son is going about his business, he has heard the commotion, people talking about the show at the temple, but people always talk, maybe he should see for himself? There are fish to catch, he has his children to feed. Not that he has a difficult life, although work can be hard, with good hard work comes good rewards. Seeing the faces of his children as they smile at the dinner table, a meal provided by the strength of his arm, the commitment of his work, and the love of a father who knows the lives that have been placed in his care, are worth every physical discomfort the efforts may produce, making it all worthwhile.

The father walks not far from his house contemplating as he goes the spectacle the show of the temple has become, recalling to himself thoughts veiled whispers of vague memories of his life in front of him; "I've heard what they say, the dancing, the music, people go in, and then don't come back for hours at a time."

My wife says that it has gotten out of hand, people lose themselves there, like slaves or addicts, "I don't see how that could possibly be?" he says silently to himself. All I know it seems to scare her what she has heard, a darker side to what others merely call entertainment. Her words of warning softly echo in his head; "Stay away from there, nothing good will come from that place!"

Ridiculous as it may seem, ghosts stories, monsters under the bed, witches dancing in the groves up in the hills, these fairy tales never seemed to scare him even as a youth, perhaps that was one benefit of being borne with a strong arm, completely confident he could take care of himself. Plus curiosity has always been a weakness of his not necessarily limited to the comings and goings of cats.

The beautiful sparkling eyes of his children he can't help but notice as his son walk's along at his feet, how he loves playing on the ground playing with him, or picking up his daughter, holding his children close to his chest, how beautiful they are. It is so easy to see his wife's eyes in them, the purity of the child's smile tickles his memory for the days of his youth, the sweet smile of his wife on their wedding day, each day is another nugget of gold so bountiful God has given him every single day of his adult life.

Thoughts cascade with each step in a moment through years of life highlights as he strokes the path along this ever seemingly darkening road. There is an air of restlessness ahead, voices even screams, seeming sirens on the wind; "is that pleasure or pain he hears?" dancing among the many busy thoroughfares he passes these days.

His earlier years were less complicated days, the pressures of responsibility were only just beginning to shine their light through the morning trees. A man only had to think of himself in those early hours, care for himself, work enough to feed himself, but the joy of a wife does bring their own comforts, contemplations, and added tasks.

Work for food, build a house, raise enough for the harvest, fish enough with the nets one has, carve and sand enough wood another, save to maybe buy a boat, all to take care of the family we both wanted. Funny how life will change one step at a time, a brick here, a table there, a baby's bottle, children's clothes, bedding, shoes, food, oh but it is so worth it, to watch my beautiful children eat and grow.

A man wonders to himself if everyone feels this way, but I certainly have seen the pleasures of my labors, the gift of love given him by an adoring wife, and loving children that count on us to provide all they need, place them on the right path in this life. But who really gave them these gifts, for only within the source of such perfection could a masterpiece of such magnificence spring?

These precious lives kept in our care, brought under the responsibility of my wife's and my protection, until they are old enough to make decisions for themselves. It is a great responsibility, their lives, growth, even health is determined by the choices we make, the work the very ground a man tills until they come to the day of accountability.

He remembers his own ceremony that wonderful Bar Mitzvah, how he so looked forward to it as a child himself. The thought of finally being old enough to make his own decisions, be responsible for himself, it seemed so freeing of thought then, how little did he know that moving into adulthood brought with it not only the accountability of self but the responsibility of everyone else who comes under your care?

"I just don't see what's all the excitement about watching the priests and priestesses carrying on." He suddenly finishes saying to himself as he walks up closer to the building now clearly displaying everything out on the steps and even into the streets, open for all to see.

The temple he was speaking of, is the newly built temple to molech, and while he had heard of this religion, if you could call it that, has been around for centuries, it is only recently that these structures have come into sight. The kings today seem more tolerant to such practices than in the past, even seem to be encouraging this carrying-on otherwise why would they build so many temples?

People come and stare for hours at the performances, a spectacle for all to see. Priests engaged in all sorts of shows, demonstrating even participating themselves in every act of vile, vice, war mimicking dances, or death acts imaginable, many things only years ago would not have been tolerated, are now being seen now on display to a docile and cheering crowd. Priestesses, the most beautiful of the land, voluptuous beyond belief openly flaunt nudity with lust-filled eyes. Calling out to other men and women, luring them with their gestures, they are all adorned with strange symbols and markings that seem to sinisterly resonate with dark meanings of their own just beyond the limit of one's awareness.

Men of strength and stature, display themselves with smirks across their faces clearly displaying the pride they have for themselves as they taunt others with their sweat-drenched gestures. Performances that mimic violence and war, aggression, even fighting displays with such ferocity it is difficult to see if it is real or merely an act? Eunuchs whose exact original sex not exactly clear to determine, engaged in all manner of sexual perversion with each other, the more flamboyant the better, desperate to bring attention to themselves.

They even engage in horrible acts with animals, the horrified inprisoned creatures stare back at them in terror understanding somewhere in their beings the evil that seems to reside here. Many even dance against cold stone statues that seem in themselves lingering on the edge of some possible supernatural movement. The more shocking and degrading, the more blood involved, the more the people's gaze mesmerized in wonder, stare, gawk, and cheer.

In the center is the huge bronze demonic statue image of molech or is it baal, it seems to be called many different things by different people? A tall bronze creature with a horned cow's head and what appears to be a human body, a rectangular cut out in its' belly revealing the constant hungry of the fire that sits within. It is a large grotesque figure of envious imagery, a beastly image with a hateful look on its face, not quite cow-like almost devilish, cow-eyed as clearly lacks any life or soul only lingers in the lifeless stare, the black slits around the eyes reflecting only the darkness that no-doubt dwells inside. Who does it hate? Seemingly everyone and everything, maybe even itself?

Hands stretched out reaching, wanting, evermore unsatisfied, grasping for something anything to quench the ever-present hunger that burns within. The large rectangle cut out of his stomach is the place they throw various sacrifices, priest's and priestesses cast various elements of precious wealth into the blazing chasm, screaming in a combination of ecstasy and pain, searing pain from the burning tentacles that reach out and touch any and all that come near. The priest must fling the treasure into the hot belly because getting too close already had caused a few to spontaneously erupt in flame as their clothes, hair, or ornamental dressing catch fire sending the unfortunate into a crumbling blaze of fire and screaming. This only seems to cause the other attendants to laugh and dance more feverishly.

The gaping maw in the belly is never satisfied, the fires cause the statue's skin to burn deeper red and hotter with every sacrifice. The tormented destruction of everything that is thrown in is evident from the gasps and radiate stares on the faces of all that stand and watch. Shadowy reflections of the flames dance across the faces of the onlookers like small menacing spirits in an endless chaotic rhythm across cheeks, eyes, and mouths. Many of the onlookers wear masks over their mouths, as do the more subservient attendants, they are clearly not leading but following the procession.

The ever-growing and constant fire within that is heating the creature to a point of almost white-hot, glowing even pulsating along the now almost moving edges seems to ripple with a life of its own. Gyrating figures all around enticing more and more onlookers, some sprint into the crowds of onlookers only to pull reluctant participants before the statue, mostly these are young children or young women that are pulled out of the crowd, alone nobody helps them as they are pulled away in grasping horror. The majority of them screaming and crying in resistance as they are drug by the priestesses, even pushes by others in the crowd. People of all ages and status, standing, sitting, kneeling even bowing low in front of the image, watching in a sort of trans, staring for hours upon end, waiting for yet again another tingle in their emotional base to spark, most of them on all fours, it is truly the earth that has them in its grip.

The most popular and beautiful are solicited into service as priests and priestesses, this service is not without compensation or costs, they receive the highest pay of the land, nearly rivaling the kings, they're every want and desires are fulfilled, power, pleasure, and even prestige. But to the costs; they pay with their servitude, it is a service for life, a blood contract for their very soul once signed they no longer have access to, only death can separate them from service once they have entered. Every bit of purity, beauty, and strength is slowly sucked out of them until only a dried-up husk of a shell remains.

All of their symbols, the demonstrations, even the words being uttered are not their own, everyone seems to know the true source of the chanting, and as a result, their every movement seems watched and scrutinized by the leaders, for they must always conform to the behavior dictated by the temple or their position will be eliminated, outcast, or worse yet find themselves on the sacrificial table. They, of course, must perform as they are instructed whether they believe in the ritual or not. They have paid with their soul, it is no longer theirs to choose, for they must bow down, and confess with their mouths the lies that the head priests instruct.

The priests and priestesses give all of their bodies, hearts, and minds to this image, the very acts they eroticize are designed to draw the onlookers in with every sight, sound, and movement. The rituals and potions that they must ingest have the severest consequence on these young beautiful bodies, marking them forever inside and out. Age and stress wear them before their time, and only when the beauty of youth seems to have left, are they discarded, penniless, without concern or ceremony.

The growing crowds of onlookers who worship them with their eyes, ears, hearts, and time, long to engage them, mimic them, even but touch one of them for the lusts and acts they impress into the audiences souls. There seems to be a repeated rhythm to the show presented, the underlying negative message hidden deep within symbolism passed in front of the eyes of the onlookers, messages hidden that repeatedly create almost undetectable small scars in the memories of everyone watching. People have no idea they are being manipulated, memories and images locked away within the deepest chambers of their minds recesses, hidden doors to secret rooms that the priests can later use when the time is right.

A priestess rushes into the crowd to pull a screaming baby from the clutches of its horrified mother. Others in the crowd now hold mother back as the priestess brings the now flailing and desperately horrified child up towards the now red hot outstretched hands of the statue. She holds the infant up between the glowing hands clearly burning herself in the process.

A man stand's off to the side gripping his small child's hand, while part of him is pulling to rush in rescue the child from the witch's grip, yet the other part remains fast as the fear for his own child keeps him from acting.

As the screams of the child, so desperate also the mother in the crowd, as well as many of the onlookers, reach a crescendo, the priestess turns and places the now dying child onto the burning hand of the demon. The very act seems to take the remaining strength from the priestess as she collapses between the searing hands of the idol, no-one steps forward to help her as she also begins to smolder igniting into flame from the heat.

A man turns to leave, his stomach already convulsing at the sight he just witnessed, suddenly jerked to a stop as he feels his own young son is being pulled back out of his grip by another priestess. A second and even a third priestess now grab the now screaming child and pull as the man thrashes, desperately gripping the hand of his child only with his one hand, because the rest of his body is being restrained by the multitude of onlookers around him not allowing him even to hardly turn or free his other arm to help.

Even as he feels his child's hand slip from his own now sweat-drenched grip, so does his thoughts fade slowly into insanity as darkness descends its veil upon the mind of our man and the devastating realization of what is coming, fear and dread constrict upon themselves somewhere in his chest, everything fades too black.

Two thousand, and twenty years later a simple man sits at his desk, and has a vision of this similar man to himself, working through his daily tasks, unabated by the constant drum of everything around him. He glances up at the TV, mesmerized by the beauty and eroticism displayed there, unaware of the symbols dangling from the ears or displayed on the gowns because his attention is not on the patterns of the dress but on the skin lying just below. Images of actors engaged in all sorts of shows, demonstrating every act of vile, vice, war, and death imaginable. Actresses, the most beautiful of the beautiful, voluptuous beyond belief, with men of strength and stature, engaged in all manner of sexual perversion, men who look like women and women doctored to look like men all speak in tones or emotions that seem to just make him feel uncomfortable. The more shocking and degrading, the more the people around him, the unseen audience, gaze in wonder, stare, gawk, and cheer.

I see our family man being brought to the image by his friends at first, then later just coming on his own, sitting more and more in front of the image. Staring into the rectangle of wonder, the rituals unfolding before him, he is hardly noticing the gradual deterioration of the events playing out in front of his eyes, the increasing images of fire, blood, and abuse of women and children being displayed. The programs seem to descend into deeper vile and vice every day, even the sporting contests he likes to watch are themselves becoming increasingly violent and angry.

The images continue to ever amplify in volume and intensity, brighter and more realistic, louder and longer, the same themes playing out on every channel long into the night. When did they all start dancing with each other naked, when did it become acceptable for the strong to abuse and rape the weak, when did the cursing just flow like filth through open sewer ditches of peoples mouths, when did the thief, the murderer, the child abuser, the criminal, the demon, Lucifer himself become the hero?

When animals were suddenly cruelly tormented and put to death for all to see, women brutalized to the cheer's and ecstasy of the onlookers, children victimized at the very hands of other children, people didn't even seem to notice the digression. When onlookers give up family, love, jobs, life, to sit there and worship, place their gold at the temple feet of these image providers, the transition was hardly noticeable.

When people start burning themselves on the white-hot hands of their god, it gives the onlookers an almost sexual feeling, while watching the pain it solicits. The audience almost erupts in orgasmic ecstasy with each ever-increasing act of human destruction. Crying for more, they will pay anything, their last coin, their pound of flesh, for one more moment of ever-increasing perversion. The most powerful of the land have become slaves to the blood as much if not more than those who perform these acts.

The priest's, the players, the leaders, the bankers constantly call for more and more, but there is no satisfaction granted the actor's plea because there is no quenching the hungering fire that burns within molech, or is it baal? So common is the burning of flesh, sacrificing of beauty, sexual perversion, it hardly has an effect on the onlookers any longer. The degradation continues, priests having sex with men, actresses with women, so common that it almost becomes the norm, almost preferred instead of the exception. Children are solicited at a gradually younger age, first against their will, and later even willfully, until the point where even babies are not safe from the clenches of the ritual. Actresses throwing their faces into the fire, witches wearing masks laying prostate naked in the image's hands, convulsing in burning pain with screams of delight. Actors wearing masks sacrificing body parts even their entire body willfully against the white-hot image, knowing the flesh is destined to burn, and only the disfigurement awaits.

Finally, the high priest turns to the audience and says; "molech demands; you give us your families, no you give us your children now because the time has come and strong is he!" The priestesses are the first to place their screaming babies in the hands of the hellish demon. Men riding on the backs of the demon baal fling their crowns off their heads, and shriek in terrorizing delight.

One after another gives their own children to the clenches of the actors and priestesses as they rip them from less loving hands. There is no safety, no kindness, no compassion, just an ever-present hunger and lust to take the young lives and use them. "Put molech in every room!" the priest screams and men rush off to obey. "Lay your children in front of him!" the priestess demands, "and watch the fire devour the virgin flesh!" she screams with a witches shrill voice.

A wife comes to our man, pleading with him to come home, take his eyes away from the hypnosis that has gripped his mind, and come back to her family, their home that has fallen apart from lack of care. Our man no longer has time, he barely has time to function, his service to his family is in direct proportion to his interest in the events away from his gaze, and right now he one hundred percent in front of this image as soon as possible, sit there in a euphoric coma all day, even falling asleep in front in front of it. He Worships' it!

His children that used to play at his feet, climb on his lap, nestle against his chest, come less and less each day, because all he does is push them away. One day they stop coming altogether, and eventually, even his wife stops coming as well, never even bothering to call him to dinner.

He is not alone, many have jumped into the fray even screaming with ecstasy as they lay their babies on the burning white hands of this filthy demon. Putting them in front of the merciless hot flames, any and all purity burned from them. Screaming in pain the sweet innocent children's cries are only drowned out by the louder insane screams of the lusting onlookers. One after another cast into the fiery maw of the filthy beast, now black with the soot of the many innocent victims within. Baby after innocent baby is thrown in without care or concern. The screams of the onlookers, why do they care, as long as these children don't interfere with their fun.

So dark is the heart of molech, so crafty is the spider baal large is its web, yet all black as soot.

He hardly feels it as his daughter is taken by the images she watches in the solace of her own room. The grips of many witches clasp her hand as they pull her mind into the shadowy realm of darkened spell-craft, sure they promise her popularity, beauty, even love, they know full well none of these are theirs to give. Suddenly screams are heard by parents only feet down the hall as a father is finally pulled from his stupor and dashes away from the images just to meet a closed door and demonic screams issuing from his sweet daughter's room.

He's a big man, made large not only from his indulgence but from the years of heavy labor he has performed. He always trusted the strength of his arms to solve any problem he might encounter. He slams against the locked door multiple times and while it should have easily yielded something more powerful than himself was barring his way. Suddenly the demonic growls cease as well as his daughter's weeping voice and the door just easily opens before him. Both his wife and he almost stare in sudden shock as the door opens by its own will. A man steps through even while gripped from behind by his wife, and only manages to reach out a single hand to take what appears to be his daughter's hand in his own.

She has become more of an animal than human, sitting on the ground, eyes staring forward in some horrific trance, looking more like a Jackal than the daughter he knew only moments ago. As she tries to pull her own hand away from his own now tear-drenched hand. Her strength has become uncontrollable, the grip sliding through his own as a shadowy veil descends upon his mind, an almost constriction seems to be occurring where his heart was, and he himself slips into darkness.

Gone forever the beautiful brown eyes of his child, our poor man stares into dark foolish loneliness. So dark is our man's heart become, black as soot.

What about him, who by her own indulgences has been left behind,
taking too long, only interested in eating they find?

The leaves and grasses now withered and grey,
unaware of the autumn storms a lost journey may sway?

What about those whom by choice or foolishness amend,
went the wrong way and willfulness descend?

Fall into the crevasse, or into the sewers distress,
only to find themselves being carried away into dark filth, dismay,
and death's recess.

Not a death of resurrection as seen from above,
a new life of winged flight and heavenly life, light, and love.

But a death of destruction where no new life can be found,

merely the disintegration of hope,

with its reintegration into soil they are bound.

"God I pray for all who have been deceived by the spirit of this demon, and I pray that not only will those people who have been captured into the service of this dark temple lift their heads and have their eyes open, but You will also grant them the wisdom of how they can bring the fight right into the enemies camp with an influx of Your Spirit, Your Will, and Your Actions. Let us turn from slaves to great warriors of Christ and take back the venues meant to enslave us, Your people, turning it into a great weapon in the army of Christ."

By Peter Colla

BOO-BOO THE SCARY STUFFED BEAR

It is said "they" are putting poison in our water, toxins in the inoculation's for our children, hiding subliminal pictures in children's films, developing GMO crop's that will kill us in a few generations, fixing our election's, replacing own our politician's with their bought slaves, working in labs to develop weaponized diseases that can wipe out large portions of the population, manipulating governments for their own destruction both from within and among each other, and even would manipulate an entire economic failure of society throughout the whole world, plunging everyone into a worldwide social and political downslide that would most likely end in total devastation, famine, war, leading to the deaths of million's, if not billion's of people, all just to keep or gain control. But the most frequently asked question is why? And if this is true, who is the "they"?

Many of the same people out there that share the same question's as to the why, often ask what possible benefit would it demonstrate for a small group of individuals, corporations, or even countries, to desire to kill so many innocents'? If even there were one or two individuals or a few that wanted to accomplish such diabolically ruthless destruction of the innocent, how could so many collaborators be organized in secret to perpetrate such an act undetected on so many levels, by many unrelated companies, and over such a long period of time? It seems impossible to think how long it would take to set such an act up, let alone pay for it?

Let us suppose there is an entity out there that utterly and entirely hates all people, and wants nothing else than to either kill, control, or enslave all mankind for one reason, because we, people are created in the image of God, and he is not.

Isaac Newton said; "energy cannot be created or destroyed merely converted from one form to another." So here is this poor, pathetic entity, this large bundle of potential energy, that by its own choice and "free-will," walked away from God, and by doing so also walked away from everything that was good, loving, light, truth, peaceful, tender, joyful, giving, healing, wise, life-filled, compassionate, satisfying, restful, and honoring. And since this entity cannot be destroyed, it was doomed to an eternity of living in the complete absence of God, you take away all good, and all you have left with is the opposite… bad. How sad the entity is when it has to exchange everything that is good for evil, love for hate, light for darkness, truth for a lie, peace for war, tenderness for harshness, joy for terror, giving for theft, healing for sickness, life for death, compassion for cruelty, satisfaction for thirst, rest for anxiety, and honor for all forms of belittlement?

We can give it a name, does it really matter which one, for even the least of mankind, being created in the image of God is infinitely superior to anything that is not. We could call it lucifer, a cockroach (fitting), or an amoeba, a wisp of air, a rock, a pretty stupid choice, the devil, Darth Vader, Ronald McDonald, or maybe something more fitting to its true ability to affect us, especially if we just decide not to let it; "Boo-Boo the imaginary killer bear hiding under our bed."

Then let us also suppose, since this creature is away from, in essence, the opposite of God, it exists within a realm that exhibit's all of those factors, bummer for him. While God loves, Boo-Boo only hates, that means everything, even himself. While God is about peace, Boo-Boo is about war, strife, and aggression. While God creates everything even life, Boo-Boo only wants to steal, destroy, and kill.

On a Quantum level, we have already determined that physically we make up the energies of the atomic structures. All the space in between "Surrounding" everything, "Creating" everything, "Holding" everything together, giving it eternal consciousness well that's God, and it is here the light is. Where does that leave the whispers of Boo-Boo? I guess the only place left is the shadow our own veiled energies might cast?

Boo-Boo can't create anything, he is only a stuffed bear, but can he steal? In John chapter 10 of the Bible, it says; *"the thief comes only to steal, and kill, and destroy."*

He "only comes to" do that, it doesn't say he actually does it. I have also heard it spoken in the church that he can steal that which was created by God, but can he really? For if he could, wouldn't he have long ago stolen everything? Or maybe can he only take what man has freely given to him by us?

Can he kill or create sickness? If he could, wouldn't he have killed all mankind, created a superbug or cancer that would have destroyed us, destroyed everything long ago? The Bible teaches in Deuteronomy, among others, that disease is the curse that comes from sin, our sin, the dark things that people do, maybe from the very words and actions that we create. Sure we are being tricked and prompted by satan, (oops Boo-Boo) but we still do it. But Boo-Boo never minds taking credit, it can add to our fear and reverence of him.

In Genesis God, Himself said; *"Cursed is the ground for thy sake,"* we sin, our dark actions have an effect on the ground, the world around us, I wrote about this in an earlier blog "Visions of Reality," with the choices of our sin diseases may result, and this dark result then prey's on the innocent and wicked alike.

So here is a Good God that gives so many diverse gifts to His children, why? Because He loves each of us more than all of the rest of the physical universe combined, more than He even loves His own life. What good Father would not gladly step in front of a bullet for his child? Every Good Father I know!

God gives us all, every one of us, the infinity of everything we can imagine, every sort of wisdom, knowledge, raining infinite droplets of blessings down on the heads of His many children as we play joyfully in the soft grasses of gardens blossomed breezes of His own breath. We get to dance through this wonderful life holding hands of other children, His own son's and daughter's, shining eyes of diamond sparkle bright in their perfect design, each and every one of them. The blessings are as infinite as the creation of the universe He has so freely given us, all for the use and benefit of us, He created it to bless us and each other, and in so doing we give glory to the giver.

Well, ok, it's getting harder and harder to see the dance through this neck-deep drudge of muck and mire our darkness has created, especially the negativity the shadows we have to wallow through all around us as we continue our slave state of being, day in and day out. We can't blame God, we created it with all of our desires. No wonder the world is at a point of regurgitating from the sickness we have polluted it with?

But then there is Boo-Boo and his other little buddies, the rest of the "Beanies," little pestering almost virus size creatures whispering into God's children's ears, coercing them to miss-use that which was designed for good. Prompting them to hold onto God's blessings in a way that is not about growth or good, but dwell's in a more diabolical outcome, one that will ultimately be bad for either the person directly or someone around him and thus ultimately for himself as well.

Yes, this creature, this immortal stuffed under the bed hiding bear Boo-Boo, has powers that men can hardly comprehend, a diabolically complex ability to manipulate on a worldly scale, either directly or through the other lessor minions he has power over. He can, attempting to mirror as God does, whisper into the ears and minds of people, louder for those who listen, a mere nudge for those who don't. It can prompt through the gifting of things it has already acquired dominion over, things of this world gold or power, but what Boo-Boo cannot do is create! For, to create would put it in a class, or image, that it is not, one with God and man.

When we people give things to Boo-Boo, yes then he can use them for the purpose of his ultimate plan; to destroy, enslave, and completely dominate over God's greatest creation, us. What a better way to pay back your enemy, than to rob, enslave, even ultimately destroy your enemies children, you start by just coercing them away!

People, on the whole, have a natural tendency to know what is good for them and what is not. They certainly wish, for the most part, to give their own children what is good and necessary for them to grow up healthy, and continue on long past their own existence. So if Boo-Boo is going to get at God he is going to have to go after God's children us, and what better way than at our children, but that means he is going to have to do it under the watchful eyes of the parent's.

Ok back to our original question, and we will stick with just one; why would corporations or nations put poison's in something like immunization's or our water?

Answer;

So here comes Boo-Boo, and he comes up with a diabolical plan, forged in the minds of his minions those greedy men, women, or families Boo-Boo manipulated centuries ago through power and selfishness, promising rule, a cold loveless crown of gold and gems, so he could manipulate them into positions of power he could use when the time was right. Boo-Boo gave them riches and power, at least the ones he had control over, all while whispering in their ears, telling them what he should have them do; *"dominion over the people, for they are under you,"* he would tell them.

"Enslave them for it is your Right by birth," Boo-Boo would lie to them, for he has no power over births or deaths, so to say someone has a Right by birth must be a lie. He would tempt them, for they so do lust for power. And when he has a tight enough grip on their thoughts he would eventually say; *"kill the children,"* for the ultimate lust for innocent blood is the perverted end of all power. But never forget, it was always their choice! These men, these puppets, when they would give him an inch, an idea, Boo-Boo wanted a death, a sacrifice, a theft, a baby thrown in a fire, some poison in a well.

Attack God's people in any and every way possible, to the ultimate enslavement and destruction of all people as a whole.

But normal men and women are not fools either, for what happens if a ruler is found to be too cruel, or too many children turn up missing, especially when the mob figures out its the rich guy up on the hill causing all this misery? The mob grabs their torches, pitchforks, and rope, storms the castle looking for someone to punish. It doesn't matter how many troops an emperor has guarded his back, if the mob decides you are dead, your goose is cooked on a spit, or dangling from a rope. Even the great Julius Caesar fell to the mob, this is the rich man's worst fear that normal people will see the skeletons he has in his closet! History is a dark teacher, full of ghost stories and tales of terror to those who live in dark places, especially when they are sitting without the luxury of a lamp.

So here we have these very rich guys that have been in Boo-Boo's pocket for centuries, they know they can't just do something that is too direct as to wake up suspicion but must maneuver in secret, through many channels, fabricate every sort of lie, using many hidden underground levels, covering their tract's and keeping their ultimate identity secret as long as possible. Such a difficult feat when the spirits that drive them are bursting at the seams for recognition, they so want to be worshiped and feared!

The higher or I might say deeper the rich man descends the more demon-like he becomes longing to control as much as they can, realizing what is the best things to control especially if you want the greatest deal of influence, answer; money, and thus be able to buy up all the various blessings of God. So they strive under Boo-Boo's promptings to own all the major banks, maybe even production of money itself, all the markets where things are done, the oil to control energy, all the wealth, they must own the narrative so only their message gets out, and they eventually lust to own, or at least control, the various courts, lawmakers and governments around the world and thus the people.

Of course, it has been only in recent times that this was even possible to control nearly all of the monies, countries, and ultimately the people of the world. Many have tried conquering the world throughout time, and I am sure through more than a prompting or two from Boo-Boo, but for the vast distances and enormous manpower it would require to not only take control but to keep it, would make it impossible to enslave the entire world at the same time. Plus there would have to be something that everyone, everywhere needed, and if you controlled this, you controlled them. Oil does allow this for the first time in history, plus having a worldwide communication system that works at nearly the speed of light doesn't hurt either.

Caesar, Montezuma, Genghis Khan, Napoleon, Hitler, Oprah, when they all realized they couldn't rule the world it wasn't long before they fell. If any one country gets too strong before total domination can occur, Boo-Boo gets working, I mean whispering, and starts destroying it from inside as well as out. Once he finds he cannot achieve his goal of world domination, adios "Muchacho's," or "Muchacha's" in some cases. One thing Boo-Boo hates worse than the children of God is the Butt-Lickers that do his bidding, he hates them because he has to use them, remember he can't do anything himself, he must have these nitwits do it for him.

Boo-Boo's ultimate plan is to bring everyone all over the entire world under his control. That is a big plan for a little bear still hiding under a bed! But he is crafty, you have to give him that!

In order for him to accomplish this, since he cannot do it himself, for he is but a stuffed bear, he must stick his "lackey," his puppet, his pathetic little GI Joe toy, in that place of total domination, it is only then that he has any hopes to rule. How sad is that he hates the puppet more than he even hates the rest of us! How do I know this? Because Boo-Boo just wants to destroy all of us but has to use a crutch to do it, everyone hates using a crutch, and Boo-Boo hates more than your average bear, he wants to not only destroy us but the crutch, the puppet Gi Joe boy-toy, he would like nothing else than to eliminate them from all existence, but again he cannot create yet wait a minute he can destroy?

Destroy what? *"Ah yes, destroy souls"* There it is, the ultimate reason why Boo-Boo does what he does; for souls. That is why he will betray puppet boy-toy, turn on him, and ultimately feed him to his own dominion of wolves when little plastic green soldier's usefulness is exhausted. It has been written so many times in History!! What a moron puppet boy little plastic GI Joe toy is!

What exactly are souls? I have written over the course of this book and others that we as people are made up of a Body, Mind, and Spirit, and while many people and philosophers mistake the spirit for the soul, they are not the same thing. The Bible compares the soul with each and every one of our very existence, we all have but one soul, our creation from even before the creation of the earth through our physical life on this earth, all our dreams the lives we may have lived within them, and unto our life after death as well as even onto eternity. I guess if Boo-Boo could ruin that soul any soul's existence by darkening it with the evil he, in essence, could destroy a person's soul? I guess if Boo-Boo could taint it with his dark whispers of blackness to the point where he dooms what was created to have eternal life to the death of that eternal life, I guess he can kill, but again it sounds like he has to have our consent.

So here is this small group of puppets that control all of the money, oil, and basic treasures of the world, it is through the money they also try to control the armies. The puppets are constantly being whispered to, for as things heat up, so do all of the many complex interactions of the cogs involved. It requires a constant bombardment of voices, like a stadium of screams and demands, pestering on the inside of the poor children's brains, that have foolishly given themselves. I am sure it must sound like a swarm of venomous insects. What started out as a greedy little tickle, ended up as a Kaleidoscope of loneliness and deprivation that could push anyone beyond the boundaries of sanity. How could a person not pity the puppets!

They strive to control first money, that's the hook, which quickly turns to power in companies such as banks, insurance, weapons, energy, communication, news, education, and the arts, later Boo-Boo wraps into control entire multi-national corporations or groups of corporations. When money exceeds the amounts they could ever hope to spend, Boo-Boo just tightens his grip by instilling terror, he places a fear in their ear that everyone wants to take it away from them, all of that bits of physicality which they feel they own, they may have built, they are entitled to.

Little do these fools know, that everything they have, everything good, was a blessing from God, and what an opportunity they might have had to really make a difference for the entire Kingdom, and ultimately in their own lives throughout eternity, had they just listened to a softer loving voice instead of Boo-Boo.

Very soon just controlling a vast multinational company is also not enough, maybe control over an entire industry might do it, or maybe a small country, but when that's not enough, a large country, or many? How can we blame these poor puppets, for he is just chasing worldly gold, like a crazed dog chasing its tail? In his heart, he really longs for but a gift from God, attempting to feel some kind of completion, but little does he know satisfaction in this life can come from one place only, and that is through doing something for which a person was designed to do. A man could own the whole world, and if it was not what God had designed, no satisfaction would come, for satisfaction comes not from Boo-Boo, only thirst for more.

Then there is Boo-Boo whispering in his ear again, find me a way to kill children, and some scientist, some businessman, comes up with the brilliant idea; we will have this or that company put mercury or some kind of dormant virus in the inoculations of children. Boo-Boo's top men make it happen! Boo-Boo whispers in the ears of other men, other puppets, what would be good to add to drinking water, because he hates water, it is just too clear? An idea comes from a man; Hydroflourosilicic acid, better known as the fluoride added to the water is actually more toxic than lead! More ideas, more money, body scanner is used to irradiate children's bodies because of some made-up terrorist threat that the average American has a greater chance of dying of a bee-sting than dying from any terrorist attack's. Dormant cancer-causing viruses are animated by the radiating (public record), and the cases of cancer in children in America go up 3000% in the last ten years. No problem Boo-Boo gets the media to lie, and blame someone else, "The wrath of God maybe." Boo-Boo is excited.

Boo-Boo talks to key people in the educational system, promising fame and wealth if they will demise a way to reduce the population, destroy the family, rewrite history, so they write about the need for population reduction, the necessity to get rid of people, all stemming on the backs of what is good for the world, environmentally. Little do they know as they conceive ways to destroy God's children they add murder and lust for blood to the already feverish state the world is in, more darkness added to the mix This world was created for man and not the other way around.

"The company you control with your money, or the Grants they rely on for their success, they will do what you tell them, or you destroy them." Boo-Boo doesn't even bother to whisper any longer, just laughs as he talks to the media, or through them, they will make sure that only the information he wants released get's out, the truth will be squashed! *"Who cares about truth, we will drown them in facts, our facts!"*

Whisper in one ear, make a suggestion in another, a promise with no intent to fulfill, maybe help somebody's career just to destroy when they are used up, build an army of puppets ruled by another puppet. There is always plenty of whisper for listening ears, find the one perfect puppet that has proven over and over to do what Boo-Boo demands, the one he can control completely, and use him. There are many ways to get what he wants these days, plenty of ears to whisper in, plenty of greedy witches eager to be used. Most will sell their devotion for much less than their fathers did, for it is gold Boo-Boo has, but souls he desires. How pathetic they all are, Boo-Boo must think, selling their souls for much less than Judas ever did.

Boo-Boo talk's to the politician's and if he doesn't directly, the men who control them with power and money do the talking. Boo-Boo holds all the blackmail cards, so getting them to listen is easy, and if he can't blackmail them, threaten them, if that doesn't work put a contract out on them. The most popular people are the easiest to turn, they all like nice things, and Boo-Boo has plenty of those.

Getting them to vote on bills forcing people to use their poison. Writing in this or that law that robs the children of God the provisions given them by the Father, and deposit's them into the bank account's or just buries it in mountain caves of the puppets he has under his thumb, child's play. Signing law's without even reading them, for they show where their devotions lie, it is not with the people, but in the thirty pieces of silver, he may give them or may not.

Boo-Boo puts the squeeze on all the people by inflicting harder and harder conditions in which they try to provide for their families. But it is never Boo-Boo, he can't do anything, but men; because of their sinful desires, that's why the squeeze happens, Boo-Boo just whispers in men's ears so they think they are profiting from it and squeeze even more.

Does nobody ever read the bible, even way back to Genesis God said; *"And unto Adam, he said, Because thou hast hearkened unto the voice of thy wife, and hast eaten of the tree, of which I commanded thee, saying, Thou shalt not eat of it: cursed is the ground for thy sake; in sorrow shalt thou eat of it all the days of thy life;"*

"Thorns also and thistles shall it bring forth to thee; and thou shalt eat the herb of the field;"

"In the sweat of thy face shalt thou eat bread, till thou return unto the ground; for out of it wast thou taken; for dust thou art, and unto dust shalt thou return."

More children contract autism, no sane person would want that, Boo-Boo does. More children get sick and die, no company of executives would stand by idly and watch their company kill millions unless they knew they could do nothing to change it, or they are in fear of saying something, *"Put fetal tissue in their food"* Boo-Boo laughs.

Families are destroyed, women are used, fathers lose hope, visionaries close their eyes, men of power become pawns, other's who once stood for honor sell their devotion for thirty pieces of silver.

What does Boo-Boo do, he just keeps whispering, well maybe by now he is screaming!

The question is not, who or why?

The answer is; how could it be any other way?

So what do we do? Well, we can storm the castle with a pitchfork and torch? Not a bad idea, but God did say; *"Vengeance is mine..."*

Ok, well if everyone started to open up their eyes and just spread the word, the light would shine into dark places, and we all know what happens; the cockroaches scatter! Or maybe each and every one of us just starts seeing a little more clearly? With each person who ascends, their universe has Light suddenly shine on the lie hiding in the shadows, darkness flees, the person takes the next step and ascension begins.

The funny thing is, as the puppets get further along these days, it would seem like the dominion dwellers are getting sloppy, or maybe they are just starting to feel like they have to communicate louder to get some kind of order in the chaos. Perhaps like some pathetic prison cellmate bragging about the number of bikes he stole before getting caught, they just seem to desire gossip (not surprising), whatever it is causing this anomaly, almost everything is readily available on the web, and miraculously right from their very hands.

Is it possible these old rich puppets hiding up in their castles or down in their not so secret bunker's think they could be safe from God when His vengeance comes knocking? Pharaoh did!

Well, hopefully, they will realize one day, that they are also children of God, and no matter how many babies have been killed no one is beyond forgiveness, but that too is between them and God? Everything that has happened has done so as predicted in the Bible, and only God knows the future, the end is already spelled out clear as day.

So the real question is do you believe a sure thing, truth, or do listen to Boo-Boo? On a quantum level, since darkness is the absence of light, no amount of absence added can in any way diminish the whole. Light in the area of God's creation, which is by the way light must prevail, for it is written in the basic formulation of the universe.

It is never too late to believe, even at the moment, you are hanging on the Cross.

WATER FALL? NO WATER ASCENSION

Water is by far the most precious commodity for life on our planet. Its usefulness as a conduit for just about every life-giving system is as unquestionable as it is nearly unfathomable. We can only begin to understate it as we take a closer look, and thus it is an invaluable tool in the Ascension process especially when it comes to health and healthcare. Merely placing our focused attention on water thereby we can see the positive instrumental value in it, has the wellbeing potential not only in the healing arena within us but everyone else throughout our existence becomes a great initial step that is easy for everyone to literally get their feet wet with.

In the natural so is it always demonstrated physically, in the spiritual it is likewise in the supernatural, and so on up the ladder unto heavenly understanding, each is the reflections of the other. "Rivers of Life" so did Jesus speak of Himself, the Message, the Word, as He spoke of spreading the good news throughout the people. But why would He use a river of water as an example? Rivers are beautiful to see, but likewise equally unstoppable in their relentless drive where they seem destined to go. Many a man has tried in vain to subdue rivers but ultimately their waters win and end up in the sea.

Jesus's first miracle as reported by His followers was the turning of water into wine. He took something common, something essential,

241

and converted it into something of physical value, pleasurable, something to be consumed, something red. Beginning and the end, God so does love to work in ordered perfection, repeating patterns that reflect the truths of His prophecies for all to see. Something red, in the beginning, using red, a call to fight perhaps, a battle against the evils that had enslaved us forever?

"In the beginning, God created the heaven and the earth. And the earth was without form and void; and darkness was upon the face of the deep. And the Spirit of God was hovering over the face of the waters."

Again the very first thing created with the earth was water, and while it is clearly stated that the earth was without form on the quantum level some sort of order was already established. Waters and its essentialness was obviously established, God doesn't talk about it just out of random coincidences, does He mention carbon, or gamma rays, or gold, or even His own short-sight-fullness for forgetting to put Fluoride in the water, He just talks about the face of the water, as if the water is looking up to Him consciously waiting for further instructions?

As it was in the beginning so must it be at the end, one of the last events He also performed was using the wine to symbolize His blood the last day of His life. The wine was involved in His first miracle at the end of the final supper, wine plays an intricate role. Wine the representation of His blood. He said specifically; *"When You drink, think of me."*

Blood is almost completely made up of water, as so is wine, but not quite as pure. It has an essence of other things mixed in that make the blood what it needs to be in order for it to give life-sustaining abilities. A small amount of hemoglobin which is a fascinatingly complex molecule, a carbon-based structure with key points of Iron, this molecule has an enormous capacity to bind with oxygen and delivers life fuel. Yet it is all the other things in the water that give it the ability to perform the various duties we need, or is this perhaps not quite so?

Water has a greater function in the kingdom than I believe we can ever comprehend. Water is used for cleansing, not only the body but also the entire world as in the flood. Water is necessary for almost every vital function in our body. Our body is almost entirely composed of water, and when all water is eliminated as in cremation only a small amount of substance is actually left. We will die of lack of water long before we die of lack of anything else. Water seems to be the key element of life.

Science would tell us that we all come from the oceans and thus from water, but I believe this world is merely a representation of our body and as we are primarily made up of water, the majority of the earth's surface is also either covered with or retains in its water in one form or another.

In my education overseas in the Netherlands, one of the areas of study was alternative medical studies, namely homeopathy, and its primary ingredient is pure water.

Homeopathy is a particularly interesting form of medicine, finding its foundations preempting the pharmaceutical medical industry we find ourselves engulfed in today, by at least two or three thousand years. It was written in the time of Hippocrates, described as healing ailments using the ability of "likes curing likes".

Without getting much into the philosophical or even into medical physiology, the premise is; that when you significantly dilute compounds in pure water, the resulting compounds can be used to cure the problems caused by the original stronger causing compounds. For example, arsenic poisoning is treated and cured by giving the patient compounds that have supposedly extremely slight amounts of arsenic in them. Remember all substances are created by God.

When I was in Europe we had an opportunity to examine not only where this process was carried out, but also a sample of these products myself. I had, even on occasion, the opportunity to receive homeopathic remedies prescribed right along with the regular pharmaceuticals when I needed to visit the Dr., and I must admit the healing process not only was faster but often with fewer side effects and downtime.

The process goes something like this; they take the particular poison, compound, or substance; arsenic, snake venom, gold, silver, a poison, or known irritant, whatever they happen to want to make into a homeopathic compound, they dissolve it in either pure water or alcohol, then press it, sift it to remove solids or impurities, and then add an extremely small amount of the pure substance to an incredibly large amount of water. After concentrating the pure initial compound they isolated from the undiluted raw precipitate, they then draw out a single drop of the resulting liquid and place it in a vat, a huge container containing maybe a thousand gallons or so of pure water, an extremely large barrel! This is then thoroughly mixed and a single drop is again drawn out, placed into another vat with water, this process is repeated four to seven times depending on the compound ending in a final vat of water with what science would say contains absolutely nothing of the original compound, not even a trace.

Yet the resulting water is then drawn out and placed in small vials and distributed to patients who suffer from various particular sicknesses, they take a number of these drops under the tongue, the result is an improvement even cure, and this treatment had been used, with success I might add, for at least the last two thousand years.

At the time I don't know how it could be possible, but when we as students blind tested a drop or two from the various vials, a person could distinctly taste a flavor or essence of the original compound. Each vial had a different distinct taste! Arsenic being the one I tried, I could really taste the specific almond-like flavor, that is typically found in arsenic poisoning, or at least an after smell in my nose, after tasting the drops even though I knew that this compound had been diluted to a billionth or maybe even many trillions of its original strength.

But I also know that as you continually make half of something even a billion times there is still a small piece left, even a trillion times make something a half or a tenth or a hundredth, there is still a little bit of that ever so small amount left. Science or chemistry tells us through various laws of delusion that particles in the water will move to areas of lesser concentration until the entire body of water has an equal distribution, and given time these distances between when not acted out upon by outside forces will always seek equilibrium.

The study of Homeopathy would possibly be a testimony to that. In the study itself, it is believed that a sort of energy exchange is passed into the water from the essence of the compound, and no matter how much you dilute it, something from the original is passed through to the rest of the pure water. Apparently, pure water has property about it that sort of draws out some of the essences almost a reflection of whatever is placed in it and disperses it throughout its entirety. Perhaps this explains why the "Face" of the water was mentioned. Is this distributional ability of the water, thus the significant cleaning ability of water as well? I believe on a quantum level the intent is expressed in the spaces between particles of energy in the water molecules and thus rapidly spread through the entire product in this case; an intent to cure Arsenic poisoning.

Water makes us clean! Water can purify, sounds Godly to me. Dr. Mike who I mentioned earlier in the book once told me he preferred to use water for the cleaning of wounds, stating that all the other products they push on us to use damage healthy tissue alongside the bacteria they are meant to eradicate, at least have the effect of reducing the structure or integrity of the tissue thus making it more vulnerable to continued germ assault, and only water has the ability to clean while not hurting the wound whatsoever.

Let us again place our attention in the quantum realm supposing that these statements about water are true, science today can only suppose and hypothesize to explain the many energies that not only hold the molecules together, and even seem to surround the various atoms making them independent of others, even though they also know vast distances compared to their relative sizes separate the fractions from their other parts in atoms or molecule as we have already stated. And since other compounds of similar structure don't have the seeming gifts water has been attributed, where exactly in the structure of the atom does this hidden ability lie?

So if we continue our examination, our ascension supposition that there is an energy surrounding and holding these compounds, molecules, and atoms together, thus making them into the significant essence they are today, this unmeasurable, invisible, unexplainable, and even unfathomable energy, almost spiritual, (again sounds kind of Godly) which is definitely strong and indestructible, being able to be split but not destroyed, then why is it not conceivable that this powerful energy could have an effect on the surrounding like energies it comes in contact with. "Energy cannot be destroyed only transferred!" Hey, Einstein said it not me!

And because we further ascend in our thinking, realizing our own immortality in the supposition, that this energy cannot be destroyed, only being be transferred as scientific illumination would teach us. Energies of such strength and significance that even just splitting them releases forces that can topple cities as demonstrated at Hiroshima. These yet unknown, unmeasurable, unseen, unfelt, only believed to be real by the faith of the observer energies... hmm Godly, are so potentially powerful then why are they literally invisible? These energies clearly demonstrate some kind of interaction as seen in homeopathy, well this raises all kinds of questions. Is there really mountain moving potentials in our mere spoken words?

If all of this is true, and I have no reason to believe otherwise, then one other fact is true; Jesus's blood was shed, his side was pierced and water gushed out. This is a fact it was documented and nobody denies this event took place.

What is also the fact is that at the moment of His death it is recorded that a great storm irrupted, to the degree where even the many Roman onlookers had to comment; "Surely this was the Son of God?" An earthquake that shook the land, and split the ground, and the great Jewish temple, ripped the veil and rain-drenched the land. But even if it didn't rain we know he was beaten almost unrecognizable, documented! A lot of blood! You would suppose that the area where whipping occurred would have to be washed, eventually!

Any rain or water would mix with his blood, if but a few drops, but all accounts tell us there was a great deal of blood and a great deal of liquid that ushered forth from His side. This, in turn, could flow over the land or soak into the ground, not destroyed only move, it would find its way into the water table eventually, which in turn would find its way to the stream, later rivers and eventually the ocean, where it would be diluted with all of the water of the world.

I guess my point is if a single drop of arsenic can be diluted in a thousand-gallon barrel of water, a drop taken from that one, and placed in another vat, over and over again, retaining enough of the essence of the original to heal the person of his infirmity, then I guess it is not inconceivable to believe that the essence of Jesus's blood, the

Creator of the entire universe, the healer of uncountable, resides in each and every drop of water we may drink.

"And He said take this cup and drink, for this is the cup symbolizing my blood, take it and think of me" I like that thought and would like to remember that image as I drink a glass of water from our own well. Amazing how much tastier, purer, and even more evidentially healing it is when I think of even this simple prayer.

Amphorae

I love my children so much, how great is this God of ours who gives so freely and provides a love that just flows from His heart. One night I was praying and an image formed in my mind as clear as the noon daylight.

Yes, my sweet friend I to have had so many visions I could hardly record them, but this one, in particular, was of a large clay vessel that was filled with a liquid.

This liquid is shown with almost a luminescent white light like the purest brightest clear white milk or perhaps the pure essence of the white sun itself. The jar or vessel that contained it was one of those old Greek olive oil containers, I couldn't at the time remember exactly what it was called, but I think it was an amphora? Or something like that, anyway as this amphora filled to the brim, it tips and spills over onto its side, spreading over the whole scene!

As the liquid spreads over the flat dark surface, it forms a sort of pool area spreading with ease over the surface. I could clearly see speckles of almost starlight shining from within the liquid, a sort of sparkles' and then dissipates softly like the remnant of fireworks in the sky! Sparklers fading from your vision like the traces left in a dark night as the bright light moves through space, so softly it fades slowly away, this is what seemed to dance across the surface of the liquid as it spread out.

God spoke to me; *"This is how my love is in you!" "And so is its effect on the world around you!" "I have one thing you are to do; Love!"*

I vaguely remember thinking; I knew how to love, and it seemed to have been held from me for a very long time, seemingly dammed up by the debris of my life, and maybe now that I think of it, by myself altogether! But maybe now it is time to see it for what it is faulty earth-filled dam holding back the vast waters God has given me each and every day?

Waterfalls are beautiful to behold, I don't believe there is anyone anywhere that would argue that but I believe on a spiritual level water cannot be associated with a fall in any way, shape, or form, and when people talk about powerful water-related anything, a more realistic vocalization of water realizations must be stated to be not waterfalls but water ascensions?

We have all walked in the wilderness, but He has promised that if we look to Him in everything, in every way, in anything, in a single thing, ascend but one single step, He will take care of the rest.

I will have received back in the full portion that which I had stolen or lost, multiplied with interest as promised! Anybody who knows me and has met my wife can clearly see that. And He keeps all of His promises!

The caterpillar sits in the crevasse of the tree resting quietly as the rain gently falls from the sky. The soft caressing of the cool touch washes over her as the water cleans from her face what little dust that may have remained from the ground. Streams of accumulated droplets flow by as our little caterpillar reaches in and drinks from this gift.

How different it tastes from waters on the ground they had such a murky musky scent, this water seems to have such a pure fresh taste. Could it be that she knows it is from on high, when she was on the groundwater seemed to come from the ground, but this is truly a gift from above? Merely understanding this truth, he gives honor to Him who creates the water, and in doing so, a prayer of recognition as she drinks again the sweet perfect water that has already begun to heal her body manifests.

BREAD

The aroma meanders through the chamber like a soft cool summer's breeze, dancing on the edge of the senses with the soft-footed gentleness of the most beautiful young princess, the whisking of flowing light garments. It touches the inner senses with a deep sense of satisfaction, feeding the hunger of a body's pure delight. The very bouquet has the amazing ability to both satisfy and illicit further hunger.

A golden loaf of light browns and earthly tans, crusted flakes, out from the warmth that bursts from within. Light penetrates within, binds to the essence of the pure white grain that rest under the surface, wrapping its arms around the bread that will not give, but sustain life. Heat, warm light, God's created gift of being presented to the body for the nourishing of its parts, given by God for all parts equally, needed, and free with love.

There is just a singe on the bottom where the bread came in contact with the fire-baked stones, heat, and fire to erupt the life-generating processes that expand this wonderful gift of God from mere elements of the earth. Life within life, grain, yeast, water, a touch of salt, and oil, all the gifts any part might need. Interesting the singe is where it has contact with the earth?

As I ponder these days of sitting at home amid the exercised COVID restrictions and the concerns regarding viral issues the apparent reports of infections, the overcrowded hospitals with their lines of infected patients streaming into the streets being hurled away because of reportedly lack of caregivers or facilities to house them, I am left with a little time to exercise a few muscles I have yet to date ever tried to flex.

Perplexing is the fact myself being a healthcare professional driving around my own city and seeing only deserted hospitals, parking lots as quiet as their counterparts the medical support complexes, with the knowledge that I myself as well as every one of the colleagues I also know, have been sent home without work. So what to do in this newfound segment of my life.

The evidential realization that something is not right with the narrative that is being presented seems to be lingering just outside the view especially when people are locked away at home and can hardly see for themselves what really is going on. I myself heard from more than one health care providing company that people are being quarantined yet do need care, and the additional fact that a large portion, especially my younger colleagues, are refusing to see them for fear of contracting the virus themselves.

Call me stupid, call me reckless, but working in my earlier career with infectious diseases the likes of the "Black Death," has given a bit of confidence regarding the infectiousness of viral or bacterial transmission, plus as I have learned in the Ascension process fear attracts attacks, and likewise, confidence often will scare even the most ominous attacker away. Like I said there is something fishy about the whole thing and the only way to really get an eye on it is to look from a higher or elevated perspective.

What do they have to gain by locking people away, closing healthcare facilities, putting people at home in fear? An interesting fact that only months before the so-called COVID outbreak occurred people in the healthcare arena started seeing a marked reduction of authorized care across the board. Doctors reported almost systematic delays in scheduling surgeries, people being prematurely discharged from hospitals, and general one on one health care was being systematically pushed aside almost in anticipation of the shutdown. Understandable that the first reported cases were in November in China, but supposedly they didn't know exactly what it was until after the new year.

Yet here we are March and suddenly pandemic reports worldwide, every country taking on the same precautionary measures, talk of closures across the board; schools, restaurants, stores, churches, public service buildings, even call centers when you had issues with paid services all on shutdown, leaving only so-called essentials such as large grocery stores, bars, and liquor stores (because they are so essential), drug stores (of course), oh and let's not forget Walmart's remain open. But what does this have to do with bread?

While I have touched on this subject before, thank God my wife returned from Europe after visiting her father in the hospital afflicted with four separate life-threatening attacks all, at the same time, her return was literally the day before President Trump closed the borders with Europe to air travel. It was a miracle she was able to go there in the first place, in such short notice, the Doctors had little hope he would even survive until she made it there, yet were the first to admit that it was an absolute miracle he recovered right after she arrived. We both knew he would heal, but again it was one of those examples; *"Lord I believe, now help me with my unbelief."* A statement we seem to be saying to ourselves more and more these days, it would seem clear the higher a person climbs the Ascension Mountain the more evident God's hand is on everything as well as the need to trust and believe in the supernatural of things.

Back to the bread; as I earlier said as soon as she returned I was instructed to go to the store and get a few things that we had run low on while she was gone, namely bread for grilled sausages and toilet paper which we had apparently run low of. Being someone who always prided himself in knowing how to stock up before a crisis. As I looked around the store it really had no sign of a run, normal products on the shelves, prices pretty much the same as always that is until I went over to the bread aisle, it was completely empty even down to the last bag of hotdog buns? Of course when I got to the toilet paper aisle the same thing, and other than really a few items seemingly short like paper towels the only other item I noticed missing was Tonic water.

I remember thinking to myself and even commenting to the cashier what an idiotic thought, when there is talk about shortages everyone suddenly gets the bright idea; "Well I better hurry to the store and buy up all the hotdog buns (because they last so long), get as much toilet paper as I can (an extremely essential item), and by the way lets not forget the Gin and Tonic?" This stuff disappeared even before the run on masks and hand sanitizer! I was almost dumbfounded to hear that it all stemmed from some report by the media that there may be a toilet paper shortage and suddenly people were buying it by the carts full!

A refreshing thought hit me that day when my dear wife sent me to the store to retrieve the bread along with other things, not that we bought our bread in the general grocery store, my wife being European likes her bread more small baker tasting, crispy, fluffy and fresh, so we often purchase it at these smaller price bakeries. But most likely if there was a run on hotdog buns then there must assuredly be one on the good stuff?

The ingredients seemed simple enough; some enriched flour, yeast, water, and salt (both of which I knew I had). Others had obviously had the same idea as me considering the shelves had already been significantly plundered from both yeast and flower, but luckily a few bags of flour still remained for me to try, and luckier still my wife had previously brought sufficient yeast home with her from home.

The basic recipe was simple enough a two to one ratio of flour to water which in my case would eventually be four cups of flour to two cups of water to achieve the sufficient size loaf for my family's needs. One and a third teaspoon of salt and a little over a one-quarter teaspoon of dried yeast, that was until I learned how to produce my own sourdough starter, sourdough being the bread of choice by my beautiful European born wife.

Instructions were simple, mix the flour, salt, and yeast, add warm water, of course, our water being well water is free of any chemical additives. Mix until a dough is thoroughly formed and then set aside for at least two hours to rise before baking for 30 minutes in a Dutch Oven at 450 degrees, a piece of parchment paper is to be placed first in the pot before the dough to ensure it doesn't stick to the pot. Apparently, a Dutch Oven is of a heavy metal construct, or cast iron pan with a lid, this was necessary to ensure the bread would have enough concentrated heat to properly bake. I use a simple metal roasting pan with a glass lid at least for now. After thirty minutes of baking time, the general instructions were to remove the lid, remove parchment paper and place it back in the oven for an additional 15 minutes or more to brown to the desired color.

After a few tries, it became apparent that letting the dough rise for at least six hours instead of only two, insured that the bread was lighter and not so dense when finished, apparently, the seventh hour is a good one for baking bread. I of course had to try letting the dough rise overnight to see how far this could be extended, but the result was a loaf of bread with too much of a yeast aroma when cooking quickly prompting my wife to advise me to keep the raising process to from five to eight hours or specifically the seventh hour for the perfect loaf.

It is apparently important to preheat the Dutch Oven pan before placing the parchment paper and dough loaf in for baking. I am not sure why, but everything I read as to baking bread required either a preheated oven, pan, or both, so I did.

Once the time of optimal resting was discovered the next few attempts only varied with mixing styles or the amounts of kneading done prior to baking. For me, I find that the minimum amount of kneading (basically folding the dough with a sprinkling of fresh flour) was necessary to ensure the loaf could be placed onto the parchment paper with minimal sticking, but I guess on a spiritual level it is nice to need something we are planning on feeding our family with. Also, I have found using my Kitchen Aid mixer with its big mixing hook works the best for mixing the dough completely in its earliest stage.

The result was what my beautiful wife has referred to as the "Perfect

Loaf!"

Anna, being born in Poland and living in western Europe, specifically Holland until I was blessed enough to find her, did prompt her upon arriving here in the US to realize that fresh-baked bread like that which she often would send me out for in Amsterdam near her home, was impossible to find in the more commercially and I must admit more mass-produced bakeries of my own home. And while the artisan shops do come close with some of their more expensive loaves, still even these seem to lack the fresh-baked flavors she was so fond of.

She was quick to point out that it is the love I seem to infuse into the bread that has a distinct difference in the product. The secret seems to be in the blessing of the ingredients, respecting God and thanking Him every step along the way, especially as they are being mixed, this not only has a direct effect on the water but seems to have an effect on the flour, taste, aroma, everything.

Ascended realizations such as blessing the base products with a verbalized thank you or thanking God for these, seem to fully release the energies being used especially water places extra positive energies into the bread baking and ultimately into the product. It wasn't long before many of my wives friends became over-eager to have a loaf on any occasion, and whenever we were invited for dinner or an evening get-together, the answer to the question of what we were to bring was always the same; "A loaf of your bread you make."

Two thousand years earlier He broke the bread gave it to his disciples and said; *"Take this, all of you, and eat of it, for this is my body, my body which has been given for you." "Take this and eat, in remembrance of me."*

The bread was broken and given to all, everyone present took a piece, receiving all they needed, all that could be given by the bread. Even as the foot sits in the dust, and has not the privilege to hear bread's crispy sound as the loaf is broken, does the foot not benefit equally as the ear? And like the hand which can feel the warmth, and has the privilege to break it, and give it, will never see its beautiful golden color, does the hand experience less? The mouth can taste this wonderful blessing, as even to the One who speaks those Words also tastes the same sweet flavors, as all that recline at the table, do any receive more or less nourishing because of their perspective?

What gift does Father have for Him, the Son, does He not receive likewise an equal gift from the Father? They all hear the Words, created by the Father; Son, sinner, and saint, all equally given, even as the rain falls on everyone's head, as every part of the body can receive equal nourishing the good energies of the bread bring. Even as the One gave, takes He also a taste, for as God gives so, does He feed in the pleasure of the gift.

Being raised in a Christian church, the act of taking communion was taught to be something of reverence, a moment of sanctification. But as I have spoken of the experience with others; a common question seems to speak through peoples heart, lingering on quivering lips as if an unspoken secret, a dark question one might hardly dare think, let alone speak; "I don't know, but have you ever felt anything significant during the act of communion"? Resting in the depths of such a question, resides a feeling of doubt, guilt for some kind of lack thereof as if belief might somehow be substantiated by the very manifest of such a question. How many souls have doubted their own beliefs as a result of the un-appearance of an emotional connection to communion?

There are many churches out there, in addition, where the taking of communion is only allowed if a number of prerequisite tasks are first completed. Rules need to be obeyed, people are told they must be or become members, given permission, a class or two might need to be taken, a prerequisite kneeling before a man, or just by being someone who happens to be appropriately dressed, and or employed. Oh, and heaven forbid if they have participated in any activities that the said church deems unforgivable, prior to wishing to participate.

I have even heard them go so far as to say; if people partake without meeting the prerequisite set of qualifiers, they even risk a dire punishment from God, even unto death. Well, I felt God prompting me to examine this for a moment.

There seems to be a number of examples of instances in which Jesus, sits and dines, or drinks with people, in any and all of these instances, I have never heard him once place any kind of admission prerequisite in any of these attendances. As a matter of fact, in most cases, He seemed to sit and dine with not only tax collectors and prostitutes, considered in that time to be the absolute bottom of society not only in cleanliness, but undeniably in the eyes of the church government at the time, but did He also not sit with the Pharisees and Sadducees who Jesus himself referred to as "A Den of Vipers?"

Or resting casually on the side of a perfect green grass carpeted hill as a few loaves and fishes are broken and given all to everyone over five thousand present, to the point of giving complete nourishment, with an abundant overfull, leaving nobody unnourished, who would but partake.

Either way in both cases there seems to be no prerequisite prompting to do anything prior to eating or drinking. Yes, He did say; *"Do this in memory of me,"* when He shared His last breaking of bread, and drink with them.

But why "think of Him" with this act?

Why not "Think of Me before you sleep" or "every time you kiss someone you love?" And while I believe there may be many reasons for the significance of breaking bread and drinking of a cup, as infinite many as there are infinite images of the Face of God all around us, one, in particular, comes to mind to this writer; if God would have us think of Him, as often as we could, even with every waking breath, what a good start would it be for His children to at least think of Him, and the sacrifice He made for each of us with something that we at least do each and every day and that is to eat and drink.

Some people need a physical representation of a supernatural act in order to bring heaven to earth into focus in their minds. People feel like Ascension or the Ascension Process will take place automatically regardless if a person is looking for it or not, but I cannot agree with that statement except with persons who are not responsible for their actions and have to be led places such as children or people who are diminished in their awareness such as extreme elderly. Yet in both cases the children and the extreme elderly I have witnessed numerous occasions where they seem to have an almost intuitive understanding of the supernatural. Children who have not yet been polluted by the darkening of this world, and the elderly who as functions seem to diminish gain others more supernatural in nature?

A real feel of something in their hand, so as to give blessing to the hand, bread is such a blessed thing. Something to the lips, as to bless the lips and more even the mouth taking in the taste and reality of the gift. Something to the ear, hearing the Word and through the sound, a realized creation of an image in our mind, not all that different than what is written about the creation of the entire universe by a "Single Spoken Work" back at the beginning of existence.

But did Jesus place any prerequisite as to who he shared bread with, who might hear, who might see? The invitation to the table, and as glorious as it must have been, there is no apparent sound of any word of restriction or exclusion. And while nobody was sent away, one did leave, turned, and ran from the presence of God. And even Jesus himself warned; *"Better it is that one was never born than to betray the Son of Man,"* for sacrificed was but the reason He came to the earth.

For it is clearly written in Luke that He shared bread and cup in the last supper, asking them to remember Him. And it wasn't until the next moment that Jesus states; *"But, Behold, the hand of him who betrayeth me is with me on the table."*

It was further written; *"the darkness came into him,"* because at that point Judas made his choice, and fled. *"For darkness looked upon light and it comprehended it not, and darkness fled."*

In understanding the ascension process regarding its relationship with Healing or Healthcare people often ask me why I write about God, Jesus, and the Bible so much, but it is clear to me the for the same reasons people must fully understand the shadows around them in order to make sense of the lies and thus venture up the path of Ascension, which by the way is merely a quest for truth, truth in every aspect of our being; Body, Mind, and Spirit.

As we climb the Ascension ladder into the stars we realize throughout the entire experience that God is essential to this illumination and understanding the many signs He has given us, in essence, reflect light on the many powers that have strived to hold this knowledge from us using every physical means at their disposal including poisoning the very waters we drink, the food we eat, sounds we hear, and even all we breathe.

God clearly shows; sharing at the table of the Lord, while one partakes of a piece, all share, all are welcome. As they take all from the same loaf, taking in the blessed life-giving energies of the bread so is a piece of the same Healing energy via words, sights, and love given to each, and each as a part of the whole enjoys and benefits in maybe a slightly different manner, but all are fed, all receive nourishment, all live.

I believe it is so throughout the entire Quantum realm, as any in the world ascends more light through the increased vibrational continuum is realized. These in their part add to the whole creating thus more positive energy throughout the entire world, universe, and eternity. All benefits, in the process fewer and fewer places are available for darkness to hide, eventually how wonderful would it be if darkness had no place left to go, perhaps the only place left is underground, hell. Everyone is important, every person a universe.

The Word that is given to a man through a man,

Who is God,

But has become man,

As to reach us all,

In loving gesture to come home.

A request to choose,

Not a command to bow,

But merely to request to remember,

The sacrifice the Prince gave each and every one of us.

That Word which is Him,

But is also part of a One as it passes through Him,

And as a part,

It is of Him if but for a moment,

Becoming Him the Word,

Resting on the edge of his tongue and soul.

The thought which is God,

Granted in His wisdom's gift,

Is life created out of light,

Baked with the fire of glory,

And resonates into existence,

For all the ears to hear.

In the ears of all that come,

The Word rests on the surface of His children,

All who would hear,

God touching the ear of each,

And forming a picture,

Creating in the mind of each of their souls.

The eyes then take each image in,

Each and every gift of The Fathers creation,

Every color-forming into beautiful picture,

Blending with their luscious desires,

Fulfilling the hunger and pains as it forms in the mind,

That loneliness that has lingered since birth's first day.

Grant to each of us,

In every part,

All that we would but need,

In our every part,

Each in its capacity to feel,

All that you would give.

Every hand that takes the bread,

Every eye that takes the gift in,

With the ears receiving of Word,

With the mouth sweet taste,

Into the body for all parts to benefit.

Is it not with any word given to any part of the body, any prophesy, any healing, and can they not be used for all of the body?

Is not every gift for the body, if it is given by God for the entire body, all to use all equal, all free?

All energy is a gift from God, we merely need to take a step up and let it illuminate us, activate as it illuminates.

By Peter Colla

ASCENDING SOUNDS

What pushes the butterfly into the ski, what revelations when on the ground presses upon him the need to ascend, is it perhaps the same consciousness that perpetuates the very idea in the first steps she takes in the world, a driving force to lift from the ground and take those first few steps, fluttered winged liftings' toward the heavens? A guiding hand from an all-loving parent, a gentle nudge to venture into realms perhaps dreamed of, but not yet experienced or even seen?

All of this magnificent power in the quantum level of awareness wrapped up in these small specks of physical energy, and remarkably everything merely looks like sound, the result of something equivalent to the spoken Word. And then to have the entire universe that makes up our real universe created to conform to the natural laws that seem to govern the systems between the individual participants of that energy with base parts that sounds like spoken sound waves lead us to the conclusion that the only difference between ideological types of individual waves is the intent infused within these. And since everything, in the beginning, was Good within the first week of creation, leaves us to only one further conclusion and that is that all negativity, bad, evil could only be laced into the system from outside of Godly sources, other creators such as ourselves, or acts performed by participants that choose a direction not necessarily good for themselves, others, or their surroundings.

Words, actions, intentions, emotions, all have the potential to add positively or negatively to the already existing energetic waves that make up our everyday awareness. The existing energies become conduits for the transmission of these intentions leading all to one purpose and that would appear to be our own Ascension or discovery of the truths within each and every one of them. And, since basically we are created in His image with the same creative abilities, we too have a responsibility for the related action our produce energies manifest?

Wow, if the Bible is merely the writings of men, what genius that these men knew without the aid of modern instrumentation and centuries of learned references, that the universe was "Spoken" into creation. So Moses without the advantage of a diploma from a knowledgeable school and the advantage of microscopic instrumentation was able to guess that everything was created from Sound when he wrote; *"God Said let there be…,"* and we are supposed to believe this was a random guess on his part, not inspired by God Himself, I think not! Everything that we see, touch, smell, feel, or even taste, can speak to the glory of God, if one will just take the time and look close, nowhere is this more evident than in science.

If everything on a quantum level boils down to basic sounds waves leaving merely the differences of these base elements residing in the interpretation and effects they have on their surrounding then one would conclude that the very words could be the most important commodities of the known universe. Is this perhaps why words, specifically; what we are being told by the TV or specifically the media is so powerful, and thus valuable?

Let's suppose for a moment, as we have already discussed, that there is some being or something out there that not only hates us with all of his essences but has the feeling that he was passed by what he feels to be a lessor creation. Unwilling to bow to beings created in the image of God Himself, and thus proving his unwillingness to bow to God Himself, and it is for this one reason satan is banished from Gods' presence. Just like darkness, when satan became darkened through the pollution of his beliefs and actions, he fled from God, from Light, and God may have not even needed to send him away, merely by creating the laws of the physical universe whereby this action was inevitable, satan desired to flee.

Dark spirits, while they have been clearly stripped of everything good, are not the essence of darkness described at the Creation per se, but they choose to dwell in darkness as preference having more in common with it, a place of lacking much less than in the light. This may explain satan's ability to come on occasion in the presence of God with his accusations of us. We can further realize the ultimate slap in God's face would be in taking God's most loved creations and causing them to turn away from Him also. Is this also why information is kept from us because by doing so we are "kept in the dark?" Perhaps this worldwide masking agenda is merely a ruse to limit the positive verbal and thus creative ability of people worldwide in a desperate attempt to stifle us, dumb us down, and enslave us.

My darling wife Anna has told me of a story from her performance dancing days in the circus where some people in Italy brought the circus a chimpanzee name Lola, who apparently had been kept in a small cage for years. The result was the chimpanzee even though it was already a few years old and should have been full-grown still was as small as a baby chimp, even though it was taken out of the cage from time to time to perform on the beaches. The restriction even in this case of merely a cage had a dramatic effect on the physical development of this animal and it wasn't until shortly after when Lola was freed in the circus did she immediately grow to a normal size chimpanzee again.

If information represents wisdom, then on a quantum level the physical energies they represent physicality are the conduits of transporting the good intention that wisdom brings. In Ascension, whether it be for wellbeing, healing, peace, healthcare, all of these emotional goals are basically the end products of God-given energetic enlightenments that are transported via various conduits of physical media.

As we have already discussed water is one of the most successful known media for transporting Godly tasks whether it be information or the performance of life-giving tasks. One other very important property water seems to have was clearly demonstrated scientifically by the studies of Masaro Emoto, whereby he cataloged positive and negative physical changes that occurred in Water when it was exposed to emotional intent.

The spoken word had a clear effect for good or bad on the water, and this had such a powerful effect that even written words placed on the beakers seemed to have the same effect. The water's positive or negative effect was solely dependent on the intentional meaning of the words regardless of what language the words were written in, or whether he could read it or not, the effects were the same. Positive words had a fresh, healthy effect on the water, while cursed words would have a clear negative or fouling effect.

Without getting into too much of the in's and out's of Dr. Emoto's research, one particular experiment that is of stellar significance to our discussion is the "three beakers of rice." In this experiment, he placed in three beakers equal amounts of pure water from the same source, he then says a blessing to one and a curse to the second one of them. He then adds equal amounts of live grains of rice into the one beaker he blessed with a simple soft prayer, the same into the second he cursed, and equal into the third this one after which he ignores.

In the water of the first one that the softly spoken blessing was done the rice seemed to grow, taking on a greenish color to the water, releasing an almost sweet healthy fragrance that when students would smell made them think of freshness or something clearly alive. The water of the cursed one turned dark and clearly the rice in it died turning dark, having the stale smell of death to it. In these two cases, the waters were clearly conduits for the prayer or curse that Dr. Emoto spoke to them. The water transported and held the intent of his spoken words in its essence, and then transmitted it into the rice even without the rice knowing whether it was positive or negative.

Interestingly in the third beaker where he ignored it altogether the rice neither thrived or died but went on to become rotten, contaminated by foreign bacteria, susceptible to outside infection, and ultimately a danger to everything around it. So in this case the withholding of information, the lack of emotional input caused even more danger than the negative one.

In my experience as a father I have had many opportunities to coach and counsel youths, in one particular experience, I had the honor of being a counselor for a group of teenage boys all run-aways now residing in a group home, a derivative of the program Teen Challenge. The majority of these boys had had their own run-in with the law, and since the parents could not, or would not any longer handle them, they were assigned, mostly by the court, to live at this facility.

One afternoon we gathered in a relaxed around the campfire discussion, and each in the group began to share what they felt was the worse experience they had at home, ultimately driving them to run away from their parents in the first place. I expected to hear tails of control, abuse, parents being too strict for these boys to handle, alcoholism, drug abuse, etc., but I was astonished to find out that each and every one of them agreed that the reason they ran away was that their parents ignored them. This single act of neglect seemed to push them not only out of the home but led them into venues that were filled with anger, crime, and acts harmful to themselves and others.

In the first beaker examples where positive or negative words were spoken, these are clearly conduits, especially in the example where a foreign written language is posted, this demonstrates the effect even if that the reader doesn't understand, or is too young yet to comprehend, still having an effect on the physiological state of the waters present. As you can see, even indirectly it does place an enormous amount of responsibility into every spoken word we may say or even write? Especially as parents if we are responsible for everything good or bad we present to our children, then likewise are we responsible for their healing especially when it comes to Body, Mind, and most importantly Spirit or Belief.

Back to a dark essence wishing to do harm even hidden among the subtleties of soft-spoken words; there are many ways old darky Boo-

Boo can accomplish this goal, through temptation, then ultimate accusation, leading to condemnation, and guilt, such as with the guilt that resides in making a small child much to embarrassed to look in his Father's face, when he or she has made a mistake and had an accident, we have all been there. Words have so much power in our lives, especially in the most formulating years.

When a child does something spoken of as wrong, makes a mistake, sometimes this so-called "wrong thing" may not even of their own choosing, such as when they might get sick or falling. Maybe they might have eaten too many Easter chocolates, or their mother gave them a piece of meat that was just a bit undercooked, children are such pure and honest believers in the complete assurance that everything their parent gives them is good, in every sense of the word, in addition, they will take these things and eat them even if they taste strange because the parent gave them, it must be good. What unbelievable trust God saw fit to entrust in us the responsibility of care for children. When it came to the caring of His precious children especially by their own parents, they seem to love even before the love is return demonstrated by the said parent? Unconditional love, babies seem to come out with it already in place.

I remember one of my children constantly getting sick from that baby milk they sell out of a can "formula," she would throw it up almost as fast as she ate it. So one day I tried a little of it in a spoon just to see, my God, it was the most disgusting thing I had ever tasted, I wouldn't mix it with dog food for the dog after that. Luckily she switched almost immediately to mashed food we made ourselves. Funny thing, every time she threw up she would look up at me with those loving eyes, how can a person not see the love of God in every child's eyes, I guess only the people who don't know what love looks like at all?

Eating something, taking into themselves something that wasn't necessarily good for them, they then throw up? They cast that bad thing out of themselves, that bad thing that shouldn't have been there in the first place. God's own built-in protections, inspires the young body to eject that foul thing before it can inflict further damage, He placed this loving protection in each person. There seem to be many protective natures, that any loving parent would gladly take the place if his or her dear child is in pain. If that only could be; "take their place," I wonder how many parents really would suffer for their children if it was even possible?

The child throws-up on himself, or on the bed, a mess occurs. Just a little mess compared to the entire life, love, smiles they bring, one that can easily be tossed in the wash or wiped from the floor. Yet, what do we do as parents most of the time; get upset at the inconvenience, raise our voice at our own frustration, maybe even punish the child for messing up the bed? The result; the poor little perfect being, can't lift her eyes, head down, eyes full of tears, fear, even to meet the eyes of her parent out of a feeling of accusation, condemnation, guilt, and shame! A scare forms in their being because of the words we have spoken in anger.

Why?

Is it because of a whisper of something or someone cruel, who is softly speaking in her ear telling our precious little child; "It's your fault, you're bad, you're not good enough!" How as a father, I would love to take a sword to the throat of that creature that spoke such words into the ear of my little child, my mercy would be measured in milliseconds! Only to realize I may have inadvertently done it myself with my own words or actions. My Father loves so much greater than this and has forgiven so much more horrific outbursts to the innocent child, He loves so much greater than I could possibly fathom, without the out-bursts, without guilt, with only the loving arms to wrap around and lift the sickened sad child, me!

Let us again suppose that God in His infinite mercy would reveal Himself in His entire creation every moment of every day, He knows the outcomes of every terrible and idolized choice we stupid men have ever done, do, or will ever do, out of our greed, our lusts, and still manages to work them all out in a masterful chess game for His ultimate victory and glory; the glory of good, light, and love! He is even so good as to then go back and give us a view of things to come, like the program of a play, a Quantum script, his prophetic word in the Revelations of things to come. That program is open for all to read, the Saints and the sinners alike. The Ascension of Illuminated truths regarding the revelations of this war we find ourselves in today.

What could be more deceptive of the devil with his lying group of storytellers in the media than to explain these observations as random, natural, and generally nothing special, the very thing the media and science attempt to do each and every moment of every day? While the devil is not omniscient, he knows the Bible better than we could ever hope to, and he knows all the prophesies and predicted outcomes, even if he hopes for an alternate ending, is it conceivable he would go so far as to try to eliminate the players as to change the possible outcome?

The devil has read the Bible, he fears what is predicted to come, with all of his being, and ultimately hates those who would play a part, especially members that end up on the winning team. He hates anybody in the universe that is better than him, and every person created in the image of God, which he wasn't is basically better than him. No wonder why wants everyone masked, changing sex, eating each other, and drinking blood.

He hates the opposing team with a level of malevolence that would make any mass murderer look like a preschool cry baby. But if Boo-Boo is unable to stop it, what then? He would be smart to put in backup plans, that could take out as many players as possible out of the opposing team, as many cheap shots as he can, and the crueler, and more destructive the better. Pay all the traitor he can, with the promise of being rulers themselves, to betray their brothers and sisters.

One thing he could do is explain these events end-time scenarios away. Make sure that if anyone even glances at something that might lead them to Ascension, explain it away as a coincidence or conspiracy theory. Put his people in charge of all the communications of the world, then make sure they repeatedly speak the lies like a repeating mantra. Take everything that seems Godly and supernatural in God's creation and events unto himself, and explain them away from a scientific point of view as spontaneously occurring from nothing. Make them understandable yet unfathomable, simple and chaotically complex, predictable and completely random, then they become uncomplicated in their evolution, naturally selected, even accidental in their unaccountability, fall in this life, steal, kill, destroy don't worry you will get another later, and ultimately point them in every direction except one having to do with God.

"Dear Lord Jesus, please allow the plans of the enemy to be discovered by your people, open the eyes of the scientists of this world and give them the courage to say no to the lies of the enemy."

VIRAL WHISPERS

The caterpillar has heard stories, a continuous narrative, repeated descriptions of how and what exactly comprises the world. Any images of the very existence of a realm above have been deemed nonsense.

More and more, images of darkness that dwells ready to spring on each of them seemingly eliciting out of nowhere fear and worry perpetrated as friends, ideas, and images are being repeated by everyone who seems to have a higher position or an elevated voice they all seem to begin to repeat the same message; "do not look up, do not venture up, but keep your face buried in the blanketed recesses of the dirt and grasses."

Doom is foretold for anyone who may think otherwise, a dark feeling reverberates through her body almost automatically causing the defensive constriction of the mind again plunging the soul into the deepest depression one can realize regardless of whether they have journeyed up or not. Is this the intent of this message?

Something deep inside our young caterpillar tells her that malevolence and lies are being told. There is an increasing awareness that these statements of lock-down, sit fast, cover your face, and don't even object, there is something sinisterly wrong with them, he can feel it inside. Others around him who dare speak up are quickly drowned out by the many voices higher up ordering everyone to stay home on flat ground, yet this seems to go against the very nature of what our little caterpillar is called to be.

A choice must be made; "do we do what we are being told or do we do what we know is right?" For this little caterpillar, if life is desired there is only one choice Truth.

In the case of disease, pandemic, "scamdemic," or whatever COVID number they happen to come up with;

Let us suppose, by our own acts of vile, vice, and sin, that darkened structures in the supernatural build and cultivated to the point where death is stockpiled in hidden away areas of the world to the point where diseases that normally would have little or no effect on the larger population, mainly because the majority of the general public would very infrequently come in contact with a large enough exposure to allow the said disease to cross the barrier of this harsh environment and find its place in men, suddenly gain enough negative intent to actually cause some real harm. Then let us also suppose that greed is tossed in making the very precautions that would hold such diseases in check, being discarded or limited because it is just not economically feasible, for that matter the people or children involved in the care of this area are not worth the cost or worse the powers-to-be actually want this to maybe reduce populations to levels of numbers they believe they can control. Disease flourishes where it shouldn't, not by God's intent, but by man's free will and greedy choices.

God knows what the outcome will be, He has seen the path and destination our own steps have led. He knows what devastation that will come out of these steps, the pestilence. He has His prophets even write about it, so those who would see, recognize the hand of God in everything around us through this most horrific sign. He even tells us when; it is at a time when men's hearts will become cold, they will kill their young, darkness will prevail on the world. It is by our own free will, by the very words of our mouths that physical sounds with intent things occur.

But the devil is also at work, he is busy spinning his own tale, taking that which he can not create, twisting it into his own dark agent of death and torment, then uses his media puppets, his Hollywood coven of priests and priestesses, or those foolish egotistic gongs we call the scientific community to talk about, write about it, spin their own natural sort of explanation that usually represents some kind of naturally occurring spontaneous cause that has happened before millions of years ago, "oh look, we survived then!" or somehow saying it is man-made, and what we make we can fix!

They make movies or a documentary, millions, no billions die, but if the star somehow survives and gets the girl, it's going to be a happy ending! They write disaster books, describe it to the hilt, even show us pictures, after plan, after scam on some far off land we hardly know exists let alone feel the sting of a just-to-dull our minds scenario. They show us faces upon insect decimated hunger ridden bodies, we forget about the overfed man that is too busy snapping photo's to help or give food to this starving child. Yes, they give us images, faces the general public can't identify with, never a small blonde hair blue-eyed baby dying of some horrific disease. They warn us with false alarms over and over, predictions and warnings that don't pan out to the point where the public stops caring, all those words, all that intent until we just stop listening. Until we have heard it so much it becomes old news, the scar is too deep, the shock is gone, the effect is nothing, no tears, no sorrow, and if it doesn't happen directly to us or our children, oh well; seen it all before. It isn't even as bad as was depicted in the latest mass destruction movie we just watched weeks earlier.

The first time we see something truly shocking, it has an almost physical effect on us. Tears, anger, people get physically ill, women weeping, grown men sobbing, these images bring us to tears, people ask why maybe look to God, most of the time they call out to God, some give up. Nobody is immune! But witness tragedy over and over in a film and the degree of emotion it inflicts becomes less and less as we seem to form a callous, our hearts become hardened. Yesterday's Columbine, today doesn't even make the back page of the newspaper!

So what is happening, where is the deceit? Let us suppose that the deceiver would have us become desensitized so that when something truly tragic occurs like children being tortured and killed for their blood, we hardly even blink because we have seen it so many times. Then to make things worse let the one spreading the deceit scientifically explain the event away as to not make it a God thing but just something natural that has been predicted for a long time. Could such things as these possibly be a form of buffer? Remember, a buffer is a chemical reaction that is an added component that is intended to reduce the volatility of the reaction, slow it, or stop it altogether.

As is in the case of pestilence God said; *"in the end, there will be pestilence, and a third of the world's population will perish…"* I wonder if He was meaning a physical death or was he referring to the death of souls?

How many movies have shown millions of people dying, how many news reports of people dead in the streets in faraway lands famine, there are video games, books, songs, the images are so common even our smallest children see them in their cartoons. Bird flu is so commonly spoken of and so misreported that even if it occurred, people would shake it off as a natural occurrence. Ebola, Aids, MRSA, none of these diseases have any shockability any longer because the media has burned them out in our senses with overplaying on the likes of mainstream media fake news to the point where we don't even care, maybe many of us have already died spiritually as a result?

"There will be a shaking of the Earth as to the like the world has never witnessed," been there, seen that! Is it possible entertainment shakings of the earth, end of days movies, predictions of massive volcanoes, they have shown so many that the interest in Honduras is at such a low that many people have forgotten that even happened. Not to mention the scientific community predicting everything from massive eruptions in Yellowstone to the Earth's axis shifting and causing massive earthquakes, depict it on TV so the shock is off when and if it occurs, and it has already been explained away as natural. Things falling from the skies hitting the oceans and causing a third of the ships to be destroyed; been there, saw that! More people die spiritually, their beliefs gone for good!

Sun turning dark, yep they made a film or two or twenty. The Moon turning red like blood, water turning to blood, wars, the complete destruction of the monetary system, fall of billions by nuclear war, the rise of an Antichrist to rule the world as a one-world government.... Been there seen that! Maybe if we are talking about people not ascending, and dying in lies they have been told the totals are completely accurate?

We have been desensitized! We have had the glory taken out of the creation to the point where everything is natural, even us. Buffers! But why? Could the mask be just another buffer?

If we are natural then we are insignificant, and if we are insignificant then we don't matter, we don't believe the things we say blessings or curses, and if our words don't matter then it doesn't matter what we call ourselves because the world will go on, and none of it matters anyway. If we don't believe our words can create then they can't! If the doctor tells us we have cancer we believe him, what does it matter he gets paid $20,000 for every chemotherapy prescribed, or $30,000 for every COVID patient diagnosed regardless if they have it or not.

And the ultimate; if it doesn't matter what we do, then we have no need for forgiveness, and if we don't need forgiveness, then why have a Savior, how can we lift our heads and look at our parent when we know we spit up in bed and feel all that guilt if there is no chance of forgiveness?

But why stop there? I mean if the devil has the media in the palm of his hand, controlling all the members of the movie industry, communications, social media, censorship, why not the drugs and foods we eat, I mean if the same few people own controlling interests in all the major industries all through its greed, vanity, lust, desire for riches, power, fame, it would only make sense that he would want to illicit that enslavement into every aspect of our daily blessings including even our food. I mean if GMOs are so good for us why do the animals refuse to eat them?

Only freely giving the greatest benefits out to those who can bring in the most worshipers to Boo-Boo himself and taking from the rest of us as much of the blessings God intended for us as he could possibly get away with. Eventually, since we have all seen it a thousand times why do they even bother even hiding it?

"Dear Lord Jesus, help your people to feel every bit as special as you designed us to be, without guilt or accusation of the enemy. Help us see every good and loving thing in each and every one of us, especially in ourselves."

FADE FROM VIEW

The movie and media productions have been one of the greatest propaganda instruments in the history of the world. Children and adults alike today believe if they see it on TV, it must be true, especially when acted out in theatrical fashion in such realistic presentation that it leaves little doubt in their minds not only could it happen so, it might have happened so, maybe it did happen so, yes it happened just like that person saw on TV. Theories that were mere speculation and hypothesis yesterday, are accepted as fact today without any validation or subsequent scientific evidence, based merely on the fact that millions have seen something on TV and now accept lies as truth, Darwinian Evolution or COVID pandemic being perfect examples. Evolution, by the way, has been proven scientifically to be untrue yet is still being taught to our children as facts.

What is amazing is the subtle messages of the enemy, one can pick up in the most popular movies these days, being paraded right before our eyes, hidden in the backdrop of images on walls or earrings with dark messages dangling from ears, but for what purpose? It would seem that they must obey the laws of reality set up by God and one of those is they need our permission, even if it is indirect, before moving forward with their plans.

Biblical names and figures being tossed out and around like they are nothing more than mythological characters of no more significance than the pagan gods of old. And to make matters worse characters of less than honorable Biblical reference are often given the loftiest or honored characterization, such as the prince of Persia being correlated to a hero, lucifer a savior. Vice versa the more honored characters of the Bible the opposite treatment; the Angel Michael, Noah, among many being portrayed as overweight bumbling buffoon's. Again oumoee to our beliefs or buffers? Does it matter the enemy wins either way?

The devil or at least the powers of the realm of darkness, from the standpoint of outcomes, when it comes to Hollywood thus far very rarely lets them win, or do they? When evil has been lifted up, glorified, spoken of with power, facilitating fear, and demonstrated its authority not only towards us but pretty much everything else especially God in these shows, when they are being heralded as infinitely more powerful than the normal person, the many stand-in's that die throughout any normal movie, who is gloried here, definitely not the normal guy?

Hollywood always portrays them as large, muscular, extremely beautiful, or looking like the classic representation of the devil; red or black soulless eyes, sharp aggressive features, horns, hoofed feet, black-winged, fire, smoke, all the power he could want or need, charismatic, literally unbeatable, not to mention very real with the overwhelming advantage. Talk about your conduits of darkness, depression of vibrations, negative energy, and descending spiritual promptings in words, sights, thoughts, even beliefs.

God in His portrayal when it comes to Hollywood, on the other hand, is nothing more than some random lofty idea that generally is only someone to be respected, soft-spoken, confusing, interested only in His own ideas and agenda's, but let's not forget unapproachable, unavailable, and most certainly not someone you can count on in a tight spot. Most certainly they make no mention of Jesus in any way, shape, or form unless of course, it's Mel Gibson, but then the rest of Hollywood ostracized him for it anyway.

Any solution to the pickle the whole world seems to have found itself in is in the hands of one or two indestructible stars that manage to either save the day by some genius discovery of the chink in the armor of the destructive force or manages to survive by the skin of his teeth and save the entire world with seconds left on the clock. Not by anything solution or salvation God might present, but by man's own wit. A couple people survive happily ever after, of course, let's not talk about the tens of thousands dead.

Movie upon regurgitation of every scenario that might take place soon; "Armageddon" God's so-called judgment is thwarted by a couple of normal oil drilling guys that save the world from a planet-killing meteor with a nuclear bomb at the last second. In the movie

"2012" the end of the world is predicted and avoided by the construction of a modern ark, everyone's safe and happy. "War of the Worlds" being compared to the apocalypse or end of time, man wins! "I Am Legend" the last man alive works to find a cure to the plague that has killed everyone, and in the middle of the show is confronted with another person who exclaims that what is happened, the death of billions is God's will to make the world a quieter place. Oh yeah, he finds the cure, everybody happy. Played over and over in movies, video games, cartoons, until there is nothing we haven't seen a thousand times. Buffers!

In healthcare this same principle is demonstrated the natural like the supernatural, take any wound and rub it over, and over and over a hundred times, and you don't even feel it anymore. See something or hear something or taste something over and over again, and eventually, it becomes so usual to the environment that it becomes part of the said environment and we stop noticing it.

There has been a flood of superhero shows lately, all these powerful beings that cannot be killed, god-like, protectors of men, heroes, saviors, and one thing they all have in common, when they come down to earth, become human, they become vulnerable, mortal, just like you and I, nothing special. They can bleed and be killed, and this killing represents a victory for the enemy never self-sacrifice for the victims. As a matter of fact, buildings full of innocent people can crumble in some epic battle but if one of the heroes dies suddenly smiles turn to tears.

In "Ironman 2" during a fight to the death Ironman, the hero, faces an evil villain that nearly destroys him, yet at one moment at the end of the fight the villain laughs and says; "If you can make the god bleed, they no longer need him, and they will hate him for it!" and laughs! I was shocked at the subtle suggestive image of the words and picture it portrayed into my mind.

In "Superman Returns" my favorite scene superman just comes back on the scene after being away for years, and the first thing he sees is a Pulitzer Prize given to his old girlfriend; "Why the World Doesn't Need Superman," then he goes on to show everyone all these miraculous things, and why they might need him. In this film as well, just at a point of vulnerability, he becomes human, which is coupled with weakness, foolishness, and possible death. If you can get Superman to bleed, why do we need him? He is stabbed in the side and thrown to his death.

Hollywood would have us believe; "If you could make superman bleed, why do we need him, he is no different than anyone else, he is just a man, throw him away!" Many have compared President Trump to Superman, others hope for the return of goodness lost perhaps in a JFK Jr. or other fallen heroes. But if we are created in the image of God, and God would dwell within us if we but ask, and if we will do even greater things than Jesus did because He is with His Father, if but a fraction of any of that is true, then Superman is within the grasp of anyone who would Ascend to the truth.

Ultimately the issue is not reducing the supernatural to earth as the goal of Ascension, more apparently is it God's plan for us to climb of our own Awareness into the infinite of the supernatural illuminating and activating everything we were created to be.

ASCENDED AND DESCENDED VIBRATIONS

Up a few steps, we climb and as I look around and hear the beauty that vibrates ever so subtly all around me, like the gentle soft sounds of the little birds chirping, or the breeze blowing slowly yet steadily through the trees, perhaps a child's laugh, or my wonderful wife's sweet voice, I am suddenly aware that each and every sound, every image, every peaceful effect it has on me, it is exactly in the right time, pitch, and presentation, exactly right where it is supposed to be in order to make a perfectly balanced picture of the gift that God has for me right at this moment throughout time and space.

Like some infinitely complex symphony of music, better than the finest Mozart, so well placed each and every note in it reverberates with perfect synchronicity containing balance throughout all the other harmonic waves in and around it. So beautiful in its composition, the perfect delivery of a moment, that the exact choice of single instrumental drum beat on key and exactly at the right time and location, discarding even the slightest fraction of a change of any of these factors would render the composition off-key, and certainly give the listener the idea that something is off, something is not just of an infinite construct. That single color in this masterful painting may be as little as the misplacement of a single flower in the garden, creates with it a feeling it just doesn't look right?

Good or bad our inputs of vibrational resonances are folded into the scene brought yet again into the harmonic balance necessary to fulfill a perfect purpose that being one melded into a perfect plan for all who take but a moment to observe. Light always wins, good always prevails, and what doesn't kill us makes us stronger all fall within the concepts of the Godly interaction spoke of above.

God sits up there and orchestrates the whole thing in the roll of a Perfect Conductor, signaling when one should be added, at which moment a drop of rain should fall, and at exactly the right place and time a note is to be struck as it gently touches the ground, volume and delivery of crescendos, and then softly taper off into infinity, they create this perfect piece of music. Yet being "The Perfect Composer," the one who creates the music, all He chooses to do is softly direct, with nothing more than the mere waving of his hand, a small and seemingly insignificant nudge, leaving it up to all of us, His musicians to play the ensembles He has given us so freely. But then again did he not give us as well the talent, the education, even gave others oh so long ago revelations of what we might hear today? They too passed on their gifts of ability to create the instruments of beauty out of simple assemblies of metal and wood, engaging the desire to teach our children, sowing the seeds of dreams, and we ascending musicians are merely the recipients of these earlier gifts.

We choose through our free will to then deliver the gifts into the world as we feel we wish according to how we desire in our own choices of action and word thus free will. We get the freedom to decide to do with that which God has freely given us for good, bad, or neutral? Delivering unto others that which has been given us adding in our own positive light, or seeding it with darkened depression? Choosing whether or not to give it in the same way it was given, the way it was created by God, or in this case The Composer intended, freely without conditions or restraint, without control and demand, without the thought; "if you don't do what I say in the future, I will take it back," no God gives us everything freely. Energy is everlasting.

For the caterpillar, the realization of truth or lie becomes one as simple of a realization as understanding what seems good for him and what seems bad. One would say it is a question between dark and light, but since the caterpillar has no eyes that concept seems only a whimsical idea fashioned from the veiled recesses of dreams or perhaps other friends who have on occasion reported images of heavenly entities, forces even entire armies of battles being waged out there depicted, yet not quite understood or seen.

A recent other very wise also ascending caterpillar who suddenly found herself journeying right alongside our fearless traveler repeated the most revealing of ancient wisdom when talking about truths realized; "You can't un-cream the coffee, once the milk has been added."

Truths, once realized fall on a young caterpillar, like rain on warm skin, they grow as ideas, beliefs, even responsibilities once illuminated can no longer be denied, ignored, and most importantly buried in the ground but must be shared with others the young climber comes in contact with, or suddenly and miraculously appear before him.

Truths like the many of these treasures that suddenly materialize can only be from God, how else would such goodness suddenly appear, this more than anything else prompts our little caterpillar to venture up, climb, ascend, realizing there is a world up there, there is an entire other life unimaginable waiting, maybe like he experienced in his dreams he can fly. He believes!

Only one other thing; "What is coffee?"

On the Quantum Level of Ascension, there seems to be a change taking place within the essence of the already produced energies effecting the God-given gifts or our collective souls, as a result of augmentations facilitated by interactions of other creators, those being the many of us. I would hypothesize that in the case of the positive, an increase in sound wave intensity takes place if even the most minute physical essences, increasing the vibrational resonance of the initial physical component to a higher level of dimensional being, an increase of illumination, whereby the nuances of this increase can clearly be seen by others who dwell in these same ascended state. With increased light, the elemental status takes on a loftier lighter existence one that elevates it beyond the mere limitations of three-dimensional time and space, in essence propelling it into a fourth-dimensional existence and beyond.

On the contrary, a negative input would then cause a decrease in vibrational status, a constricting of the density of the sound emission, a grounding even condensing effect compared to other like entities, a cooling of emotional states, and an inward focusing effect of the life systems it touches. These only take and never give, vampires of life and soul energies. If the light of God leads to immortality, then the center darkening effect of sin leads to death; *"The wages of sin is death."*

The other option of course is to take that which has been given all of us and stick it in a jar, burying it in the ground, selfishly hoarding, removing the beauty of creation from sight. One might think this is a bit of a buffer type reaction, yet it is through the depressing of that which God gave all of us the perpetrator solicits an act of actually stealing from God Himself.

How sad would it have been if any of Mozart's concertos had been hidden away, buried in the ground for nobody ever to hear? I have known rich men who take vast treasures and lock them away, they are placed in places, like a masterpiece being locked up in a vault, not to be viewed or displayed even for others to enjoy from afar but are hidden away, removed from circulation, buried until all memory of their existence disappears from memory. A selfish rich man doesn't steal from others and hoards it then away because he wants something for himself, he does it because he doesn't want others to have it.

As we have already examined; the removal of God's created gifts and the subsequent ignoring them has but one outcome and that is the rotting or degradation of the original to the point of becoming harmful and even toxic; *"Store not your treasures where there is worms, or rust, or thieves to steal, but store your treasure in heaven where there is no worm, no rust, no thief, for where your treasures are there your heart will be also."*

Is it not so with the Descended life?

God gives us this miraculous gift each and every day, breath upon breath, every cool sweet drink of water, warn light to bath our skin, to fill our cells with its warming energies, every blessing our heart can possibly think or our bodies could possibly taste or feel, and we decide how then to deliver the gift back out into the world in turn for others too to enjoy. Like a beautiful garden, of which we have been so blessed to enjoy, the seed turns to life and with God's blessing of water feeds others with its bountiful beauty. A garden of life where countless colors of flowers, subtle soft smells, and radiant light reflections bathe us in the warm light of love, peace, and abundance, each and every moment is a place of healing for those who dare to believe. And we dance through it by stepping on the perfect stones our Father also provides, free to experience and even take one or another flower along with us as we go.

Some of us run and others crawl, some dance, many walk a few run, an even greater few fly, yet some poor seemingly rich souls sit their fat asses down and do nothing else but pick every flower in sight or reach, gripping them hard and suffocating them in their sweaty chubby hands, picking everything they can get their grips on until nothing is left except a cold dry and barren dirt, nothing remains in their hands except wilted strangled and mangled rot of decayed soil.

Many rich people have been given so much, life abundant free of strife, only seeming to suffer from the fear that others may try to take from them that which God has so freely given them, the gold, love, food, everything warm and convenient, the so many gifts they have received. It is pride that convinces them; no, they created these things themselves. Ask the majority of them and they will angrily say; "No one has given me anything, I built it, took it, accumulated it all myself, with no help from anyone."

When is enough, enough; even the great kings of old had not even close to the abundance of the simple poor of today? This is the curse of depressed thought, focusing all their attention on the few specks of energy they think they possess, only to lust for everything they don't. What do they do, do they share this gift, do they hold it up for all to see, lifting it up in splendid demonstration as to honor in practiced reproduction of symphony, "The Composer," who created

303

it for all to enjoy? Or do they sit back and self indulge caring only for themselves, sharing only the slightest fraction of what they have been given to give the impression to everyone around that they really are charitable, when in reality, in the darkened veils of their own hearts, they know they share really nothing, no time, no blessing, no gold, not even with their own children, any display of giving is merely again a chance to parade themselves for glory?

How many men stuff gold down their own throats like some gorged hot dog eater, consuming everything, all the goods gifts, even unto their very children. Drinking the innocent blood of one after another, never getting enough until they are so bloated inside they bust from high pressures, blockage of life-giving systems, or cancerous rebellion of their own body parts, weighed down by the heaviness of the golden ball and chain they have placed themselves around their own legs. Always fearing the fall, the eventual reconciled throwing to the ground and its unyielding receptions of hard stone to the justly meted greed with breaking bone, exploding from the inside in delicate hearts vessel or subtle brains aneurysms, changing forever a beautiful flower of a child into a withered crumpled husk of withered dust and sand. Depression of vibration until it mimics death, buried in the dry desert ground like some long-forgotten mummy carcass.

Or worse yet do they take His melody with them, His gift, His gold, that they buried it in the yard, stuffed in the garage, shoved under their beds or down their throats, I think not? The only talent they seem to have is an uncanny ability use their remaining God-given talent, breath, and gifts in order to accumulate, control, and horde as much of the gifts around them that God gave to all of us to share for themselves, like some crazed fat cat who frantically strives to hold all the marbles it can in its greedy paws. Did they create these marbles, did they form this gold from nothing, did they take the songs of The Words and form from nothing the spectacular illuminations that God sprinkled this wondrous world with, for all men to enjoy? No, they did not, no matter how much they try to convince themselves, or lie to all around them that they did when they go, they go alone.

One can always see the darkened souls of these kinds of men and women when they step into the light when the light shines on their dark hidden realms. Just look in their eyes, darkness is what you see. From their depressed vibrational state, only the cost and mud, and blood, and fear is available for them to hear, the low rumble like some grinding engine far off in the depths of the ground.

Let me describe what they look like, for I have seen the creature close up; they drool their abundance like un-chewed food from their mouths, as they snicker watching others around them starve. They boast as they give, giving only what they no longer want, the refuge or garbage they would have thrown out anyway. Or often when they do give, they take from others and then put their own names on the gift as to place themselves in the place of honor, acting, lying that they are the ones giving. They impress others around them, but only others who know the truth to lie for them, as to not let best friends or family know that they really pay nothing. Acting like they've paid much, then enjoying the charity of others as they take advantage of other men who truly demonstrate charitable giving, he never sits on the board of a cause unless he can siphon out the most for himself. The poor rich man never gives more than he takes.

And while they may have been blessed initially from God with what they have, for people who descend accumulation of more always result only as of theft. They steal the knowledge, the business, the souls of people from others, from their mentors, and even their friends, and deep down they know that everything they have they stole, and this is why they are incapable of enjoying it, no matter how much they get. They become like a dark void ever trying to fill that void with more and more, but darkness added to darkness makes nothing, and this endless quest can't be quenched no matter how much is taken. They are unhappy, depressed, full of cancer, heart problems, their faces fall in perpetual signs of sadness and depression slowly mimicking the sadness they feed it each and every day one dirty fat-ridden stinking golden spoon at a time. Followers of demons such as baal always begin to look like the image of them in time.

Depressed souls strive to enslave all around them, first giving what was intended by God to be shared, but using it to control only to take back when they no longer can use them or when the control is resisted. How sad they yearn to control even those who only love them, do they think so terribly of themselves that they feel they can only buy love, even from their wife, or husband, employees, or children? How sad is the mother who would eat her own children to survive, to live the life of lust instead of joy? You can spot the greedy a mile away, they don't even share with their wives, their children, only enough to make themselves look good. They don't realize with every golden shackle they form to enslave others they weigh themselves down as well until they are so heavy and burdened they can hardly move from the weight and pain of arthritis as it stabs through their back and legs and hands.

They respect "no-one, and nobody" around them, because they are to busy only regarding themselves. They hate, especially those who have less than they, but then again they hate those who have more, add to this self-hatred and that pretty much counts for everyone.

Why is this? Freud says it is easier to hate others we hurt than to think ourselves capable of being someone who would hurt another individual. Perhaps deep down these rich people know they are supposed to share with others, God's blessing, their money, light, time, but they don't, so rather than feel bad, it is just easier to hate those around, especially when they see them happier than themselves.

The poor descended man never has time for anyone but himself, and sadly time races by! How sad with each and every one of them do you hear them say; "I wish I had done this, or I wish I done that, something good, spent more time with my kids, more time with my spouse, did something worth remembering... But mostly; I wish I spent more time with living, my life." What a waste!

It is not so with the truly rich man or woman, the Ascended soul, the person who is rich in spirit and light, for they share with their spouse, friends, even strangers, and always with children without conditions, without demands to be paid back, without the need to be paid in love, for this man knows that his gift, his love came not from himself but was a blessing from Above, and in same, he must share it with others. But he can't even give it away fast enough, for every truly generous person I have ever met that gives, just keeps getting more from God. It is said God cannot be in debt to anyone, you can't out-give God!

It's not just money, but love, forgiveness, compassion, prayer, and time!

Men, women, who give their time to their children to the ones they love, their wife, husband, they find their time stretches turning minutes into weeks, and days into years, entire lives can be changed by the insertion of themselves into the lives around them. For, God gave us also the gift of our own life so we would share it with others. The very act of giving is the Ascended enhancement of energetic systems.

This is the climbing of Ascension through Revelations into higher dimensional awareness and realization.

Shall we continue the journey?

Rolling majestic hills crested with outcroppings of sands and stone, miles of valleys and rivers, greens, browns, and reds all lines in ordered placement, painted in such a perfect canvas as to leave no doubt as to who is the artist. How grand is the view from the air, no shadows to block your view except perhaps those of the clouds flying just a bit higher and on slightly out of reach? A long way down, how free the feeling of gliding along the airways of height, gently turning, soaring, dipping, and ascending at the very whim of thought.

From this birds-eye view, a person can almost feel the subtle changes in altitude as we sore higher and then dip lower, a bird-like sensation breeze blowing on your skin, the feeling of the air flowing by, in an invisible pool of currents and streams, pushing against your skin as the forces of air thrusts hard up in their upward lift, ever wrestling with the forces of gravity that seem to keep our feet firmly on the ground. Far below small shapes, are those buildings, vehicles, or just some rocks, loose lying materials of all shapes and sizes both useful and discarded, awaiting a future point when they will become useful again, needed for some function by the children of God?

"Is this how it feels, to be a bird?" the small seven-year-old boy says to

himself, but also out loud, not only in a nonchalant manner but with such self-confidence and absolute assurance that at any moment some invisible companion will just materialize and answer his question without a single break in step.

"I have flown many times in my dreams, and I can wait for the day when just like my dreams, I will launch off into the air and not worry about the landing back on the ground."

He walks, yet so much more meanders in a nonchalant manner, lending the observer to the conclusion that this small boy is completely and utterly at peace in the endeavor he is engaged upon. He could be anyone in the world, a prince wandering through his kingdom, a content husband dreaming of his beloved wife, a free spirit without a care, content and happy, quite different from those that present themselves from day to day alone. Not a worry in the world and completely oblivious to the surrounding noises or even so much as the world and all the complexities that are yet to infiltrate into the private bubble of a universe that this young lad has captured and made his own.

"Yes it is, but so much more!" says the strong yet southing voice, clear and deep, resting within his head and at the same time permeating every part of his soul. The voice is one the young tow-headed boy has heard his whole life, a calming voice, one filled with complete acceptance in a world of often un-acceptance, somewhere down deep

this young lad knows in the innermost part of his chest, in the very heart of his soul that this voice is not his own, it is of another, One greater, One older, One always right, always true, but most importantly loving… complete peace…God.

"Let me show you, close your eyes and walk, let the feeling of the air flowing under your hands listening with the subtle changes to the ground beneath, as you and not your feet pass over."

The boy closes his eyes because as he had so many other times in his life, he completely trusts the voice, knowing instinctively that this voice has only his best interests at heart.

"There is an order of things in the world, you can not always see them, one thing feels like this, but it is really that. A good thing might seem good, but can be bad, and a tough thing, one that almost seems unbearable will almost always be a very, very good thing."

"And while you feel alone, you are never alone, and not in any way do you ever experience anything that you don't in some way experience something altogether different."

"When you hear it, smell it, taste it, see or feel it, that single part of the world becomes a part of you and your own private world, forever with you, becoming a small piece of who you are and what you will become forever."

" So be careful and choose well."

"What is forever?" the small boy says while continuing with eyes closed.

"That is such a good question; what do you see with your eyes closed?"

"Nothing, an orange or red glow, maybe something, shapes sparkles I don't know."

"How high is up, left or right, or even down, can you see the edge?"

"No"

"As it is with you, so is it with Me, without end, up and down, left and right....forever!"

A small smile crosses the child's face as he hears the sweet words caress his lonely heart, and he almost coos in some gentle response, one that no other living soul in the entire universe is aware of except the one who spoke to him. The child knows He not only hears the sweet sound, but feels every emotional inkling with all the importance, significance, and depth that his very breath indicates, and He loves the child for it, but oh so much more than a normal love, for the child is the very essence of that Being,

He who created the entire universe for him, His dear baby child, His son, His daughter, His light, He would give it all for them, He has! and would have given it all again, if only for him alone, so great is the love of a Father for His child, nothing and no one can keep a Fathers love from His children if they but reach up and take it.

This heavenly interaction, which was most likely only as brief as a blink of an eye, was as real and significant as an entire creation to the one who decides for Himself, what and exactly when anything is important. Yet the boy moves on oblivious, other than just in a very childlike needing way, as unaware as the baby is to the source of the milk in the bottle but ever so thankful for the satisfaction and elimination of the pain within the body when hunger is vanquished.

Any feeling or awareness the child may have felt from this interaction floats by nearly as unaware as the ground passing under. This doesn't stop him, and as he walks for what seems to be forever, eyes closed not slowing for a moment. What initially started with a small sense of apprehension quickly turns into nervous fear laced wonder. All this conversation passed in a blink, between steps, and as the boy realizes he is still walking with his eyes closed, he briefly resists the temptation to open his eyes, even as fear begins to wrap its tentacles around the very fabric of his thoughts.

"Don't worry, I won't let u get hurt, I will always be with you, I have always been with you, and nothing or anything can ever keep me from you, because I love you so much, my precious sweet child."

"Open your eyes now and stop!"

The young boy stops only inches from a crevice he knew was ahead but was sure it was far to the left of where he was walking, yet he had strayed much farther off the normal path than he had ever expected. The crevice was not extremely deep but may have injured him had he fell in unexpectedly?

The boy was me, but now that you have read these words, and they have become part of you, the child is you.

MEESTER; I CAN FLY

"Meester, I know I can fly, I have done it many times in my dreams. It is as natural as walking, most of the time I am just walking or even running, but suddenly I remember I can hover, or even fly up and above the others who seem oblivious to my actions."

I speak to a man who we will call Peter, a mentor, a teacher, a friend, a man who divulges wisdom unto everyone he comes in contact with, not for pay or praise but because that which has been freely given him, that light which shines from the essence of his spirit is clear to anyone who is looking. He is not a "Meester" because of a diploma or title given him by a corrupt or bought system, but because he has the Godly wisdom of experience in the subject he is consulted in.

"Describe what you remember," the Meester says to me with a wise and knowing yet interestingly curious look on his face.

"When I was younger the dreams would often take on pretty much the same image; I would be running almost trying to catch my step. This seemed to be a common issue with me because I would try to run and it was as if my muscles, especially my calves, would push me up rather than forward. This had the effect of making my gate appear to be more like a bouncing rather than propelling me forward with speed as was my desire."

"A sort of bouncing gazelle-like prancing would appear, and this left me in my dreams often frustrated as it became difficult to control my run for speed rather than this bouncing motion. What was strange is as I remember in my own real-life especially in my youth, it was difficult for me to get into a rhythm of running when it would come up to trying to speed up, and the same frustration I seemed to have managed to get my own gate pattern to one of forwarding acceleration rather than the bouncing that seemed to occur?"

People even critically commented to me when I was quite young, even my own parents scolding me that I bounced along when I walked, often prompting me to walk straight without this bounce in my step.

Back to the dream; *"When I would run and basically resign myself to this bouncing step, I often started to push off increasingly higher and higher until some of the steps would be so high I would begin to worry that I was falling too far down and might get hurt. Some of the jumping steps were much higher than a house, even multiple stories high."*

"Yet I would never get hurt upon landing merely make a step and bounce gain even higher than the last. Ultimately the steps would bring me so high I would sore through the air seemingly for long distances and then come back down just to repeat it again."

"As the heights seem to almost be cloud high, I again would come down toward the ground accelerating with the fall but this time I would, in my mind seem to

say; No, and not quite touch the ground but go back up into the air as if from my own will."

"It is at this point I would remember that I could do this up and down motion through the air merely by thinking of it or concentrating on it. My motions up and down, always directed in a forward direction, would glide up and over as well as under objects high in the air, like telephone wires, tree branches, clouds, even other objects that seemed to be in the air, yet I have no idea what they were or even who put them there. They seemed to be like fences in the sky."

"Sometimes I would lean forward in a prone position flat on my stomach, stretch out my arms above my head and reach forward with my thoughts, causing my whole body to go the direction my mind and my hands were reaching. Gravity was not something that seemed to pull on me, but a force that I could push out of myself by free will."

"I would dive down, arms and head first, merely to stretch out one arm and this would cause me to turn the opposite way or the other. Two arms down, I go down, two arms up and up I go! Straight out and the harder I push my arms the faster I go or higher I climb."

"Sometimes I can bring my arms in and I will just hover there hi above the trees seemingly sitting in the clouds. I was never afraid of heights."

"With most of my dreams as I sit up in the clouds or in the trees there seems to be a purpose, sometimes I am watching people, even as they seem to be looking for

me? But nobody on the ground seems to be looking in the air for me as if they cannot contemplate I could be up in the air."

"This ability seems to be refined over time to include even the most simple floating over large areas of steps or a repeating decision to float down the stairs instead of stepping on them one at a time? A sort of ability to just decide, instead of walking, to float over the steps, yards, even hundreds of yards before taking a normal step again."

"Sometimes this floating sensation has the effect of placing me just above the people who are walking along with their normal daily tasks, amazingly they don't seem to notice me floating, none of them ever look up at me or make any kind of gesture that leads me to the idea they have any idea I am there?"

The Meester looks at me and with a look of understanding or perhaps even an experienced grin says; *"This is not a memory, or a simple dream, finding yourself in some kind of place other than here, but a vision of what is to come. There will come a day when the abilities you remember in that spiritual dream will weave into the tapestry of your physical life, where the physical flows through memories and resides in the spiritual. When walking on water or flying through the air become realizations no more difficult to remember than waking up and walking to the bathroom in the morning."*

Ascension is like unto a focusing of awareness, a memory of spiritual abilities. As we take our first steps as a child off the ground and onto the higher dwelling realm of walking, yet unknown abilities transcend into newfound adventures bringing our perspectives higher into vantage points not unlike flying or floating through the air. These seemingly childlike first steps, while scary and unsure, secure in our physical memories confidence that we are no longer bound to the earth crawling on all fours but destined to the heavens of which like the unknown and incalculable vastness of the world before us stretches out into infinity as we begin to step and then fly through the garden of our life.

As it is with steps, health is realized in the dwelling of spiritual awareness, the many irritants that find themselves on the ground, or residing in the dust of the earth have little effect on the hands and face of those who sour through the skies. They see them below knowing them for what they really are; merely particles of dust or grains of sand bound to the ground and easily ignored as our life passes them by in our journey.

Oh sure, dust can be kicked up, especially when a great deal of activity is associated with the mix? But fear not, one only has to close their eyes for a moment and wait for the irritant to pass, knowing it is but dust and can really not harm you, only if you focus your attention on it. Plus there is always a little water a person can wash their hands or face with to clear away any dust that might have touched them or attached itself to them in their journey.

"Meester, I know I can fly, I have done it many times in my dreams. It is as natural as walking, most of the time I am just walking or even running, but suddenly as a

caterpillar, I remember I can do neither, yet here I am finding I can hover, or even fly up and above the others who seem oblivious to my actions."

A flutter of a wing, dancing colors that I sing, a bright morning that swims through the sky,

I know what I see, or what I might be, floating gently across clouds tumbling by.

For ilse as I do, in winged flutter life's new, a soft message does rest in my head,

Pure love joy abounds, with new life it has found, rests softly in the warm warmth of my bed.

For I know I do dream, yet know not does it seem, these bright images that flutter are noble en true,

With new life Angels delight, soft ripples of candled light, God's vast ocean before me of freedoms, majestic kingdoms, and infinities are blue.

GARDEN OF PIGMENTS

So are we all speckled by the seeming random brushstrokes of God, butterfly wings, unique colored hairs across the body of the caterpillar, snowflakes, fingerprints, even the irises of our eyes those being so specifically individualized no two are identical, each painted with the uniqueness of specific subtleties that can only beckon to one conclusion; as individually unique, and perfectly endowed with specific observable vibrational eccentricities, it can only further be deduced that if God would take such measures to individualize each and every aspect of His creation, and then make it known to us, it would signify a specific and infinitely perfect role or plan each and every one of us plays in this masterpiece of a garden he has so skillfully painted.

"Silver or Gold, I have not, but what I have I give unto you" a nice thing to say, and while we certainly are not the first to say it, or even to put it into practice, when it comes to sharing the gifts God has given us, we are more than eager than ever to try this decree.

God's gift of a Garden of Healing has found its place in the everyday life of this couple of Health and Wellness instructors since the very moment it began to spring up. Both Anna and I have spent the greatest part of our lives, at least lately, helping people realize the more spiritual side of Health and Wellness, perhaps create a better healthcare application, and through this realization, insight to counter the affliction and infirmities that have gone unchecked attacking many of us especially the last few years.

The many visitors who have come to our garden, some of which, brought to tears by the splendor from the natural beauty that presents itself, a God-inspired oasis in the middle of the desert, all find it miraculous that such growth could arise in only a few couple years. While we have planted many of the fruiting trees of papayas, nuts, apricots, guavas, citrus, apples, and berries of all sorts, many of the other plants merely spontaneously sprung up, growing to astonishing heights in even the last few months.

This Garden of Healing montage was taken up by us, it came to be known to us that the gardens planted by our own hands would provide with its own fruit, when combined with our meals a supply of the needed healing nourishment people could used for their own specific medical and psychological ailments when they visited. Only to later find it scientifically confirmed that it had been established in researchable proof; when people grow their own plants, especially with love and blessings, the plants secrete specific enzymes that will counter the afflictions the people residing there may encounter. It is as if the plants somehow know what ailments their residents may have and then prepare accordingly; this almost proves the symbiotic relationship God has established for the earth towards us when he created it for all of mankind.

Along with this, there is a peacefulness in our garden that can only be described as mesmerizing, even our chickens roam carelessly, as do the many bunnies and sparrows that frequent the grasses or the leaf's of the ground cover, its blanketing cool colors always provide the most gentle receptive breezes and sweet scents in the otherwise stark dry desert. A Kaleidoscope of healing colors and sounds that refreshes the very heart of each breath taken.

The caterpillar looks down from on-high takes in a deep breath of the beautiful scents that fill his very heart from the garden below. How wonderful is the caressing vibrations that gently water his mouth tastes, fresh smells of greens and flowering buds, the warmth of fresh-baked break cooling on the window sill, soft creatures of peace meandering about each eagerly receiving the food God has for them this and every day? A balance of harmony seems to lift her thoughts up even higher into the cool flowing streams of cloud tinted skies.

Dreams of light and goodness almost solidify in the scents and tastes of purity beckon as he ascends even higher still. One could almost imagine being able to just lift off into the air right now, a clear realization takes ahold; it is not yet time, soon, have patience, keep climbing, keep helping others too, this journey is not yet a destination but methodical voyages that will encompass this life, finally result in one dying to the concerns of the ground, and ultimately being reborn to the effortless adventures of the air.

We have made it our mission to help people realize the spiritual significance in the health and wellness of their lives. Addiction Rehabilitation, cancer, and PTSD being among the many chronic physical issues we have seen the greatest success in treating with spiritual therapies. Our instructions are simple, help people realize the greatest significance this spiritual visualization has on their Healing, Health, and overall Wellness, then give them real tools to facilitate their own Ascension type recovery with merely the vast natural abundance God has so graciously given all of us. Light is one of the best tools available, this, combined with the voice seems to be the most powerful weapon we have in our tool belt of options.

On the quantum level the variations of photon wavelengths that make up the garden of colors we are bathed with every day within the visual spectrum, vary by only the slightest fraction of a degree between the colors we see with our eyes. These energies not only bathe our bodies but flood our eyes with images that hold within them intended nuances that reside within the realm of belief.

On the health and wellness front, it has been understood for centuries that colors possibly play an active role in a person's spiritual wellness and thus overall well-being prompting many of the customs associated with colors such as lighter clothing in the spring and summer, or the gifting of bright colored flowers for happy or joyous celebrations. Dark colors that elicit fear or colors that mimic blood all have powerful intentions subtly assigned to them when brought into the perspective of certain objects, actions, or words.

Certain colors have also been known to compliment people's skin tones thus prompting some people to wear certain colors actually aiding in their health, while others have an opposite effect. Colors have for centuries adorned men and women's faces as a means to solicit in advance the intentions the person has for future activities.

Auras have been speculated to be the visual representations of the energies of our spirit. There have been visual recordings using various apparatus that can record these radiating energies, noticeably colors are associated with them and the colors are said to correspond with the spiritual and emotional states of the individuals being recorded. These energies, while being often dismissed as merely heat signatures do not follow patterns that are observed under infrared camera observations, and seem to follow the patterns across the board for the accepted interpretations.

In Quantum Awareness colors can play a key role for those who wish to examine these energies and likewise interpret the information they may be reporting. First, back to auras, it has been observed that people who engage in more spiritual activities especially within the self-examination category have been known to display measurable aura's far outside the distance normally measured by the typical individuals that are merely busy with their day to day lives. This observation matches my own image of broadening awareness in a whirlwind model as the person's attention elevates into the spiritual, so does the expanse of consciousness also expand and even intensify.

On a quantum level light waves can increase in two fashions; in intensity whereby the waves gain in strength and thus brightens of color, and or in frequency whereby increases or decreases of wavelength results in variations of observable colors. Science will tell us that we are only able to visibly see the smallest portion of the electromagnetic spectrum of the energy around us, and a vast majority of things possibly out there, existing within the same space are undetectable because their energies are vibrating in unobservable wavelengths which we cannot see or hear.

In the examinations of Anna and I, we have observed that there is a specific color associated with many significant things in our lives. My wife Anna has this particular God-given skill to see in her mind's eye the specific color associated with people's names, numbers, emotions, days or months of the year, even sicknesses, or spiritual status names. It would seem on a Quantum level that even with particular names of people or things, they all have a sort of vibrational compensation granted them, speaking to a specific purpose, and clearly demonstrating the ordered perfection of all of God's creation.

This specific information could be invaluable in the treatment of afflictions especially when a health practitioner considers not only the Body and Mind aspects of health issues but more importantly the spiritual or belief aspects. If the spirit is infinitely more significant than the physical merely by pure spatial calculations, then a belief based application of health care should have an equally infinitely greater capacity for success.

Over the last few years as we have practiced helping people with their health issues, we have seen enormous almost supernatural gains being made in technologies, the internet, and many other physical venues across the globe within the healthcare system or more significantly the media within society, education, what is being constantly told to people. Yet there seems to be an increasing fear and dread surrounding health-related issues.

When I was educated in the 80's we were taught that people "suffered from" illnesses, they came "down with" colds or flues, they afflicted with heart "attacks," this or that infirmity, describing what was clear to everyone as something from outside the person trying to hurt them. But today people are led to believe they "have" these issues, the issue is "inside" them, they have "become" the sickness, "I Am" this or that, or worse yet, they were created with some kind of flaw just waiting to betray them like a time-bomb, metastasize, or somehow change them into something harmful to themselves or others around them. The worst thing a "Creator" can do is claim something with their own mouth, this energetic construct positive or negative goes out into the physical universe affecting and ever so slightly changing the entire universe forever. When enough people believe they or the world is sick, they become sick!

This "I am" doom that we have been brainwashed into believing we have become, really only has one purpose and that is to convince us we are not sovereign beings that God stated we were created in the image of God, but merely slaves to a system that will tell us who we are, and what we can expect, no more. In essence, the healthcare system has no interest in healing, merely enslaving people into their oil-based, poisonous institution, and then keep us in by thereby telling us our only hope is to follow the programs they have set up, with the insurance or "assurance" they have our best interests in their hands, only the doctor knows what is wrong with you, and they tell the doctors what the definitions and solution options are.

When I, as a health care practitioner discovered they were lying to us about one thing, how could I trust them that they were not lying about everything? But the good news is as we Ascend in our consciousness we embrace within ourselves increased vibrational states merely by the intention of our creative ascension ability. It is this increased illuminated status that the Deep State, the powers that would subjugate us, the Satanic evil of this world, understand all too well, and so desperately wants to keep out of our hands. They also know it is by their own choices to Digress in vibrational status, that they can never obtain even the levels we have already been given freely by God. It is for this reason that this information is so desperately withheld from us by the bosses, the rich, using media brainwashing, false education, chemical poisoning of our water, air, and even food, or by herd vaccination, any way possible to inhibit our collective realization of the illumination of times we live in.

On the Quantum level, a decrease of light-wave intensity has the result of dimming the strength of the visible brightness of the light. Depression, stress, worry, and any gambit of other negative emotions have the same effect on the spiritual auras' of people. When people focus intensely on the physicality of the earth a constricting or physical focus in the smallest of spaces, right to the very base of the ground before them occurs. Concentrating one's attention on the dust of the earth, this focus on the dirt causes them to miss all the blessings happening around them each and every day.

Now add onto that the decreasing intensification of negative energies; hatred, abuse, addiction, lies, or worry and the result is an almost black hole effect whereby the spirit of the individual doesn't only sink into the earth but constricts into a singularity where no light, comfort, or peace can penetrate. The true death of the soul occurs.

Ascension of awareness is the counter to this digressing constriction, and no willing soul is beyond redemption, except those who have willingly sold their souls to evil, forfeiting and no longer possessing a soul to ascend with.

It is our contention that in the near future light will be able to be passed into a system or body at specific frequencies or colors that will counter the issues a person may be suffering from. It will be the job of the health care practitioner to help the individual to realize the corresponding attacking spiritual essences frequency and then by administering a likewise counter frequency to facilitate healing.

Perhaps this can be facilitated in the form of a tank or some kind of submergible apparatus, and if breathing liquid could be incorporated then it would be possible to transmit the essential healing energies inside the body to affect the tissues without having to be shielded by the skin. Perhaps this could also be combined with alike frequency sound to have a further strengthening effect on all of the body's molecular components.

But of course, if we Ascend into a high enough frequency state we should be able merely by pure will effectively activate, repair, clean, and illuminate any and all structures of our own bodies and thus activate the many areas of our brains or DNA that have until now been depressed, inactivated, or held in limbo by our own miss-beliefs, and the poisons of the world.

We invite you, our friends to come to visit our garden
And dabble in discussions of Ascending displays,

And as you experience its awakening into healthier vitalities,

You will not but help witness its childlike play.

And if we decide together to embrace new frontiers

With healing and therapies arts,

Casting off fears,

And shedding off tears,

You may find yourself Baking Bread,

Or painting a picture instead,

Or perhaps dancing in grassy pools as your body's mends,

Your energies ascend,

And by God's Grace,

Your spirit takes flight as high as stars up in space.

By Peter Colla

FIGHTING GOLIATH'S

As we examine the Quantum Levels of Awareness in health and wellness one cannot help but notice the absolute infinitesimally small stature of the majority of the attacking agents especially when we are speaking of infectious agents such as viruses, toxic pollutants, or even intended dark curses when compared to the mere vast size of our bodies, and that's not even considering the almost infinite status of our spiritual potentials. Yet it would seem that especially the last couple of decades the world's media has increasingly placed, through fear programming and relentless doomsday scenarios, almost giant-like indestructibility onto every sort of affliction, to the point where the majority of people once being told they have this or that ailment just give up, give in, and accepts it.

These sicknesses, which in most symptomatic cases merely result in an inconvenience to the person, and only in the most severe cases when left untreated or mistreated for long periods of time, could ever result in anything that actually could be considered life-threatening. The majority of these such as cancer, people often become truly sick not from the actual tumors but from the treatments given them consequently, and ultimately die from other issues they acquire because of the now severely depressed immune systems. I have personally known people who have died within moments of hearing they had a severe disease long before the actual problem could ever spread throughout their body and attack the vital organs to cause death, once they seemingly believe they have something it actually manifests in them, COVID being a perfect example of this.

In such an accusation based hysteria, I credit the media, the doctors, the Big-Pharma, the most vocal that props up the reputations, gloom, and doom regarding these almost inconceivably small bugs to the point where the rest of us people have become so afraid of these bullies that the mere mention of them places us into a complete state of mind of submission being one of acceptance of the fact, as well as the course of action, they decide to place on us without question or accountability. Kind of like a bully does when the young child runs into him on the way home from school. I have written in past publications regarding the comparison of bullies with afflictions, but to properly examine the quantum awareness of sicknesses as well as our own infinite abilities to overcome it is necessary for me to bring back an earlier story and expand upon it to properly make my point.

Bullies demonstrate themselves in many forms, not always limited to the pimple-faced somewhat overweight boys, large in stature for no other reason than the fact that at least once having been held back in the early stages of his education experience, and hereby gives them the illusion that they are actually bigger than others, their whole stature is base on an illusion. This demonstrative characterization not necessarily earned by themselves but placed upon them by the exaggerations of others, aka the mouthpiece, who might wish to somehow benefit from such dark glorifications. We will call them the groupies, media harlot, talking heads, basically the want-a-be butt-licking idiots that stand next to the bully repeating everything that comes out of his mouth like some half-wit parrot.

Lacking as much in the stature department as they do in compassion, the Bully always seems to present themselves with a dark heart that drives them to particular behaviors of cruelty, perpetrated against what their attending mouthpiece crew has deemed weaker or defenseless opponents. Popping up in vulnerable even hidden locations, often present themselves at times only for reasons known to their own jealous desires or those who have viciously sent them.

Once said bully is spotted, or at least finds himself within striking range, one of three responses for the would-be victim must follow; these choices include either "turn and run," a second which seems to happen in most cases just "stand there and take it" until the beating is over, or the third and often most frightening option "fight back." Let us examine each on its merits?

Turning and running represents a physical changing of direction from the path in which one has been set. When a person turns their back on something, it becomes difficult, if not impossible, to see it thus becoming blind to everything that lies down that particular path they were on only moments before. On the quantum level if we believe our very name or birthdate is ordered even in the stars, one must assume that the energies that represent our physicality have been placed on a particular path for a reason, destiny, and purpose to fulfill an integral part of the total masterpiece of the whole, and likewise, evil entities that would alter that path are not doing it for our best interest or even for that of the whole, but for some plot known best by themselves to deny us the gifts God would grant us, and perhaps hoard for themselves, said gift, residing down the path we were on?

Turning one's back on the attacker puts the child in a particularly vulnerable position, by presenting one's back they invite attack without defense, blind to any blows, tail tucked in pathetic attempt to protect private parts in the backside of running retreat, it becomes impossible to even dodge a haymaker blow that might find pay dirt as we turn to flee. Protecting private parts, now that's a statement; trying in some desperate way to protect a person's destiny, their not yet conceived future, even maybe their future children, holding tightly to any hope that not only pain will be avoided, but maybe other daybreaks warmth still might be found shining on their face, if only through survival.

"Turning and Running" demonstrates and grants most assured defeat if not today for many more days down the road when the same tuck tail and run posture is assuredly repeated!

But let us make one thing clear, we are talking about a bully here, not standing and fighting battles we are not equipped, nor called to fight against in our own proper time by Him who would command us could be considered by most peoples assessments as foolish. Running, and while in certain cases especially undeniable and overpowering attacks, survival can in itself find certain qualities of victory, but for the sake of the bullying, we can assume that God will never place His children who seek Him in a place where defeat is possible.

For, He has said in many places throughout the Bible; *"I will give you all you need!"*

Other applicable promises are tied to overcoming such as; *"But my God shall supply all your needs according to His riches in glory by Jesus Christ."* *"Seek ye first the kingdom of God, and His righteousness, and all things shall be given unto you."*

Notice He says; *"seek ye first,"* so by assumption, if we are seeking first, looking up to God, doing what we are supposed to, in each and every one of our steps, then we can also assume by His promise, that He will give us all we need to overcome any challenge as well as any attack that presents itself on this path.

But again, God also doesn't honor the footsteps of fools. If we by our own selfish desires and sin find ourselves not only off the path but knee-deep in the camp of the enemy, then getting everything we need to overcome may just reside in a pair of good legs and enough oxygen in the blood supply to get us out of there with barely our skin.

Back to the bully. Running is defeat, and results in two things that only a good God could even remotely turn to positive; it reduces the value, the stature of our would-be hero in the eyes of most of the groupies watching, those eyes of the child himself is the greatest effected. A shift of energies takes place and all the energetic physicality that makes up this particular person becomes a bit diminished as the result, they the victims, in essence, believe themselves to be less than they were only moments before. Popular phrases that one will often hear include; *"Once a coward always a coward," "You chicken,"* or *"Run piggy run"* these just being a few terms, that have been associated with people who flee. God's ability to even turn this into positive is without dispute, for no other reason than just because He said so, but we will have to reserve this topic for future writing. Most importantly in this scenario the person doing the running believes a sort of diminishing has taken place in their entire being, this belief-based spiritual change is the most devastating effect on us.

The second effect of running and one that seems to be further perpetuated by those who promote the bully in the first place is that it builds the confidence of said bully. Making it more likely he will just do his mouthing-off again, louder next time, more often, and cause even more damage in the direct vicinity. This digression or increase in negative energy is the very elemental energy that feeds the demon. Creatures that have had all goodness, light, love, peace, or compassion taken from them, have only negative energies available such as hate or fear in which to realize some recognition of gain. Fear becomes the food or drug of the bully.

So confident becomes the bully, that in time he doesn't even care if other people learn the truth of him, he becomes overconfident in his own elevated status, he could care less if victims of his past knowledge, or where he has been in the past, so much so that he doesn't even look back. And why should he, only the conquered reside behind him? But it is in his confidence that he exposes his weakness.

The medical community, the system as a whole would have us choose the second platform of performance, the "just bend over and take it one." It has gotten to the point that even to question the absolute authority of their recommendations as to how to deal with affliction bullies is met with aggressive opposition, basically; *"Put your mask on and shut up," "if you don't do what I say you could lose your insurance,"* oh by the way *"take the vaccine, even if you have heard it may be dangerous."*

Taking a hit, on a Quantum Awareness level would be the equivalent of realizing that the only way these depressing energies could possibly have an effect on you or any member of your family is because you turn a blind eye to what they are attempting to do. The mere focusing of your attention on the truth has the effect of illuminating the situation, increasing instead of decreasing your vibrational status in this particular area of physical energy existence, and by increasing the light to the specific energy location, darkness has no choice but has to flee! This is where we find the final glorious and optimal choice; "Stand and fight!" "Standing and Fighting" grants and demonstrates certain absolute victorious parts! Victory is victory!

By definition first, a person must stand; get up, rise, look up, take that first step in Quantitative Awareness that brings the soul, and those they care for, out of the valley and up the slope of the Godly Mountain, never to return. Now with this image carries a meaning of an immediate and direct increase in stature and almost heavenly perspective allowing the mountain climber to look back down and get a clear vision or reality as to what really is going on down there. When a person rises to the occasion they grow larger and stronger, their vibrations increase in intensity and frequency, and indirect counter-reaction, their opponent must decrease, remember for "every action in the universe there is an equal and opposite reaction," if by no other means then just simple vantage point. As a person being attacked gets higher, the object against which one stands and views in the visual appearance spectrum becomes smaller.

To stand also implies to find a firm foundation, one can only successfully achieve a solid foundation if they press against something also firm, the rock being the strongest, but make no mistake even deep foundations in the sand, the key being deep, can be a significant pillar for resistance. God describes studying the Word as finding a deep foundation or building on the rock, looking for ourselves and not just believing what the mouthpieces are telling us, learning truths and thus discovering spiritual Truths, increases our own light within energizing dormant portions of our own being, all must apply.

As I have already stated the physical changes that one will benefit from in standing and fighting, those being first an increase of the defender, and a decrease of the attacker are invaluable and absolute. These are immediate and Godly provisions given by the natural laws that nobody can deny, promised to each and every one of us, it is these provisions that the enemy would so desperately deny us in our very existence. It is, for this reason, all of there would be solutions aka pain pills, sedatives, tension relievers have a dumbing down, clouding of the mind, a sort of placing veils over the eyes of people affect on who choose to use them.

There is movement in dark entities as well, and that nightmarish direction is backward into a realm the giant never looks at because he has no experience there, it's called retreating or fleeing.

Let us examine further a historical event of overcoming a Bully, nothing demonstrates the power of supernatural belief over the physical like the depiction of David and Goliath especially in the area of supernatural effects, those just under the skin.

What must have gone through Goliath's mind, and maybe even that dark hole which represents his heart, when David walked out there unto the lonely battle plane? And we might even possibly take a glance at what may have been going on supernaturally, in and around the environment, just outside our vibrational awareness to see. Remember on a quantum level Goliath is only slightly bigger than the smallest virus, but in the eyes of all the people, there he was a monster not only in status but reputation. Then up steps a little boy!

First, In Goliath's challenging experience everyone who had ever faced him at least was full-grown, armed and armored, battle-trained and confident at least at first but all ran. Only the poor unfortunate's that he may have been chased down, who might have fought back in some kind of pathetic defense did so as he dished out his cruel blows, moving if at all, always in a groveling fashion away from him. For an oversized opponent, forward motion has its advantages, forward momentum of any type is a force that must be resisted, held in check, overcome, and eventually overpowered in order to turn into a retreating and eventually defeated posture into anything that might resemble victory. A very difficult situation when facing something that big, no maybe the largest warrior to ever step up in history.

So when Goliath saw someone step up and faced him, even just a boy moving towards him rather than away, there is the slightest chance that doubts from witnessing something new and yet unseen must have at least tickled the edges of his senses. It wasn't tickling the hordes of the supernatural cronies, the on-looking mouthpieces, the hopeful for a crumb butt-lickers watching, for the wave of force that shot through their ranks in the quantum realm as Godly light was suddenly introduced, most assuredly shook them to their black bones. We shall call it the wave of righteous fear, a blast of Truth that would mimic the initial blast of an atomic bomb in the supernatural. Kind of like, suddenly lighting a dark cave with flair the size of the sun.

Goliath was bigger than anyone, so fighting from a height advantage in downward blows allowed him to engage much stronger muscle groups than having to fight upward. Goliath was used to only forward motion, using his imposing size, weight, and great strength to do most of his work for him. It was said it took four men to carry his shield, not that he ever used it, this is signified by the fact that others carried it for him anyway. Most of the people he had ever fought by the time he caught up to them were so afraid they barely offered any resistance, merely laid there and whimpered as the Bully dished out his cruel blows.

When David stood his ground, the increased advantage, even if it had been but a slight decreasing effect on Goliath, was a decrease none-the-less! Anyone who participates in any kind of top-sports activity, or fighting, will tell you momentum is a powerful thing, and when someone starts a downward or decreasing trend, it is ultimately coupled with some kind of loss and or pain, by the time the person realizes the shift of momentum has already occurred it is usually too late, the match is over.

Next, David not only took Goliath's insults and threats but laughed at them and responded with his own, backed by the power, confidence, and increased vibrational resonance granted him by the Creator of the Universe! Oops! Suddenly Goliath's words that usually made his opponents quiver, made this person laugh, but notice Goliath wasn't laughing, he was to busy shaking from The Lion's Roar, the flash of blinding light, the thunderclap he just heard! Something was seriously wrong here for Goliath, and for the first time in his life, he might have even felt a twinge of fear, that cold chill in the back of his neck, going right down his spine, and if he wasn't, he sure-as-hell should have been!

Momentum shifting from Goliath moving forward his whole life, to being suddenly held in check, someone stepping up, the great Goliath shrinking in stature, and getting less than expected result from his threats, even resulting in further diminishing on the bullies part. Momentum had definitely shifted!

Goliath threw out his last desperate comments, not at the boy but to the others watching trying to weaken David's now definitely increasing stature with statements such as; *"You come at me like a dog, with a stick."* His comment was not as much of a joke, but a feeble attempt to redirect everyone watching and maybe even himself that what he saw with his own eyes wasn't reality, but lies, they love or hate to spout their lies even up to the end, for it was designed to make David believe he is ill-equipped to the task. But really who is he really trying to convince, because God Himself who created everything equipped David with everything he needed to overcome, and Goliath's negative energies spouting out of his yap would have no effect in the brightened illuminated realms of David's realized truths.

David's faith and the trust he had everything he would need from God to defeat this man, threw the insult right back stating that Goliath's weapons were nothing compared to that of the Living God. And if Goliath's eyes weren't wide with fear at the power of these words, they were the moment the giant took but a single step forward and David started running straight towards him!

At every turn, victory was accomplished, and the actual deliverance had not even been dealt out yet in everyone's eyes, for, as it is in the natural so is it in the supernatural, there was no doubt as to the sudden cease and immediate reversal of the momentum. The snowball was already rolling downhill, and with every step, it grew!

I can imagine on the barren plane of the supernatural where a horde of demonic legions, the cronies, the groupies, stood up until then confidently moving comfortably forward against the children of God, riding on the backside of Goliath's image, the attack's and effect's of the constant bombardment of fear, doubt, hopelessness, rejection, abandonment, and doom, must have been nearly overpowering to the soldiers of any army including God's army.

But the moment they registered the blast of light created by the image of someone actually attacking Goliath many a troop probably were so gripped in paralyzing oppression, not to mention being now way too busy protecting their soft underbellies in some kind of fetal self-comfort, to even pick up the sword and shield that lied only hands reach from them, for them the end was already in the cards. I can hardly imagine the hot blast that must have flowed over them like boiling anointing oil as the demon horde immediately stopped the attack posture, withdrawing into their own defensive positioning at the sign of the sudden and direct momentum shift exploding in front of them, like the explosion a thousand suns of bright holy light!

I can almost hear thousands of smaller demons squealing and running in every direction almost immediately as the light went on! "A Scattering of the Roaches" does apply here very nicely! There must have also been an immediate chaotic withdrawing of the more herd animal type troops, first pulling back hard a few of the leaders may be interlocking the shields in some kind of desperate counter defensive. This had no doubt, sent earthquake-like shock waves of physical twinge up the spines of not only Goliath but all of the Philistine troops assembled, cold and lonely was its chill as all the supernatural dark forces they had so depended on were running like frightened bugs, disappearing the moment the light turns on.

A direct opposite effect in the good-guys camp, the white hats, a sort of instantaneously counter anointing, the refreshing warmth that thrusts power and confidence into the souls and bodies of the Israeli army, as they saw fear manifest in the eyes of their enemies, the empowerment that confidence grants erupt in their very hearts. They too felt the blast of light, but for them instead of frightening it was empowering.

But I also know when David charged, any demons of herd animal status, the entire front lines, dropped everything and ran, even trampling those who were not as fortunate to get out of the way. That's what herd animals do when someone charges, doesn't matter how big they are, they cut and run. Ripples of fear and fire-filled Godly retribution sent choking shivers through the remaining demonic soldiers, and this feeling was backed by the absolute power and presence of the God who created the universe.

The Stone, the hurdling of the rock, the spoken manifestation, the small representation of the word of God, even in its simplest form, was all it took to close the final pages the floodgates of God's deliverance. David could have thrown anything a spear, a thermonuclear missile, or a simple stone, the giant was already doomed, so throwing the simplest small seemingly insignificant thing out a single small piece of the Word was all it took. This is a clear demonstration of even the slightest smallest word in the quantum realm can be spoken against any giants when backed by the belief of truth resulting in the same effect and likewise vanquishing of darkness.

Once contact was made the end-game was immediate and sealed. Down onto his face, Goliath fell, back exposed, demons of all ranks were running for their lives, very much emulated in the natural as the armies of the Philistine also broke ranks and ran.

At this point, all that remained was the mopping up! David casually walks up and takes Goliath's head with his own sword, his victory prize to present to the King. The armies of the Living God pursue now in frenzied strength, I am sure empowered by the angelic horde that wraps themselves in and around all of the arms and souls of the Lord's army until all of the opposing force has been hunted down and killed. The Bible speaks of bodies being scattered across the countryside. It took a little time, and effort, but the victory was granted long before the army was destroyed, the moment David stepped up.

All we have to do is say no to these dark forces, these diseases, turn on the light and they have no choice but to flee.

FLYING IN THE FOURTH DIMENSION

Was it a dream? Close your eyes and tell me if you don't have similar experiences?

I dreamed a dream that I know must be true, for memories are sure and skies colored of blue.

At the start of the day, I am asked by a Little One; *"describe to me an example of my body as it would perform during the day and how that is different depending on what I intend to do today?"*

I seem to sit between that world between dream and awake more often now, perhaps it is because of Ascension, and perhaps because it is from the desire to do so? The Image comes into my vision before me of a gauge, one a person might see on the outside of a machine measuring the level of fuel inside, this one was resting in the air floating as if in glass that shimmered with expressions of thoughts. It had a clear glass window in the front, and inside a bubble which marked the fuel level, also a line across the center measuring the levels of fuel being used.

Then the Voice of God says to me;

"The fuel is your Life's Source it is very similar to the energy of the sun and is being used and dispersed throughout the day. Place the guide at the level you wish to use for the day; the more you wish to do actively, the higher you place the guide at the beginning of the day and the more you will have available throughout the single day's creation. Place your attention on that level you wish and I will fill you with lights life energy that will propel you through the dimensions of that day."

I seemed to just have the understanding and memory of the fact that the guide gauge is first placed at the top of some kind of invisible chart being held out in front of me. The whole thing resembles a chart, and I just know that this is the display of everything that will happen to me today, the height of the place of the gauge depends on the intention of the use of that day.

The highest intention would not only be some kind of extremely active physical day like someone who would be competing in physical sports, a game or some kind of training, maybe even only working at a physically strenuous job, but someone who is very spiritually active as well, expanding to the concerns and consequences of physicality around them as in-store for them that day. These high place settings require a collecting of the highest amounts of fuels for processing throughout the day like having the gas peddle pushed down to get the most fuel in. Somehow I knew this would activate until now non-implemented DNA receptors, allowing these to be mobilized whereby these energies can be received and stored for the up and coming elevations of thought.

If we were just planning on having a more mild merely physical or rudimentary day and knew energy needed to be stored up as reserves for future heavy or busier higher activities we also would place the gauge high and then more fuels would be collected, but the excess fuels would be drawn off throughout the day and placed into a storage holding area in close proximity surrounding the person like an aura.

If the gauge was placed at a middle position it would mean that no significant event was planned and just a small amount of normal usage would proceed, but as the day progressed the gauge could move up and down on the chart depending on the day's change of activities. Sudden or unexpectedly busy strenuously physical, mental, and most importantly spiritual activities would demand the most usage, thus the gauge could be lifted up to accommodate by us at will.

Likewise, if the person is needing to rest the gauge would move down to the lowest position where the least fuel would be processed and very little fuel if any would be placed into storage, only using the minimal fuel to replenish the mechanisms used that day. Somehow in my dream, I just know these things as if they are memories from many days past.

"The energy of the day's creation is freely given to each and every one of you

regardless of whether you are gathering sticks for a fire, oil for lamps, or a feast to lavish the tables of Kings, it is really, all the same, you merely have to decide what you wish to do with it, how you wish to share it, and most importantly how you consider it."

The dream fades…

As we have already seen various vibrational aspects of being are associated with diverse frequencies of energetic resonances and the fact that all physical experiences of this universe are made up of the same basic elementals components, the only real difference within these anomalies is "Intent." These are increases or decreases based on the associated emotional states, we happen to be the observers in this adding or subtracting of volume or wave speeds making our observed resonances dependent on our own acceptance of these oscillations, intent is the only possible when we are there to receive it, giving awareness for the differences in energy polarity. We just get to decide ourselves whether we focus on them or not, what effect it may have on us, and how much this has to do mainly with our vast belief systems our eventual path towards or away from God.

The question is often asked; do the emotional states cause these vibrational anomalies, or do the vibrational resonances cause the emotions that manifest within us? And while this seems like a chicken and egg question the truth is we as free-will created spiritual beings choose to assimilate the vibrational levels purely by our own concentrated awareness or focus. Of course energies from the outside good and bad have an effect on us, but how much of an effect is based on how we chose to react.

Of course, spiritual energy transferences can be passed on to us from non-living energy systems as we have already discussed in the case of water, poisons, viruses, or even harsh words, and these slight increases or decreases in energetic status could without a doubt have an effect on our emotional, our health and wellness, our health care effectiveness, literally our physical and mental status, but again the decision to accept them or not often resides in our own ideologies of whether we believe them or not? This may account for the placebo effect people have with taking medications when they believe one function, but in the physical, another is presented, their belief often outweighs the physical.

Large steps or multi-level leaps in the vibrational resonance of a being cannot be experienced, especially in many multiple levels, merely by sheer will, at least not while we are in what is referred to be only the third dimension. Higher-dimensional beings or individuals that are aware of this wisdom and live in a higher vibrational awareness status's can through their concentrated focus change the very levels of vibration merely by pure will, yet this process does take discipline, meditative concentration, and training, only to be accomplished by those who have learned the ability through years of self-discipline and spiritual reflection. The exception to this rule is those blessed few that have been given this skill directly from God and seem to understand as well as precipitate these transitional actions by pure will almost instinctively.

But before we delve into the in and outs of vibrational shifts, and the consequential health benefits arrived from these shifts, I believe it is prudent to understand the idiosyncrasies of the various dimensions to better understand the environments we are dealing with. For the purpose of this book, I will only briefly describe the various aspects of dimensions starting with the third dimension and upward to further correlate them to the understanding of Quantum Ascension in health and wellness.

Because we are considering the Mind, Body, and Spirit (or Belief) aspect of the Quantum existence it is important to also examine the dimensional realization from each of these three perspectives to understand fully the significance of entering into other dimensions as well as how this might present itself in the healthcare environment.

Without getting too much into the physics of our descriptions it is important for the reader to understands that we are born, live, exist and unless we ascend even die in the third dimension. This third dimension is what we call our physical reality consisting of height, width, and depth of physical space. We have an understanding that time passes by because we accumulate information in the form of memories. But more than this it is the combined data arrived from thoughts, tastes, smells, every sensation our body feels, even those of dreams, realms not yet experienced or thought physically possible flow into a grandiose garden of memories, the mansion of many rooms, this entire accumulation of experiences we call our life. In simple terms, the third dimension represents the dimension of the body.

Any physical location within this realm of the third-dimensional universe can be determined simply by plotting the height, width, and depth of three points, regardless if we are speaking of galaxies or even the smallest point in a single atom. But when we move into the realms of the mind these constants and the laws of 3D space begin to get a bit insufficient.

Three-dimensional space and the physical particles within must observe all the physical laws that reside within the physical universe. Time, electromagnetic reactions such as the feelings of heat and cold, movements, even physicalities of which it speaks to the awareness reside within the reactions of sentient beings and all find a place within the physical constants of the third dimension. All the reactions of the body, the many gambits of symptoms we address when afflicted, even the all encumbrance pain, which is itself a reactionary signal of which we will talk later, all must respond in the physical in orderly reactions based on the many constant physical laws. These are all properties that consist of elements of the third dimension and thus are the very systems that keep its constants as well as imprison its people who are stuck there.

People have throughout history labeled and classified hundreds even thousands of physical laws, constants, Godly truths, and rules of thumb such as; "Love thy Neighbor," "Action-reaction," "Karma," "Do unto others…," "Laws of Thermodynamics," "Laws of Attraction," "What goes up must come down," "Face-mask's Don't Do Shit," you name it, all the basic rules that seem in 3D to create order in the universe are also available for all of us to use. Create in our trust that with each step we take, through this physical universe, the results of a subsequent step forward on the path of which we call the garden of our soul, a firm placement of the foot and next step will result.

All of these believed laws dictate a set conclusion in the trusted reactions that match expectations placed within our minds by the experiences and observations of the past both verbal and experiential. This is where education and media programming can be so influential. Believing the lie that we are merely accidental creations of some primordial pool somewhere far off in uncountable years past, could result in taking away any faith in a higher plan for us, hiding from our sight any real potential destined growth, instead of the arbitrary and unrealizable evolution that we are told is out of our hands. These arbitrary teachings deny the created perfection of us and the universe for that matter, keep us staring to the physical and deny the very existence of God.

Imagining the differences in dimensions, let us put it in terms that people who may still be dwelling exclusively in third dimension existence require as we paint a simple picture and then describe possible hypothetical experiences people will have as they pass into these various realms of this climb.

Imagine our whole life is an experience of living in a deep valley, not all that dissimilar to the one described earlier but instead of a deep valley like river canyon, a vast gentle sloping valley lined by far off mountains so distant that people deep within can't even see them over the hedge-line of weeds they have grown throughout their days. My own Valley of the Sun, Phoenix Arizona upbringing was quite similar to this, the gentle slope to the river in the middle and the vast flat distances in between left the unknowing child, such as myself, no idea they were living in a valley but gave the illusion of flat even ground. Had I not been constantly told we lived in a valley, I would have had no idea, that was of course until it rained and the vast rivers of water would flow past my house?

For the people who are in the valley, it is difficult to even imagine that they are actually in a valley. The slope downward is so gentle many can hardly believe they are slowly rolling down towards the more congested valley center. This slow falling manifestation often occurs when they are asleep, they usually have their attention constantly on either on someone or something in their immediate surroundings, focused on some desire they have within their line of sight, which happens to be often-times themselves, the result is the slow descend downwards.

When in this state it is difficult to see far off in front or behind one's self when you focus is on what seems to be flat ground, staring at the little stones at your feet, especially if it is so busy in our surroundings as things seem to be these days. On flat-ground, or from a lower vantage point, it is difficult, if not nearly impossible, to see an attack coming even if it is but a few hundred yards away, of course, if we are asleep it is completely impossible. All sicknesses and attacks reside in the realms of the third dimension. If the physicality of the body is limited to the physical laws of the third dimension, then the realizations of truths through the mind become the pathway to and through the fourth dimension.

In earlier writings, I have described sicknesses and infirmities, not as affliction we have or become, as we have been brainwashed recently, but as attacks inflicted upon unsuspecting or sometimes expecting victims from outside much like an attacking animal or insect coming at you and biting with malevolence.

People who are locked in the third dimension, the day to day considerations of life, work, the desires of their personal physical needs, create a basic and often mundane experience with others around them, the accumulations or physical baubles obtained from the shifting sands that surround them and others, create a fixed field of awareness so focused and busy with the third dimension, they don't have time to even consider a fourth dimension can exist. These are the imprisoned people of the third dimension; their heads are down, their attention is focused on the now, usually unwilling to even hear anything that might take their focus away from what they happen to be concentrating on at the moment they are being addressed.

I have found, as a health care provider, that people who are suffering from afflictions, or under some kind of attack either physical, mental, or spiritual, usually display this focused inattention on the smallest of personal physical spaces. Three-dimensional people are so stuck in the reality of the now, they believe the world is exactly how it has already been presented to them, they are convinced of being basically powerless to change it, so they might as well take it, hopefully, adapt if they can, yet often just submissively willing to suffer through it until they by death or mercies sake are freed from this jail. If the fourth dimension is the place of awareness that healing is possible, then to perform good and proper healthcare a provider must aid in the deliverance of the afflicted from the third into the fourth dimension.

Rising out of the stigma of three-dimensional thinking requires first an act of realization that the way the world has been presented to us is not necessarily true, a realization that we have basically been lied to, or there is at least more to this life than we are being led to believe. Of course, there are many people who overcome difficulties, cruel, or evil attacks, and it is through this overcoming that the first steps of ascension are made, these people are often living examples of what is referred to; *"What doesn't kill us makes us stronger,"* or *"God turns all things to good,"* both Godly laws of the universe that further demonstrate the reality of this and other dimensions.

Basically, the journey into the fourth dimension is a journey primarily of the mind. This ascension can fall on the footsteps of study, personal growth, reflection, and or spiritual growth, as well as any infinite other directions where an ascending soul climbs out of the valley and begins through a few simple questions; *"If they lied about this, then what else are they lying about?"* And the almost immediate follow-up questions; *""Why would they lie, and who is the "they," that are behind the lies?""*

Regardless of the questions, the particulars of the lies, or the first realizations, an ascension takes place when the person lifts their head to the truth, begins a spiritual climb up the slopes of the surrounding mountains, and thereby has a clearer vision of what was transpiring in the valley below. While he or she can clearly see those below them, as well the newfound heights of which they now dwell, for some odd reason those below cannot seem to see them, maybe because the valley-dwellers all have their heads down looking at the ground for baubles in the sand or other things?

The Mountain Ascender's have, by the pure realization of their experience, moved into the Fourth Dimension. Things seem brighter as they move up out of the smog of the valley, the air is fresher, the day seems brighter, life becomes one more observational than just experientially consumption-based. The afflictions of the valley, the arrows, and rocks being hurtled around don't seem to reach up the slopes, even the words, accusations, and screams being launched from below seem to have lost all volume as from steadily greater climbing heights fade to mere whispers. When one realizes the truth, lies no longer have any effect.

The many attacks going on back in the valley, when people are up on the slopes are easy to see and now much easier to deal with, if they even have to deal with them at all? And in the case of health, a birds-eye perspective is granted allowing people to really see the true nature of afflictions, the negative energy shadows become visible and how insignificantly small these former giants really are. Healing occurs as spontaneous regenerations of dormant functions spring back to life bathed by the light and fed by the waters of God's perfect day. Belief starts to take hold of perhaps other miracles only yet dreamed of.

As concerns for friends and family members back in the valley begins to weigh on the hearts of the Ascenders, it is possible for those to descend back down from the fourth to the third to help those asleep or the many too busy with their heads buried in the sand to notice the signs occurring in the heavens around them, compassion grows in the entire universe. It is almost impossible for those stuck in the third to manifest effects on the people of the fourth from their descended viewpoint as much as they might try, tragedy loves company, yet the only true tragedy is the one's who pull their hands away or refuse to look up when help is offered. If the fourth dimension is simply one of the mind and truth, then the realm of the spirit and miracles must be the fifth?

People of the fourth dimension increase in more than just spiritual height as their ascension takes place, an increase in vibration status takes effect within them in many of the physiological mechanisms that we have already spoken of. This increase in vibration has a direct physiological effect on each of them causing the activation of dormant DNA that had been yet suppressed either by generational programming or recent negative infusion since they were children while they still dwelled in 3D. Using any one of the many realizations of the natural gifts God has given them as well as the new wisdom delivered through the ascension process a cleansing of impurities is accomplished resulting in even further increases of DNA activations, a sort of illumination activation and transformation occurs propelling them ever so higher into the realm of the Heavenly perceptions.

A common occurrence in people who Ascend is revelations of past, present, and even future events, visualizations of places even worlds unknown to us, visions, dreams of abilities that defy the natural laws of the third and even fourth dimensions. Conversations with malevolent beings such as angels or God Himself, quietly discarded as the soft imaginations of the past come in much clearer as trust and belief is added to the signal strength. For it is written by God; *"In the last days, I will pour out my Spirit on all people. Your sons and daughters will prophesy. Your young men will see visions, and your old men will dream dreams."*

It is also perhaps with the increased frequency of vibration that the people of lower vibration seem to cease seeing the climbers of consciousness, hardly hearing them, or more tragically finding anything in common with them any longer. Many of the higher seeking adventurers and patriots have lost jobs, friends, even love ones as they suddenly find they are no longer understood, especially when their newfound truths seem to go against the narrative the system constantly pushes.

It would seem in particular with people who have chosen to descend instead of ascending, there is a hatred that develops whereby these descended people are almost driven to attack, slander, even attempt to destroy individuals who have ascended for no other reason than merely out of hatred, this is nowhere more visible than a recently clear political arena of our own country.

While people of the third dimension may have dreams and visions of abilities in the fourth, it is the people of the fourth who begin to realize that many of those dreams and visions may actually be possible? Up the mountain, they climb ever ascending in truth, wisdom, and realization onward a steady illumination of accumulated truth occurs. The true meaning of the Words; *"We are created in the Image of God,"* becomes not only an understanding but manifested in their life. There are many truths in the ascension of the fourth dimension but all of them seem to circle back to the one essential word; Belief. Accumulation, consumption, and the things of the third dimension no longer are of importance, only the realization of the ultimate truth; "other people are important" there is really only one law *"Love God with all your heart, and love your neighbor as yourself."*

As we increasingly become aware of the Godly majesty of everything around us it becomes of the greatest concern for the All within everyone else around us. This influx of love and compassion can only come out of God and seems to be a further attraction to climb even further up into the now dreamed of fifth-dimension.

As we increasingly see God in everything around us, we, in turn, see others and even ourselves as God does, and a basic fact is revealed; that we are created perfect, it is only through the tainting of the earth that we darken or become increasingly polluted. Maybe this is why babies smell so fresh and pure especially when they are so little?

While we are on the subject of little ones, I always found it astonishing that children seem to have a pure sense of seeing into the supernatural, sensing good and evil without having any input, they're undeniable belief in God almost comes natural especially when they are young and have not yet been tainted or fed darkness. Perhaps this is why God Himself told us to come to Him as little children?

Ascension in the fourth dimension is basically a reduction of focus on the physical, a steady increase of self-reflection and everything Godly around us, an eventual decrease even in ourselves, a death of the old, and a sort of born again experience into Truth, resulting in an increase in how God views the world through us. This brings a whole new meaning to; *"Give unto others"* in the higher fourth dimension you have no choice but to do so. If energy is the food of the third dimension, Truth is the food of the fourth, and if this is true, then what is the food of the fifth, perhaps Belief?

In the areas of Ascension of Health and Healthcare dwelling in the fourth gives us the realization of the truths in front of the shadow of lies brainwashed into us while in the valley, a clear picture of what is real. It is this knowledge that gives us all the weapons to combat the many sicknesses and afflictions attacking the people of today. As we climb the ascension path the realization that we have everything we have ever needed to thwart any of these afflictions right at our fingertips, and all we had to do was reach out and claim them, this truth becomes empowering? With this newfound confidence, fear flees and with it any chance the enemy has of overcoming us.

Forth dimension Ascension in Health, Wellness, and Healthcare is nothing more than a simple awakening of the truth, a realization and vanquishing of the fear from the lies spoken to us, the acknowledgment of many warning signals the body gives us, the understanding of the true direction or purpose of these attacks, our own responsibilities in allowing them to happen to us, the forgiveness of the innocent parties involved, and the resolve to fight and win. All this positive wisdom brings with it the responsibility, and then ultimately the unquestionable desire, to share these newfound treasures with as many other people as are willing to listen.

As I stated above, while wisdom is being downloaded, and the increase in vibrational status is being granted, a transformation through activation of our very human potential is being thus materialized. And while we are still limited to the physical laws of the universe within the fourth dimension it is after this metamorphosis takes place in newfound activation, the implementation of higher energies into our being, and the transformation into everything we were created to be materialize, that a sort of caterpillar transformed into a butterfly is realized, whereby we can literally then fly into the heavens.

As in the transformation of a caterpillar into a butterfly, a temporary cocooning takes place where the body, the whole world of the caterpillar enters a stasis, a time of biological chaos, a sort of dying to the old self and rebirth to the new. The body must reject the toxins accumulated in the third, this can be experienced by the ascending in many various physical symptoms; ringing in the ears, pressure points, sudden aches, and pains, even expelling of poisons in drastic fashion such as coughing or even vomiting, these are not signs of sickness but an ejection of unneeded and unwanted negative factors from the body. A restructuring to the very bone occurs in our little caterpillar.

While the ascent is within the realm of the fourth dimension the cocoon and dying to the old self becomes the destination. God in His infinite wisdom has seen it fit to protect the vulnerable caterpillar as this death and rebirth process occurs. I am sure if we had eyes to see, we would clearly see all the Angels our heavenly Father has assigned to insure protection from attack as this most difficult and delicate juncture of the masterpiece is being painted.

This experience is exactly what so many people throughout the world seem to be experiencing simultaneously today. Soon we will reach the critical mass as the combined massively positive energies of the many overwhelm the small negative desires of the few and a breach of activation, illumination, revelation, call it what you will, must occur propelling all who are willing into this new realm, into the very limitlessness of space.

This is the transition into the fifth dimension, which we will speak of later.

By Peter Colla

ASCENSION OUT OF SPIRITUAL ENSLAVEMENT

As we further examine the Ascension process specifically observing elemental qualities of existence revealed to us either in the physical or mental realms of awareness, and perhaps even a few revelations within the symbolic abstractions of spiritual visions, we cannot properly investigate the highlighted hues of this master painting without first setting down the darker backgrounds of vibrational resonances, those dark pigments that make up the shadowy kingdom.

As we stated earlier in our discussion the Ascension process is a step-by-step climb that begins with a single act of merely setting our attention on Truth. "All Truth comes from God," and likewise any observed truths are subsequently merely reflections or apparitions of various aspects of God Himself. If that be the case, what is the descending process or the process that I have coined "Descension," it too resembles a step by step process but downward instead of upward, but how exactly does this process begin in the spirit?

It is obvious that if a true descending takes place then something is facilitating this reduction in the quantum realm. Knowing darkness is the absence of light, stacking components of darkness on top of each other does not produce a diminishing effect any more than stacking zeros upon each other can finally add up to even a single fraction of one. But something is going on that facilitates the reduction of energetic vibrational volume or reduced or compressed frequency speed creating a muffled or dampening of the vibrational frequencies of those who descend.

As we return to our valley model those who are firmly grounded or trapped in the third dimension over time do through mere consumption slowly degenerate back into the base element from which we were formed. This slowing down, aging, dilapidation, rotting as it where, seems to be a product of the assimilation of lifeless accumulations, a build-up of negative energy oscillations within their energetic space-time awareness, or muffling of the visual and audible capacity of life-enhancing energies that would and could heal, stimulate, or illuminate the Godly immortal structures already present.

In the health and wellness arenas, especially the health care system we find ourselves in these days, it would seem that suppression of awareness appears to be the goal of the majority of treatment models presented. Nowhere is this more evident than in pain suppression. It is this health care practitioner's contention that pain is not the villain it has been promoted to be, but merely a God-given signaling system of our body, to alert us of any and all acts of malcontent against us. Understanding this, thus honors the system, allows the person to extract all the information this warning system is designed to solicit, after which the pain can immediately turn off, confident of a job well done.

I must admit for the majority of my medical therapeutic career the larger portions of my own treatments primarily consisted of various techniques to facilitate pain reduction or other less irritating symptom suppression. Symptom suppression and overall dumbing down of the senses seems to be the goal of almost every pharmaceutical medication out there, regardless if we are talking about pain medication, sleeping aids, anti-depressants, anti-infectious, or even medication that are supposed to help children with autistic or depression issues, the hidden goal seems to be a numbing of the person's ability to fully sense their environment around them.

The majority of patients who are willing to speak of anti-depressant medication effects almost unanimously describe an almost tunneling reaction whereby the whole world, at least your awareness of it, seems to be limited to what you see down the end of a dark tunnel or a deep well. Even sounds, tastes, every form of feeling appears like it is muffled by tons of earth, veils, or being covered in blankets, a limitation effect is placed on emotions, the ability to feel or express with any kind of sensitivity, making a person almost emotionally dead and numb to everyone and everything around them, the emotional desert, themselves included.

But why this almost obsessing need to dumb down our senses with medical treatments by the medical system, and more importantly what do they have to gain by us having a more numb awareness of the world? But then again what do they have to gain by us wearing masks?

I can remember the days early in the career as a young health care provider, one with fonder reflection, a gentler time, when thoughts, study, and adventure all resided within the same sounds as of waters crashing against the stem of a boat sailing to yet unknown lands. Knowledge and experiences were as magical as the soft breezes that gently touched a young man's face. There too, resided understanding that everything presented was good, enveloped in truth, and drifted in the depths of peacefulness, this gave way to a view to a calmer reflection of tender gentler care that one knew must reside at the foundation of health care.

Men and women soft of touch, being firm of conviction, rendered all types of healing arts with an air of professionalism, given not for prestige or money, even as this most usually and almost assuredly followed, but for the deep desires to merely help other people in need. This desire being the driving force that released spiritual blessings into the sacrifice of reaching out a helping hand, a man could find a special calling, giving a sweeter meaning to a life that without would most assuredly lack taste or spice, a bland dish without; unpalatable. The true meaning and more importantly the honor that came with the title Doctor, Meester, Wise Man, even

Medicine Man was one earned through experience and not merely bought from some Cracker Jack box of one or another educational system of greed, lies, or deceit.

In the past men and women who answered such a deep-seated calling, they might actually catch a glimpse of the life dwelling within the very eyes of the many he or she might help in this world, this was often the reward which far exceeded any payments of gold. Bringing perhaps aid through the seemingly impossible trials of sickness as well as despair, the many affliction's that are so often brought to some even themselves, finding in return a quenching of water to the dry mouth of life's desert chapped lips.

Was it not a simpler time when people paid for the medical services they needed, a fair price for the time spent, and while I may be giving up my age by saying so, many times people who were even a little short, might bring in eggs or a baby pig, or maybe do a little work on leaking plumbing in the Doctor's basement as a payment in like, and to this medical caregiver; payment of such was just fine! House calls were not reserved merely to treat the sick, but the doctor of a community would make his rounds checking out the many people he served, examining them and advising all to keep the community healthy, only bringing the afflicted into his own clinic or home when ongoing care was needed.

It was the gratitude expressed in the smile of a woman when she finally came to the realization her child was going to be fine, or the injury to her husband wasn't as bad as suspected. And while the two chickens or newly finished quilt hardly made up for the relief they found, ever happy was she to know that the Doctor or the kind woman Meester, who had been such a God-send, would sit for many a warm night inside the arms of that quilt it took her so many hours to produce, maybe presenting but a fraction of the warmth her own love ones produce for her.

Over the course of but a few years, it was as sudden as a thief in the night, maybe beginning as a dark mold slowly growing in dark damp hidden place, who's dark tentacles only show their intent long after the roots sit so far throughout the walls and foundation, nearly nothing can remove them. This creature of dark-hearted stealth started slithering its evil talons hidden right in plain view, only inches from the bare innocent feet of our children. Enter the insurance companies, the heartless snakes, who creep in with their seemingly innocent statement; "give us a little of your money each month for medical insurance so you can be insured, or assured, that when you have medical needs, the money will be there to help pay the medical bills, the care will assuredly come, we will pay them?" But that is not exactly what was delivered.

Let me reiterate, what I have written many times in the past, within the boundaries of the next few paragraphs, this part of the story the media refuses to bring to our attention even though they are quite knowledgeable about it themselves. You see the media derives an enormous amount of money from the promotion, mass re-education, and ultimately the realization of the expansion of the system these advertisers promote. I am aware of this information because I have wallowed in it for nearly thirty years, myself being a medical provider with my own private practice, as well as working through various specialties within this field for this entire time. I have witnessed the degradation of a profession, of a calling, of the industry, almost as it has withered in front of me, like watching a piece of fruit decay and eventually die right in front of my eyes, all the while also seeing the attempts of the media to place the blame where it shouldn't have even been, on the health care providers.

Let us find a villain so we can point the finger of accusation at, and granted a small fraction of truth can be shown that the Doctor's must ultimately know because they are often sited as the villains, but again this is merely an attempt to sway the attention away from the true culprits; the insurance companies and the Big-Pharma who actually control them, the narrative, the education, even the research, what medicines that will be used, what products go in the medicines, and ultimately what are the true goals of treatments we receive. When I say Insurance and Big Pharma, people to have a tendency to then look at individual companies as individuals not quite realizing that they too are merely puppets for higher controlling agents who have made sure not only have these specific companies "they" happen to own control the industry, but "their people" are placed in high ranking positions, and most importantly that these companies do their sinister bidding without question.

It astonishes me how many people have been duped, or are being blindfolded to the corruption, either way, most people have no idea of the truth regarding how little the insurance Big-Pharma companies really care for them, no the truth is, they care for only one thing, taking total control of as many people as they can, sucking all the life, wealth and dignity out of them, and fulfilling the bidding of the ultimate boss who even controls the families on top. They do this bidding by setting as many of us regular people to slavery as possible, plus get paid for it in this process.

The spirit that drives them has a bit of another goal; stealing from God His children's First Fruits, those gifts of our labors, those He intended so desperately for us to use for our families, our own life, and His kingdom, as blessings for our lives, our health, our wellness, our very children. The system tricks us through imposed poverty to take from each other, and by dumbing down our expressions of love instead of sharing with each other, thereby cons us into giving our gifts to a greedy spirit who only wants to invoke fear to steal from God, while controlling and enslaving all of God's children.

Medical Insurance really did not become a term of common knowledge even in the insurance agencies themselves until the second half of the twentieth century, finding its foundation on the heels of accident insurance. This event followed a series of dangerous endeavors that seemed to injure or kill many people, while sensationalized and basically used by the media to sell papers, early life insurance companies would capitalize on titanic fears in order to make people became scared by these earlier disasters, such as The Titanic, ultimately prompting them to purchase insurance policies, believing they are buying "assurance" against a future accident that might occur and most assuredly leave a person's family ruined. Soon the insurance companies saw the huge profits that could be generated by receiving small premiums, especially after they played and even fed on these fears, but there were still just so many of these tragedies to go around, plus people were quick to forget, and even if they didn't it only affected a small portion of the public, the rich.

At about this same time, early twentieth century, a push was being made initially throughout America, but later through Europe as well, to step away from more natural water-based medications of plants, flowers, natural oils, and move more towards the exclusive use of synthesized chemicals dissolved in crude oil or petroleum-based products in all of the medications recommended, distributed or produced. Petroleum oils are toxic to the system causing a slow degeneration of our own ability to fight off afflictions, diseases, or allergic contaminants and thus make us susceptible to an ever-increasing array of bodily reactions. Toxicity has by its own spiritual intention, a health depressing motive, placed within the very meaning of the word it represents and thus has in the Quantum realm reducing effects countering the very life-giving energies light, health and love may illicit? This suppressing effect is exactly the intent of its producers.

It is was also about this same time a huge media propaganda campaign was initiated to basically scare the public into the need to stop trusting in God for their health security, but rather in an entity that has through lofty promises, itself boldly attempted to provide security even in the event of the most tragic and fear-driven event; and that was death. So maybe innocently or perhaps by design, the life insurance companies have tried to usurp for almost one hundred years the security only God can give, the security over death. When this worked, why not try it with other areas; fire, transportation, or auto, home security, mortgage, renting, business, loans, and eventual heath itself? Today there is insurance offered for every conceivable event where outcomes are predicted, policies sold and outcomes insured, in essence, these companies have the audacity to take the place of God.

While God was increasingly removed from us in conjunction with the health care arena, more and more treatments were implemented, dark and evil names used, many with hidden satanic or occult symbolisms right in plain sight, medicines prescribed, and chemicals synthesized to dumb us down ever reducing our ability to ascend, see the light, or look to the heavens. Hospitals and other higher places of learning were initially all associated with God or the church, yet the schools increasingly pressed a belief system that placed no consideration on God, faith, or healing, as a matter of fact, the opposite was jammed down the throats of its students. Is this coincidence or a diabolical plot? What possible reason could a satanic entity have for trying desperately to limit everyone's ability to ascend, and what better way than to place some kind of inhibitor in every medication we use including even the very first inoculations of our babies right out of the womb?

It is first important to realize that the same families that control the banks, oil, federal reserve, weapons manufacturing, who are the major stockholders in all of the Fortune Five-hundred companies, including the media, pretty much lust to control everything and every Creation under the sun, that same Creation of which God had originally intended for us, every one of us. These happen to be the same that also started the major insurance and pharmaceutical companies, or have obtained at least a controlling interest in every one of them, worldwide.

It was not long after insurance companies started providing comprehensive medical insurance, as a matter of fact only a very short time, by the early eighties, that these same insurance companies began a campaign to acquire ownership of all the hospitals, and within a couple of years, by only 1983 had already purchased 20% of all the hospitals in the United States, and today own more than 90% of the rest. Why?

This brilliantly corrupt and devilishly Judas-kiss move grants three very important components for success, as well as guarantees expansion of the control of the entire medical industry; implementation of fear of a problem, as well as the sole assimilation of production responsibility location of the cure, but also ensures isolation of the locations of primary care sit behind the observing eye of the public and now with the implementation of HPPA ensures nobody can look inside to see what goes on unless they choose to let them. Let me further explain;

Now let's say you are a greedy old man who owns an insurance, petroleum, or pharmaceutical company, maybe all three, or worse yet a dark spirit whispering in his ear, and promise the old fat cat the goal is to make enormous amounts of money at the expense of the general public, but really all the spirit wants is control; the problem is, if said company is a public traded company, (and why wouldn't you want it to be public and generate a profit, you want to control the markets as well), there becomes a need to not show to much profit, a darker more destructive agenda or heaven forbid complacency between these industries! First and foremost, for the justification of increasing premiums and reducing payable services can only be believed by the public, if hardship is demonstrated, stating a necessity to raise rates, controls, or mandatory participation such as with vaccines, must be made. But more importantly, is the absolute must, to make certain the peasants don't learn the truth, grab pitchforks and look for a public burning, after realizing the vast amounts of Gods blessings that have all been stolen, from our own health at the cost of our vulnerable parents, or from the very mouths of our children!

So where to hide those enormous bundles of stolen gold? Answer; buy the people who they pay the most money to, then pay it to them, thus themselves! As of today, insurance companies or at least the subsidiaries thereof, own almost "all" of the major hospital's in the US, and are presently attempting to acquire the larger firms of general practitioners (Doctors), as well as specialist, and if not the insurance companies, then the pharmaceuticals. But we should not forget who owns the major pharmaceutical companies as well, yes the same people who own the banks and insurance companies, they have many names; Bilderbergs, Illuminati, The Thirteen Families, The Venetians, Masons, Satanists, The Micky Mouse Club, call them what you will they print the money, collect the taxes, and decide what scraps are left for the rest of us to fight over! We will call this Implementation!

So the greedy old man, concocting this brilliantly treacherous plan; buys up the hospital's, uses the media to drive fear into the people with images in Hollywood and commercials, drives the bills up so high the public becomes scared of absolute ruination if we find ourselves or the need to send our children into such a place for life-saving care, funnel huge portion's of insurance premium sums of money to him, paying without question ridiculous fees such $250.00 for the little plastic bucket, or a one and half inch tube of toothpaste, the same products you can buy at "The Dollar Store" for much less than a dollar. Show fewer profits on the insurance company's books, and what a bonus; *"Blame rising cost of insurance premiums on rising health care fees charged by the Doctors, and the stupid peasants will only have to look at their own medical bills to see the enormous cost,"* there is our old not-so friend Boo-Boo blabbing again. Blame the individual Doctor the one who is supposed to render care or health advice; *"see he is rich, it must be his fault,"* sit back and watch the sheep hide at home scared of the big bad bogeyman that has already been proven to be no less harmful than the common cold.

Is it such a coincidence that about the same time the insurance companies began to obtain the hospitals, that the rates of the hospitals and all the care surrounding surgeries went through the roof; the early to mid-eighties! The greatest fringe benefit of this scare factor; people seeing the enormous costs of a typical hospital stay, or an operation, become so scared, they hardly dare live without insurance. Fear is a powerful weapon to bring the populous under servitude, bring them to their knees, then convince them to give their money, even before it gets into their hands, first fruits, their sacrifice that is brought to the altar of the "one who gives assurance" the insurance company, instead of being used for the children of God, or His kingdom as intended.

I have been practicing medicine for thirty-five years in my own strangled practice, but the amount I got paid from health insurance, regardless of what I charge, had not gone up a cent! They, the insurance companies keep us, providers, settling for these frozen rates year in and year out because of contracts; HMO's, PPO's, Industrial Insurance, and the like, and if we have a desire to renegotiate the rate, their answer always is; *"if you don't want the contract, the guy down the street will take our clients." "If you don't treat the way we say you're out." "If you don't repeat the lies you know to be false, and we know to be so, you can't talk to our patients."* The newest order in a long list of lies; *"If you don't label everybody COVID, or wear the ridiculous mask, we will run you out of the business and do everything in our power to ruin you."* Assimilation!

Even today the hospitals sit at the center of the controversy; the majority of medical providers were all told to go home and sit tight as the hospitals prepare for the massive overflow of COVID patients. But anyone who might have access to the truth or courage to look for themselves saw the hospitals were all ghost towns, empty parking lots, taped off for so-called renovations. The images we as masses were given, long lines of cars and people being tested prove merely to be staged by the media. Every health care provider I know that is still seeing people know the truth; that every patient that dies, regardless of why is labeled COVID, every patient that is billed to the insurance for anything is added the diagnosis COVID. The reported deaths regardless of what other factors are involved; heart attack, COVID, old age, COVID, death by cancer, COVID, suicide, COVID, overdose, common cold, auto accident, fall off a horse, it doesn't matter COVID. Who are the orders coming from? I don't believe for a moment all the Doctors across the country would risk their license just to make a few extra dollars? No, they are being ordered to lie, and someone powerful enough to also order their silence. Who has the most to gain by this ongoing perpetuation of a lie? I believe we should start by looking at who has gained the most since the lockdown?

You see my dear brothers and sisters, Insurance-Big-Pharma companies care less how many providers or contracting doctors they have, as a matter of fact, the fewer the better, shut down the hospitals, the doctor's offices, send everyone to the pharmacy for their pills, the small clinics who cares, what does it matter, but it is more than just money, its control, and what better way to control than by fear? More waiting time for our appointments means more time to sit at home in fear, fear the test, wait in fear for the result, less billed visits totally means more money in the books, the ultimate home run; people give up out of frustration when the clinic tells us there is at least one-month waiting list. Extra bonus; no more hospital visitation of loved ones means the regular people don't get to see what's really going on, who cares their loved ones are sitting alone in those stark hospital rooms alone, wondering in fear if they have been forgotten?

The industry knows full well on the Quantum level fear, depression, loneliness makes us susceptible to more illness not less. They know isolation kills little babies, so placing people into isolation is not help them get better it is rob, kill, and destroy!

Amazing how all these false gods want the same thing; control, steal our first fruits, and ultimately spread fear and destruction. In the early kingdoms of Mesopotamia, Egypt, Babylon, Rome, just to name a few, Mitra, a figure of a woman with a crown of light, looking mysteriously like the Statue of Liberty, adorned in golden jewelry, was worshiped by laying gold, crops, or the first fruits of one's labors at her feet, for the assurance of getting through the next years harvest. Insurance against destruction, a promise to give it your first fruits now and she will take care of you in the time of need. Sounds familiar? Does it surprise anyone, that the image of Mitra was the symbol used by the initial founding companies for life insurance that later turned into the health insurance companies of today? Look it up!

Most insurance companies have no problem writing a check to deliver death and darkness into the vein through chemo, paying upwards of $10,000 per inter-venous chemotherapy treatment, or paying for an abortion. But to ask them to pay for a woman to have an early preventative natural medication, if it's not on the computer screen as approved treatments you can forget it, even if she feels a small lump, or wants to save money in future care, no chance! Or an extra visit for a man trying to rehabilitate his back so he can return to work and support his family, perhaps treat another body part that may ensure he doesn't injure himself again when he does go back, no way.

You want the truth, I have seen it all; demographic denial, approval based purely on where in town people live, authorizing care then enacting denials to the patient to scare them into quitting, bumping up patient responsibility or co-pays until the so-called partial payment represents almost the entire bill. The supposed losing of information merely to stall approval, then waiting until the period of care is exhausted only to then make the approval knowing full well the care can no longer take place in the specified time frame, even throwing claims in the garbage to push out processing times and press costs from the provider's side. All of these practices have been reported to me by patients who themselves worked for these companies only to quit when their consciousness became too much to bear.

Another common trick is hiring secondary management companies that deny everything, creating a situation where the company itself doesn't even have to take the blame for the denials. And on and on it goes, tricks after tricks designed for one thing; lie after lie, betrayal after betrayal, treachery upon malice, to steal more from the people in what was promised to be a paid in advance benefit, place them in a position of unknowing and fear, poison them with meds that dumb them down and keep their heads in the dust, while they hold the gold in the fat coffins of the money changers that call themselves the insurance companies rich fat cats. If you dare bring your complaints they casually laugh and say; "If you don't like it then sue us, as they hang up." Why wouldn't they; if they can't beat you they will buy your lawyer, if they can't buy him then the Judge, if not him then the politician who controls the Judge, either way, they will win. If none of these possibilities work then they will commence to killing!

The common people are the victims of veils and blankets slowly descending over them without even knowing it, this initiates the Descension process in the spirit. Of course, the villain who is profiting from what he knows is a lie, cruelty, despair of his fellow man, treason against his own home against humanity itself, or even the poisoning of children, he already dwells at a level so far down the Descending tunnel it is hard to believe any light whatsoever could reach him, leaving only hate, greed, depression, and despair as his or her cellmates.

If all gifts come from God, then so did all the knowledge that was given to our fathers and mothers in the form of advances in health care are also among the gifts meant for everyone. While Doctors should be paid an honest fee for their services, companies have no right holding back real cures or suppressing technologies, delving out those gifts given to our children at such exorbitant fees that it would cost and put a family into lifetime ruination merely to perform a service that saves a child or wife's life. A doctor has a gift, of this no one doubts, and they should be paid for their gift according to supply and demand, but what gift does the $250 tube of toothpaste provide?

Doctors or any other healthcare provider should have the right to set those prices of their care, not insurance companies or their cloned servants the hospitals, and let the doctor look into the face of the child he is treating to see if his own eyes can live with the price he places on that service.

What is right with a system that through government mandate forces participation? Forcing people to participate in a system that itself demands them to bow down and give homage to a spiritual entity that only use the synthesized medication they know full-well cause any number of other issues, and then demands a stifled dumbed down obedience like a voiceless clone wearing a mask to dare not speak its bidding, the eyes behind the mask being the only sign that fear resides. We call this Isolation!

What are we to do? Trust again in God, for by Whom, and only through Him healing comes. Turn away from the dependency of Insurance spirit, and call for true health care reform; a return to a fair price for a fair product, putting an end to a few using those gifts God gave our fathers; treatments for the aiding in the healing of children, and share again that which people need for a fair price. A return to a fair price for a fair product in hospitals, where they are held accountable for costs that are nothing short of stealing. A return to only natural products and treatments known to heal without side effects, instead of paying billions to the technocracy of the health care management unsavory system, a jail that doesn't work to free anyone but merely keep people behind bars. An end to agencies whose sole purpose is to cut costs at the expense of care, no, use those monies for the people whose costs are greater than can be paid under normal circumstances. Reward doctors for helping to keep people healthy, give the people all the answers they need for life, liberty, and the pursuit of happiness without a price tag, wasn't that in an Amendment at one time in our Constitution? The people will decide what is a fair price for a fair service, they do it now with their cars and their dogs.

Help people towards the only true source of healing and that is Ascension to the truths of God.

Look to the days of the country Doctor, when almost every form of care was given at the office, a simple remedy or tea was enough to solve most ailments, instead of some oil-based pill that while it helps with one symptom causes five others. And the cost, well if you didn't have the money, for the most part, a chicken or baby pig or quilted blanket, or a heartfelt thank you was enough.

Sickness, depression, affliction, these are all attacks that have the effect of reducing our vibrational status, the last thing a person needs is adding to their physicality more negative energies and dark intentions that only seem to facilitate one common agenda and that is to numb the senses and further reduce the average person's ability to look up and ascend. For God's sake take the mask off!

GRACE IS THE SOUND MY EYE SEES

As the Ascension process expands and in this revelation realizations of higher frequency illuminations becomes evident, further possibilities of physical probability, some only dreamed about before, become not only plausible but themselves in fact manifest. An ever-increasingly clear view of the world left behind perpetuates themselves in the frequencies below as by the sheer energy of the spirit; belief, truth, God, all of these Heavenly resonances seem by the mere creative ability of the spirit to form a past that can somehow manifest the present dreamed of yesterday.

As we have already stated throughout this book and the many other writings I have already published, the Quantum Ascension is the process whereby a sort of facilitation of energies primarily connected to "Belief" are used for various aspects of our own individual growth in health and wellness. It is the realization that the environment within the spiritual is infinitely greater than that which resides in the mind, while the mind or thoughts are also almost infinitely greater than the mere physicality of the body that being of one single moment of time. That through the realizations of God's promised laws that we have come to realize as truths, activation of our awareness can occur resulting in the further development of unrealized, stifled, inactive, or underdeveloped skills we may already have possessed from creation.

This activation while continuing in the physical realm of light, frequencies, and energy, may, in fact, perpetuate itself with a complete metamorphosis of the individual into a higher functioning status whereby issues that once plagued us in the valley no longer have any effect on the physicality of the existence we are experiencing now. Spiritual considerations and focused thoughts become realized as further activations of spiritual abilities manifest.

As we have discussed earlier in this writing only a fraction of our own brain or DNA strands are activated throughout our lives, some scientists estimate as much as ninety percent of both of these functional potentials lie dormant but as these functions begin to activate what does this look like?

A few days ago I was sitting drinking coffee with my lovely wife, discussing the concept of "Worship" when we read it in the pages of the book we are reading together? To be honest, the concept, as well as the practice, seemed to be something I have struggled with perhaps the majority of my adult life, or at least from the time I can say that I have been actively engaged in the arena of at least trying to "follow God."

What exactly is worship? And while I had the privilege in my own past to play a musical instrument and be a part of a "worship service" band, I can say that the actual feeling of worship as well as the desire to enter into it, seemed to escape me. Plus reading passages in the Bible where statements are made of people or angels worshiping God for extended periods of time, even weeks or years, not only baffled me but is some cases even scared me, as I contemplated the translations of my own guilt-laden boredom with the mere twenty or thirty minutes I had in the church as well as many times falling asleep, now expanded to periods over months if not more?

I went to bed or perhaps relaxed, and as I began to dose off an image came into my head from my own young family life experience, and I felt God may have been answering my own questions, even one I hardly realized I asked. I have an overwhelming feeling to put that image onto paper after discussing it with Anna this morning.

In my dream I am transported and see before me, my own small child Grace as a baby, sitting on the floor in front of me. What is amazing, the image I can see is one where I am looking at the scene from directly behind her and I can at the same time also see myself sitting on the couch off to her right watching her play? A sort of out of body experience is taking place, that or I am somehow transported back to witness the event that I also remember myself in the past? Regardless, I am clearly there watching myself watch my child.

I say I can see myself because I am sort of watching her, and watching myself watch her even as the scene unfolds before me. There is a look on my own face sitting on the couch, as I watch my sweet child just sit there, playing before me; of pure happiness. And while I probably couldn't do it justice, let's just say I don't think I could ever remember seeing myself as happy as I witness myself at this moment. But perhaps the only word that I could possibly come up with, that could even remotely describe the look on my own face I am witnessing is utter bliss.

My little daughter cannot be even a year old yet, because she doesn't seem to be old enough to stand up on her own, but she is sitting unsupported. She is from the vantage point I am observing, right now behind her, clearly sitting looking or playing with something in her hands.

My own eye must have the supernatural ability to simultaneously look from behind her and at the same time, not only see what she is examining in her precious hands but also the look on her face as she examines it? She is just sitting there looking at a simple small rectangular toy, perhaps a small woodblock over and over in her hand as she looks at it, studying it, and turns it over again and again examining each side as if the new side is suddenly and excitedly being found new again.

Her face is one of complete contemplation but also happy and smiling satisfaction as she looks at the block, turns it over, looks at the other side, and then looks at the other side again, studying it and smiling in her thorough exam. I think I even softly hear her quiet voice a soft cooing sound as she again discovers a new side. "Hmmm, Ohhh, Shhh, Hmmm" The words she says soft are as relaxing to my ear as the wave of symphonic images that bathe my sight in beauty, love, and joy.

I am myself amazed at her complete peacefulness and thoroughness she places on this simple item, locking her gaze, not wanting to miss a single atom of the precious treasure that has suddenly found its way into her hands. Over and over she turns the block examining it and excited again to find a new different side, color, or image carved on it.

For a moment she almost seemed to get so enamored by her activity she nearly forgot I was there, but suddenly she stops and turns, needing to make sure I still was. She looks up to me sitting on the couch next to her, watching her. She gives me a happy satisfied smile, almost as a response to me watching her, and just as quickly returns her gaze to the object of her attention. Because just as fast she looked at me, she was is right back looking at the block, again starting to rotate it around in her hand as she examines one side and then another.

Again my spiritual eye goes back to myself sitting on the couch and the look on my own face as I seem to realize myself she is just making sure I am still there; her father, safely watching her as she plays. A wave of personal satisfaction as my own fatherly self seems to know that she must have thought, at least realized with the look on her face; "Yep, dad is still there, I am safe, protected, loved, even being watched."

Again she suddenly stops, but this time reaches out with the outstretched arm to show her dad on the couch the block in her hand. Looking up at him and lifting it up, she smiles at me clearly wishing to show the wonderful treasure she has just discovered.

I cannot begin to describe the feeling I see on my own face as I look at the wonderful smiling bright loving eyes of my child, reaching up and wanting to share her new discovery with me, her precious treasure. At this moment she is giving me a true experience a true gift in my own life, one I will cherish as a true treasure, a gem, a real golden nugget, and love all wrapped up in a single "wonder"-"full" wooden block.

This I feel in my heart and realize immediately in my own thoughts; "Is the Definition of True Worship." God does the exact same thing with each and every one of us as we sit and discover the world He created for all of us. And like I saw myself, He watches with infinitely more love than I could possibly comprehend as He watches all of us as mere children examining the simple wooden blocks he gives us each day.

And if I can sit there and feel a wave of utter joy as she holds up the block to share the new discovery with me, how much infinitely more does our own father feel when we take but a moment in our busy lives and hold up our own discoveries to Him?

God loves to watch us experience his gifts, loves it more when we look to make sure He watching and loves it the most when we reach out and share our wooden blocks with Him. *"Help me Lord to remember you are watching, eager, and loving in the discoveries we have each day, help me remember to take the moment to reach out and show you."*

As the spirit ascends visions increase that expands beyond the limits of time and space. Perhaps the caterpillar as he or she ascends the tree, as they ascend, begin to dream of times when they ultimately will fly?

As we ascend up the ranks of spiritual considerations and our focus broadens into the clouds that await us, this manifestation of expanding consciousness brings with it added burdens that result from our more lofty view of the world. With the higher vantage point of the mountainside, it becomes clearer all of the happenings going on below in the valley. We begin to see not only the real perspective of the environment we were living in only moments before, but catch a glimpse of the true nature of surrounding players. We see all of our friends still in the valley and more importantly, the enemy can also be seen as they muster various attack postures against friends still below.

With each truth that is made known, and the wisdom revealed related to the "who's" and even "why's," patterns emerge suddenly understanding erupts in our minds revealing clearly what is really going on down there. With these newfound understandings come with it a concern for the many friends, loved ones, even strangers left behind still sitting in the valley, unaware, who might fall prey to the plots and attacks these dark entities are clearly perpetrating.

The first desire is to shout back at each of our friends, trying to describe the picture we so clearly see, but this is often met with denial, disregard, and in some cases even angered insults. It is almost impossible for people to believe someone or something is mustering to attack them in the valley when they have no idea they are even in a valley in the first place? Right now the world is as it has been presented to them, and they are busy with the particular task in their hands, unable to even imagine the picture we might be describing since they have never seen it or even imagined it could be?

"You want to help your friends, you cannot do it merely by telling them the truths of what is going on around them, you must show them, and this means you must go and get them, bring them up the mountain and show them for themselves so they too can see."

My mind is suddenly brought to another child the same age taken from its mother and father perhaps only moments before birth. Now sitting in a cold cage, down in the dark recesses of a descended prison. Cold, dark, damp, void of any love, or compassion, she sits with her back to the door of the cage afraid almost to look back out of fear that evil will appear again to torment and abuse her.

She is nervously wringing her hands not in play or examination but in fear as the screams and moaning cries of others lash across her young skin, their echoing pleas continuously bring her attention back to the distant darkness, not looking to see if a loving father is watching but silently gasping a prayer her tormentor is not. Her skin bare the marks of abuse's past, the filth of neglect is the only garment her you brushed skin wears, but her eyes are clear even in fear emitting the purity that resides deep within.

Silently my mind's eye can see her, the terror in her eye, the fear so strong she dares not cry until she realizes the sound of perhaps her own cage being open and demon hands reaching mercilessly for her, seizing her yet again for some cruel and painful purpose. She clearly shakes, wringing her hands nervously, her body twists as she desperately tries to turn away yet her neck and head turn towards the sounds in fears cursed spell. Even as the sounds of other cages are suddenly unlatched followed by immediate screams of terror other children are making, a shudder shoots through her young body unable to release the fear it might have been hers?

My own spirit is filled with rage as I realize this could be my own child, sitting there in terror, with no hope or help, merely fear that life is not discovery but torment, not something that is enjoyed but something desperate to end. It fills me with rage as the thought that someone could do such a thing, and others know, support, even approve of such evil. I feel powerless to do anything, my spirit wants to rip these demon ghouls to pieces, but I feel powerless even to begin to see how. It is mercy for me I only have a glimpse before my eye returns to my writing before me, this too is Grace. If this image is true something must be done, and while I can't storm these facilities, gun in hand, wanting desperately to dispense some kind of Godly vengeance on those who would do this to a child such as mine, I feel I must do something?

Perhaps by writing it, telling it, screaming it from the rooftops, or publishing it, in the spirit another light turns on, another person learns the truth, another wave of positive energy cascades out into the universe increasing the Godly energy in the quantum, increasing the entire ocean of being ever so fractionally so the realization of rescue becomes reality. The strength and courage of great men and women being led by our great President who has long battled for, and are even now battling all over the world to free these captive children, girls and boys, women, and even men who are being held, victimized, tormented, abused and used for the dark talons of these creatures.

Ascension brings with it the visualization of the whole painting we as people have created in this world, and as we slowly see more vibrant colors of the surroundings, hear clearer the hidden sounds of angels singing in the chirping sounds of a mornings dawn, so do we also see the shadowed darkened hues of deep dark crimsons blood reds laid down layer upon layer until they look black to the observer. In the shadows, there are still screams that have been muffled within deep-hidden recesses from view, but if we concentrate enough and not ignore the dark but set our God enlightened attention on it even for a moment we will also find that as we do, so does God through us, and the rescue is already underway, the darkness must flee, and the battle has already been won.

By Peter Colla

Q

The caterpillar ascends and as he climbs realizes that the dangers that plagued him below are disappearing from not only view but from concern, there is an air surrounding him that something wonderful is about to happen. In his now more recurring dreams, she flies and with it, a realization that fears once believed is no longer a danger in the world this freedom perpetuates. He ascends, and yes she does become an increasing target for the creatures of Heavenliness, they see him but since she doesn't yet have eyes, he can only sense them when they are close to touching him. A balance of revelation occurs, the peacefulness and nurturing, on one hand, balances with the desire to fight against the dark forces that would set to destroy everything she holds true and love in the world below.

There is more of a concern and an almost increasing love to go back down and help others who remained seemingly unaware of the revelations visible from above, perhaps help them lift their own heads from the dust or encourage them to themselves step up for the long climb up into the heavens.

This is quite an illumination of its own and since the caterpillar has no eyes there is no possible explanation how she can know the truths being revealed to him, leaving only one truths they all come from

God. Be it as it may, the higher he ascends the more truths seem to be understood, images and hidden pieces of a puzzle, secrets revealed that have only tickled the hairs on the back of her neck when he still dwelled in the dust and grasses of the earth's ground.

God in his grace grants to our caterpillar a time of protection, encircling around him a protective shell, a cocoon of strength, as its body has time to activate and grow into the marvelous winged masterpiece of perfected majesty, she is granted a safe and warm high place in the trees basking in the sunlight of another perfectly dawned day. The realization of everything below sounding like the echoing rumblings of the night thunders, fall away as the Ascent produces a yin and yang spinning of the senses. At first, these physiological activations create an almost dizzy sensation as her body copes with rapid changes God's light seems already to have magnified. What does this period of dreams, physical change, and literally a soul change resemble when one not only doesn't have the eyes yet to see it but has no experiences in the physical below to draw perspective from, one can only imagine? Yet imaginations explode and dreams materialize as realizations of heightened clarity press our little caterpillar until the destination is achieved and metamorphosis begins, continues, and is complete?

Two thousand years ago our society as a whole experienced a manifested descending of sorts whereby God Himself came to earth with a single purpose and that was to demonstrate a manor in which the rest of us might ascend up to the heavens into everlasting life, wisdom, and accord with God Himself. This was demonstrated by the sacrificial death and resurrection of Jesus, forever creating in the physical-spiritual continuum the essence of Godly manifested Light, His very illuminated resurrected being, the realization that each of us can for ourselves raise into this same heavenly essence if we so desire merely by lifting up our heads, recognizing the Truth revealed and making that first step up the mountain was promised and delivered for all of us to experience.

A quantum shift occurred where Godly light perpetuated out into the universe eliciting abilities witnessed by many, noted by few and acknowledged over the whole world for all time, and all to see. As these manifesting energies radiated out throughout the entire known universe in the physical, mental, and spiritual realms, Godly light permeated everyone and everything. Abilities such as healings merely by commanding them, men walking on water, the dead rising, the blind seeing, the deaf having their ears opened, nothing was impossible, even the dark spirits that plagued so many for so long cried in fear when commanded to leave.

Ascension on a quantum level was manifested as absolute and immediate as the spoken words that created the entire universe one moment begun, and in the next instant existed for all time. Science has long proven even simple sounds, the words we speak, once spoken are forever spreading out weakening but never disappearing completely; how many times can something be halved before it is zero, half of anything even the fraction of a single atom is still something.

One of the many anomalies of Christianity, the New Testament, and the accounted depictions of the miracles and words of Jesus is the fact that the first three books of the New Testament; Matthew, Mark, and Luke all seem to follow the same basic order and name specifically the same miracles as examples even though Luke himself states he was not a direct witness of the events first hand? It is commonly believed that in the earliest writings of the accounts of Jesus, someone may have penned a single text, perhaps one of the direct witnessing twelve, or maybe even by Jesus Himself, and it was this original document that was later repeated by many of the twelve Apostles as documentation to take with them as they spread across the globe and repeated the message of Christ in every direction.

This original document which has been reported witnessed, especially in the earliest records of the church, yet now is believed lost or perhaps hidden away, carried the single name and simple designation of a simple letter; Q. The Book of Q has stood the test of centuries to be believed to be this single text, and while many have searched, and many more do believe it may have once existed, there is but one common belief when it is described as either being original or merely an imagined document, and that it represents the basic "Truth" or original account of the life, acts, and words of Jesus.

A book of basic truth called Q leaves us with any number of questions including; does it exist, who and why was it hidden, and finally why call it Q. A basic single program, a simple perhaps chronological list of events, and perhaps a simple plan from which others could be facilitated for one purpose and that was the spreading of the message of God Himself out throughout the whole world and unto everybody who is willing or wanting to see.

I am not intending this book to be a documentary of research into the legitimacy of Q, or even dare to attempt to convince anyone of the truths of the Bible, I am not worthy, but all I can do is relate my own experience in this process, report what I have learned, seen, and come to understand, and perhaps each of you reading this will search for yourself the truths, understand them in your heart and further ascend to see more. Ascension is the understanding of truth, and the quest to find more. For me, this rests in my own related experiences to the belief of stories in the Bible, whether they were true or not, and then the understanding of who is fighting against these truths and why.

For me, Peter, my introduction to the truth, as with many others usually requires an almost rock bottom experience whereby the looking up desperation move is a life or death choice. It started perhaps many years ago on the very cusp of the death, in a tragic car accident of my then-pregnant wife Hilly only a day before she was due to deliver our second child. She died on the 11th day of the 11th month in the 11th year we were together, and for people who seek out the hidden messages of numbers will without a doubt immediately be drawn to the significance of 11, 11, 11, but I myself will not get into that yet in this book.

Truths then, and revelations about God as they presented themselves to me, not all at once, but as seemingly unrelated puzzle pieces that at first merely tickled my curiosity to learn more, only later to assemble into a picture that demonstrated to me absolutely God's face and the ascended vision He had for each of us willing to look. It was because of these witnessed truths that I felt obligated to inject spiritual considerations into the healthcare practices I was engaged with. It was also the aggressive counter push by the system even when it was obvious all that was occurring was people were getting better and the system was saving money, that I realized I must be on to something, thus pressing even more for investigation of additional truths.

People who wish to learn more about my own realizations of truth can read about them, for I have written many pages describing the events, experiences, teachers, and teachings along the way. The transformation from a simple healthcare provider to spiritual therapist and writer, or aiding people in true healing was the result of asking for myself the why's, who's, and what more's, these revelations presented to a simple man as I climbed out of the valley, wondering in myself the same living the greatest portion of my then long few years in the dark.

One experience related to this tragic beginning is relative to this book and stems from one of the first writings I had ever published called "We Are All Flowers." And while I have included this earlier writing in my other publications, long ago I promised God it would always be included in any writing I published.

We Are All Flowers

I knew a man once, a long time ago, he was a younger man, naive yet full of faith. Faith in God but also in the world! This man always loved God, even walked and talked with Him his whole life, but often knew not how to show it.

Then one day he found himself in a far-off land, and the last thing he expected happened; God decided to bless him by allowing our young traveler to meet one of God's "truly wonderful flowers!"

It didn't take long for this man to fall in love with the flower, because everyone who ever met her loved her. But another true miracle occurred, she actually loved him as well! Giving up school, home, family, even country, in a place that didn't speak his language, for a gift given by God didn't seem like a sacrifice at all, but more a privilege.

Days and nights filled with laughter, most of the time at nothing at all, coupled with the sweet scent of fresh dew on newly blossomed flowers, the misty morn of a cool spring's day, so was her breath. A touch so soft yet graced with strength, that it lit a flame in this man's heart that encircled said heart as gently as a warm feather bed snuggles shoulders on a cold winter's night.

Every curl, every curve, the every glance, her mere touch was as perfect as the speckling of beauty marks on her legs that randomly adorned her being like the stars of the sky. Perfect, maybe not by world's standards, but to him as perfect as any glorious creation his young eyes had yet witnessed.

How sweet it was to sit across a crowded room and have her look at him, mouth a word, and he would know exactly everything she said. How sweet was it to come from a feast every day that was her, and be so full he couldn't even glance at another morsel.

She was his love, she was his heart, she was his friend, she was his life. She became and was his wife!

A man would risk, even sacrifice his life, gladly!, to protect the precious pearl, that God has blessed him with. She does as well; risks her own, sacrificing body, risking life to joyfully bring a child into the world.

Blessings beyond imagination!

Some would say our young traveler had it all; when you have everything you need, all the extras are just extra, and really only amount to simple pleasures that rain down from God as simple flakes of snow in a perfect winter's scene.

But suddenly one day which should have been glorious, being only a single one before the scheduled day of birth of their second child, joy turned to tragedy! A stranger who would rush to beat a red light would cross her path, and life for her, as well as the child, would disappear from her blue eyes. Or so he was told then?

To understand the depth of what he experienced, only those that have experienced similar losses can feel the pain, and through this common feeling, this tragic experience, can relate to what he went through after that horrific day.

When I say those of similar loss, I mean someone who has a part of themselves taken from this world.

Not to diminish anyone's loss, whether it is a parent, a dear friend, or close love one, but nothing seems to compare to the loss of a spouse or child! This may very well be due to the fact that a child is created with a piece of ourselves. In the same way, when two people become one flesh as is the case in such a marriage.

The loss of either of these kinds of individuals in our lives can leave us not only depressed at this loss but left with a sense of utter and unexplainable incompleteness. We feel like a part of us is missing, and no matter what we do, we can't seem to find a fill to that lost part!

Why he asked?!!! But heard no answer.

Our young traveler, our angry, confused, guilt-ridden, tired young believer, would enter the wilderness, wander with fist in air, kicking rocks, head down, eyes turned away from the glare of a day that has become various shades of grey.

Days turned into weeks, which turned into years. Relationships came and went, and with them came various levels of betrayal even from those who pledged their deepest devotion.

Funny how a man can just slowly walk into a "Death Valley," slowly descending, unknowingly most of the time, until he finds himself so far below the "Sea" level, that he can hardly imagine a way out. When all seems lost and giving up becomes something our blessed, not so young man possibly looks at for the first time in his life, finally, out of desperation, he calls out to Jesus for help and Jesus answers! In a bathtub of all places!

The climb out is a rapid ascent when God shows the path! Three things happen when you get to the other side, at the top of the mountain ridge that crests the edge of the valley; one, you can look back and see the whole valley, giving a clear picture of the whole valley and what exactly it was, and two, it doesn't look so big as it did when you were deep in, and third, a person might even thank Him for the experience of overcoming, the task won, the lesson learned! But lessons like life were just beginning.

God is so good! Not only does He rescue His child when called, He blesses our traveler with the answer to his "why?" question that has haunted him all the previous eleven years of his wilderness walk.

One day he was asked by a female friend who had also had a tragic loss of a child that hard question. When she heard of his loss she turned as with tears in her eyes said; *"If God loves as you say He does, then how do you explain the loss of an innocent person such as your wife or child, or my baby?"*

At this point, our new recruit in God's army believed himself to be a "Born Again Believer" and knew Jesus lived in his heart, but the answer to that question he had never quite heard!

He closed his eyes and asked Jesus for wisdom, and low and behold; Jesus spoke in his mind.

An image immediately appeared and I will repeat it in these words as stated to her now all those years ago;

I softly spoke into her ear; "I just had the vision in my mind of a beautiful field of flowers, mostly reds, but also yellows, violets, and whites, appear like a picture before me in my mind eye. In the middle of a sweeping hill lined valley meadow, stood a shady tree, large, full leafed, quite inviting and peaceful! You know the kind, they show on a travel brochure to Tuscany, Italy or someplace like that?"

"Peaceful, restful, perfect in order and design, balanced majesty of symphonic grace as the breeze gently flows over blossoms, like the caressing waves of green-tinted shore."

"The voice of Jesus just said in my head;"

"Consider the flowers;"

"Some lie in the middle of the field, where the Sun is strong and the soil is deep, plenty of water, safe."

"Some lie under the trees, a good safe place but not as much sun, they just don't seem to grow as well."

"Some lie in the rocks, where the soil is thin and water spars, they do not grow well at all, a seemingly poor life."

"Some lie in the weeds, where life is hard and struggle seems to be a daily event, their short life choked out sometimes cruelly."

"And some lie on the road, where the wagon comes by and snuffs out their life suddenly!"

"You are all those flowers in that field! You are all flowers to me; some you are strong, some of you are weak, some of you are tall, some are small, all equal, all loved, all perfect."

"Yours is not to understand why this one lies here, or that one there, in my most perfect field, yours is to Thank Me!, for the time you got spend with another of my most precious flowers!"

Our young believer then understood and had an overwhelming realization that he needed to "Thank God" for two things; for all the precious time he got to spend in his life with such a beautiful creation as one of God's precious flowers, his wife and even unborn child. If it was but a moment, it was infinitely better than to have never had known them at all!

And two; that Jesus loves him enough to let me see the rest of the beauty of this gift we call our life, seeing not only our place in it, but His hand in every sight, sound, taste, and breath we share. If God didn't have all of the flowers in their perfect place, and in their perfect color, we wouldn't have the even more glorious field!

The true picture of life, as He sees it, and as we experience it.

This traveler was me!

God is faithful, I have had precious time with one of His most precious flowers.

That was many years ago, praise God I have also had since been promised restoration, and God always keeps His promises. A flower? Could God have another for me, and allow me to be one for her!

The answer is Yes!

"Dear Jesus; Allow me to not only see myself as one of your precious flowers, but all those around me, grant me the vision and sight as you see us, and in turn experience the same love you have for each of us, equal, and perfect."

I wrote this for my departed wife Hilly and our daughter Petra Colla who never got to see a single day out of her mother's womb never knew her father, never got to play hold up a block and show it to me.

All these years later, all this climbing, two steps up and one back down, an ascension of my own is finally realized at least enough to give some kind of account for others perhaps to see.

The caterpillar climbs and along the way, dreams descend upon him, and for me, all I can do is relate what I saw, for others, it may be different, we are all different flowers, each alike yet placed in slightly different locations in this vast beautiful garden God has created. For this caterpillar, a recurring image as I have already written of earlier was the flying experience, and while I will not expand on that idea or image again, I would like to add that memory has carved into my mind those experiences, while I know I was only dreaming, seem so real and vivid they were that many are clearer memories than the physical ones the many days or so-called real experiences only now a few years past?

One image or dream stands out and I feel compelled to repeat it, for I believe it is important for the reader to understand any of the potential gifts and with it, the consequences of receiving these gifts may bring. I had already by this time been promised restoration of everything that I had lost or stolen from me, and I believed God had told me this either directly, or indirectly through others? This restoration had not yet occurred, and as I aged it seemed increasingly unlikely that it would be possible.

Along the many now numerous times in my dreams when flying occurred, an almost Superman-like flying would be experienced where I could fly merely by thinking, reaching out, or remembering.

Never in these dreams did I ever experience any other of the typical Superman qualities; the strength, the X-ray vision, perhaps the only thing that I seemed to also experience, was a sense of indestructibility when hitting things or landing after a great fall. Also, I seem to always be engaged in something that was for good, looking for someone, or helping someone?

On one occasion I remember now eleven years ago a Superman flying dream stands out and I believe it is relevant to include it; one day I dreamt that I was standing in a room almost like I was preparing to go out to perform some kind of military assignment or another, and small little grandmother lady maybe barely four feet tall was standing on wooden stepping stool before me adjusting my clothes, I was wearing the Superman suit cape and all, but different than any I had ever seen deep shades of dark blues and darkened earth-tone reds. This little old lady could barely reach up on her tiptoes to adjust the shoulders. I don't know how I knew it but the little old lady; I felt she was the Holy Ghost, she was wearing light tan colored linen very old almost simple eleventh-century style woven cloth?

Then I hear the voice of God clearly say; *"If you knew going forward, you may have to be alone, would you go anyway?"*

I remember seeing myself standing there, looking down, a look of sadness seemed to be on my face, as the realization I may have to be alone was considered. I knew in my dream what I lost, and I also knew I desired to have it back, but as I stood there I can clearly remember thinking about it for seemingly a long time, although it may have only been an instant.

Then remember finally lifting my head slightly and looking at the old woman and simply saying; "Yes." Then I woke up.

The caterpillar climbs and with each step, there is a realization that takes place; one, the higher you climb the more you die to old wants and desires of the ground and earth. Things below just are not important to you any longer. And when I say die, it is as if the desires for them leave you almost as they fade from view. Of course, old habits are hard to lose, yet in many of these caterpillar's cases, old behaviors or even foods seem to make you ill to try them again?

But the second realization is a bit harder to stomach; the higher you go the lonelier it becomes. Many of the friends, some loved-ones, colleagues, even close family don't seem to understand you any longer, they look at you and think you may have gone crazy? It is a journey most may have to do alone? This factor is one of the strongest for turning people back down, giving up, or denying the very existence of the Ascension, and without getting into too much of it right now we will just call it; "The Fear of Man."

Back to Q. About four and a half years ago when I was continuing the Ascending investigations of applying God into the Health and Wellness of treatments another anomaly occurred of which sparked attention into politics, which was for me as far from my interest as the dark side of the moon, and this was the appearance of then-candidate for President Donald Trump. Things were said, ideas were mentioned, controversies promised to be investigated, exposed, and even eliminated as this candidate seemed to cross a line never before attempted. Now I can honestly say prior to this I had never given President Trump one thought or another, and other than seeing him on "The Apprentice," never really liked him much or not, I really didn't have an opinion.

But suddenly something appeared; a deep aggressive posture against him without a solid reason, an almost hate-driven campaign against Donald Trump from the media, what seemed at the time to be the controlling powers of our country, and pretty much everyone else that already enjoyed a position of elitism? Since I was on my own cusp of ruthless attacks, lies, and destructive acts for no other reason than what appeared to simply be hate, I began to identify with what this guy was going through and solicited me more to actually listen to what he was saying rather than just what they were telling me about him.

Out of the growing support I suddenly began to see a simple sign repeated itself at rallies, reports, messages, and following; that being the single letter "Q." What an odd symbol to represent some kind of message, seemingly repeatedly demonstrated, yet unfathomable to me. As God opened my eyes with each investigation into the things quickly coming to light another step up the ascension, another truth revealed, and more importantly another piece of a massive puzzle started forming seemingly from unrelated pieces I may have only glimpsed at my whole now nearly thirty-year ascension.

I am not going to get into the proof, politics, predictions, claims, or disclaims of any of the many "Gates" such as; "Pizza Gate," "Obama Gate," the CCP, the Vatican, "Election Fraud," "BLM," COVID hoax or not, Media Lies, Big-Corporate Big-Pharma involvement, the list goes on almost forever. Pieces of puzzles some seen, some experienced, others merely dreamed of all spread themselves with increasing frequency and almost mystical regularity into position, whereby a larger more complex image starts to manifest, an increase of clarity that maybe all of these unrelated and seemingly insignificant little pieces perhaps could all come together and reveal some yet hidden truth.

On the quantum level, we have already demonstrated that all positive energy, of which Truth is comprised, comes from God. And if we will further extrapolate, all positive intentions having the same increasing ascending potential of vibrational intensification likewise must then be of Godly origin or at least Godly destination. One can further conclude if a person seeks to reveal truths, speaks of God in a positive light, or works to improve the qualities of those around them especially without any apparent personal gain to themselves, then the only conclusion is they must be on the side of good, truth, love, and thus God. We are all active participants in the wonderful universe God has created for all of us to experience Him through and thus discover our own potentials, the only difference is our own personal free will choices.

All of these enlightenments these days, all of the illuminations, the Revelations that seem to be exploding around us, and with them the seeming hate-based objections, the masking, the lies, the hiding of the truth, the censoring unwillingness to reveal truths, all this does is lay credence to the authenticity of the truths? As more and more people step forward and bring the light upon hidden secrets, and more people see the truths, take their own single steps in ascension, and thereby see more, again patterns appear, symbols become statements, each of us as vessels of water become influenced merely by the intention behind these symbols and choices are made to Ascend, fixate once gaze on the dirt, or even descend, it all remains ultimately our free will a single decision to look at and for Truth, or live, ignore and ultimately choose the lie?

I have no idea if Q represents a person, penned by a single person, a group of people, a predicted rise of a fallen King or a Superman for that matter, or maybe a program set forward through masterful illuminated knowledge that could only be obtained through supernatural intervention, but as I experience my own observations with it these revelations that are first spoken of like soft whispers, later predicted with almost prophetic accuracy, and ultimately brought to Light with righteous indignation, I can not help but believe the entire idea behind Q is nothing more than a simple infinitely complex movement for the assimilation of Truth.

A crack forms in the cocoon and the caterpillar who now realizes something dramatically different is going on, not only in the world of her dreams but in the visions that are manifesting right before his eyes even as the first rays of light penetrate into its once safe haven of growth. What once was a dark world filled with fear, danger, and deep restricted movement is now filled with light, bright colors, truths about the real world around her which is full of freedom and potential one has only before dared to dream of, yet now seems imminent.

A new dimension seems to be unfolding right in front of us. Restorations' of hopes and dreams only dared prayed for in the past, enlightenments of the satanic parties involved, those who have perpetrated many or perhaps all of the attacks in the past on all of us, as well as the others, especially the innocent. A dimension where the limitations of the ground no longer apply, while vision perpetuates and bodies enhance, which have now only just begun to activate, ascended bodies will manifest themselves with powers only spoken of in the dreams of visionaries past. The Ascended create with them new destinies arising where they as Remnants can fly forth eager to engage the hostile foe, willing to serve in the aid of those who might yet only today begin their ascending steps, spreading messages of truth, tender touches of healing sounds, bringing with them heavenly justice, silently waiting for their specific assignments from Him who created all and holds the victory and the plan in the palm of His hand.

Hope to see you on the other side.

"Behold the Great and Mighty Day of the Lord, it is upon you, and it is... Vengeance."

Made in the USA
Las Vegas, NV
21 January 2022

42010427R00256